STOP ACTING RICH

STOP ACTING RICH

... And Start

Living Like a

Real Millionaire

THOMAS J. STANLEY, Ph.D.

WILEY

John Wiley & Sons, Inc.

Published by John Wiley & Sons, Inc., Hoboken, New Jersey.
Published simultaneously in Canada.

For general information on our other products and services or for technical support, please contact our Customer Care Department within the United States at (800) 762-2974, outside the United States at (317) 572-3993 or fax (317) 572-4002.

Wiley also publishes its books in a variety of electronic formats. Some content that appears in print may not be available in electronic books. For more information about Wiley products, visit our web site at www.wiley.com.

Library of Congress Cataloging-in-Publication Data
Stanley, Thomas J.
    Stop acting rich : . . . and start living like a real millionaire / Thomas J. Stanley.
        p. cm.
    Includes index.
    Summary: "A leading expert on the affluent reveals the real way to build wealth With well over two million of his books sold, and huge praise from many media outlets, Dr. Thomas J. Stanley is a recognized and highly respected authority on the wealthy, their behavior, and their thinking. Now, in Stop Acting Rich, he details how the less affluent have fallen into the elite luxury brand trap that keeps them from truly acquiring wealth and details how to get out of it by emulating the working rich as opposed to the super elite. A defensive strategy for tough times, Stop Acting Rich will show you how to live like Warren Buffett-a rich, happy life-through accumulating more wealth and using it to achieve the type of financial freedom that will create true happiness and fulfillment. Puts wealth in perspective and shows you how to live rich without spending more Details why we spend lavishly and how to stop this destructive cycle Discusses how being "rich" means more than just big houses and luxury cars Other titles by Stanley: The Millionaire Mind and The Millionaire Next Door It's time to understand why we buy what we buy, so that we can start accumulating, rather than depleting, wealth. Stop Acting Rich shows you exactly what it takes to achieve this elusive goal"—Provided by publisher.
    ISBN 978-0-470-48255-1
    1. Wealth—United States. 2. Rich people—United States. 3. Finance, Personal—United States. I. Title.
    HC110.W4S734 2009
    332.015'01—dc22
                                                                                        2009023406

For Anna, Ryan, and Kate

Contents

List of Tables		*ix*
Preface		*xi*
Chapter 1	The Difference between Being Rich and Acting Rich	1
Chapter 2	Everything You Think about Rich Is Wrong	33
Chapter 3	Do the Shoes Make the Man?	59
Chapter 4	Brother, Do You Have the Time?	83
Chapter 5	Keeping Up with Your Spirits	115
Chapter 6	The Grapes of Wrath	145
Chapter 7	The Road to Happiness	171
Chapter 8	Getting Out of the Poorhouse	209
Chapter 9	All that Glitters Is Not the Millionaire's Goal	235
Appendix A	The Nationwide Search for Millionaires	245
Appendix B	The Millionaire Profile	247

Contents

Notes   251

Acknowledgments   257

About the Author   259

Index   261

List of Tables

Table 2.1 Homeowners in America: High Income versus High
Net Worth?   44

Table 2.2 Homes of Millionaires in America: Average
Value by Augmented Net Worth   48

Table 2.3 Neighborhood Defined Consumption Lifestyles
Where Millionaires Reside   50

Table 2.4 Wealth-Producing Characteristics of Selected
Occupations: High Income versus High Net Worth   53

Table 2.5 Top 20 Ancestry Groups Who Own/Occupy
Homes Valued at $1 Million or More:
Total Number versus Concentration   57

Table 3.1 Price Paid by Millionaires for Their Most Recent
Haircut   60

Table 4.1 Top 10 Brands of Watches Worn by Millionaires   91

Table 6.1 Price of Wine Served by Millionaires   153

Table 6.2 Prices Paid for Wine Contained Inside the
Homes of Millionaires   154

Table 6.3   Wine Inventory Owned by Millionaires   155

Table 6.4   Price Typically Paid by Millionaires for Their
Dinner at the Restaurant They Dine at Most
Frequently   157

Table 7.1   Stores for Clothing and Accessories Patronized
by Millionaires According to the Most Recent
Make of Motor Vehicles Acquired   199

Table 7.2   Makes of Motor Vehicles Acquired by
Millionaires   203

Table 7.3   Popular Models of Motor Vehicles Acquired by
Millionaires   205

Table 8.1   Profile of Happy versus Unhappy High-Income-
Producing Baby Boomers   224

Preface

Thirty years ago, I first defined the blue collar affluent, aka the millionaire next door, in a speech and paper that I delivered on behalf of the New York Stock Exchange. This began a lifetime journey of identifying and profiling the myths and realities of the rich.

I discovered that not all millionaires have high social status. In fact, those who are among the least productive in transforming their incomes into wealth are in the higher-status occupations. In a 1980 national study of multimillionaires, I found that half of the millionaires in America do not live in upscale neighborhoods. In 1988, I wrote my first book, *Marketing to the Affluent*, which essentially discussed how to market to the "millionaire next door." After reading it, one of my colleagues at Georgia State University, Dr. David Schwartz, author of the perennial mega-bestseller *The Magic of Thinking Big*, suggested that I broaden my work to appeal to a much larger general audience. I followed Dave's advice and wrote *The Millionaire Next Door* (1996), which answered the question: Who is the typical millionaire in America? This bestselling book exploded many common myths about the wealthy in America, revealing that their low-profile and frugal lifestyle were pervasive among this group.

After the success of *The Millionaire Next Door*, I continued my research with *The Millionaire Mind* (2000). In this book, I revealed the factors that millionaires, who had three times the wealth as those in *The Millionaire*

Next Door, reported as being most important in explaining their economic success. Among those factors were integrity, discipline, social skills, a supportive spouse, leadership qualities, and having a love for one's vocation. Among the least important were luck, investing in the stock market, and having high academic achievement. I responded to the numerous queries I received from women about their lack of representation in my books by writing *Millionaire Women Next Door* in 2004. Women in business succeed because they work harder and are more frugal than their male counterparts. Women who fail in business typically love their product but not their business.

In *Stop Acting Rich . . . And Start Living Like a Real Millionaire*, I detail why so many people who are not rich hyperspend on luxuries. Often they think that collecting these expensive toys will enhance their overall satisfaction with life. But, as you will read in detail, happiness in life has little to do with what you wear, drive, eat, or drink. The people with the greatest satisfaction are those who live below their means. Even during the recent peaks of income production, the residential real estate market, and the bull stock market when the main survey for this book was undertaken, these millionaires maintained their habits of thrift and frugality. (See Appendix A for the survey details and Appendix B for the profile of millionaires.) In other words, increasing asset values did not cause the majority of wealthy people to hyperspend.

So who are hyperspenders really emulating? They are merely mimicking the behaviors of people like themselves, who are not rich but act in ways they think the economically successful people act.

Why is it that some people worth $10 million, $20 million, or even $30 million own few or no luxuries whatsoever? They know that satisfaction in life is not a function of what you can buy in a store. As you will come to learn in these pages, these people were conditioned by their parents to live below their means and were taught how to invest and manage money effectively. Accordingly, the billions of dollars poured into the marketing hype associated with promoting status products have had little effect on their consumption lifestyle. Also these people tend to associate with others who have similar attitudes, interests and activities, and beliefs.

The reason why so many homeowners today are having a difficult time making ends meet goes way beyond mortgage payments. When you trade up to a more expensive home, there is pressure for you to spend more on every conceivable product and service. Nothing has a greater impact on your wealth and your consumption than your choice of house and neighborhood. If you live in a pricey home in an exclusive community, you will spend more than you should and your ability to save and build wealth will be compromised. My research has found that most people who live in million-dollar homes are not millionaires. They may be high-income producers but, by trying to emulate glittering rich millionaires, they are living a treadmill existence. In the United States, there are three times more millionaires living in homes that have a market value of under $300,000 than there are living in homes valued at $1 million or more.

Given the recent reversals in the market value of stocks and homes, you may be asking: Is the millionaire market dead? While completing this book, a newspaper writer called and asked me what I thought about a published study claiming that the number of millionaires had significantly declined during the 2008–2009 period. I told her that I disagreed with these findings. Since 1980, I have consistently found that most millionaires do not have all of their wealth tied up in their stock portfolios or in their homes. When the investment gurus talk about diversification, they show how very parochial they are. Real safety is not in a diversified stock portfolio. One of the reasons that real millionaires are economically successful is that they think differently. Many a millionaire has told me that true diversity has much to do with controlling one's investments; no one can control the stock market. But you can, for example, control your own business, private investments, and money you lend to private parties. Not at any time during the past 30 years have I found that the typical million-aire had more than 30 percent of his wealth invested in publicly traded stocks. More often it is in the low to mid-20 percent range. These percent-ages are consistent with those found in studies conducted by the Internal Revenue Service, which has the best data set on millionaires in the world.

In a way, the credit crisis of 2008–2009 is serving as something of an intervention. But for the treatment to work, you must take a cold hard look at your balance sheet and at your life, and determine if you would be wealthier if you would stop acting rich. It is my hope to show you that you can stop acting rich and still enjoy life to the fullest by living like a real millionaire.

Disclaimer

This publication is designed to provide accurate and authoritative infor-mation in regard to the subject matter covered. It is sold with the under-standing that neither the author nor the publisher is engaged in rendering legal, investment, accounting, or other professional services. If legal advice or other expert assistance is required, the services of a competent profes-sional person should be sought.

This entire project was underwritten by the author. His views and interpretations of the findings may not necessarily be the same as those of the organizations that market the brands that are mentioned in this work. Except for two speeches given to BMW dealers in the late 1980s and a summer job at a Chevrolet dealership in his youth, the author has never been employed or compensated in any way by these organizations.

1

The Difference between Being Rich and Acting Rich

Anyone who lives within their means suffers from a lack of imagination.

—Oscar Wilde

While in his early teens, my dad worked as a paperboy, covering two newspaper routes: the blue route and the white route. Most of his "blue" customers lived in working- or lower-middle-class (blue-collar) neighborhoods located to the east and south of his parents' home. The "white" route included middle- to upper-middle-class (white-collar) customers who, for the most part, occupied nice and neat single-family homes to the west and north. Both routes contained roughly the same number of subscribers. Contrary to what you might think, my father found that the "blue" route was the more financially lucrative of the two. Customers were significantly more likely to pay on time, tip their paperboy, and provide him with a Christmas bonus.

Why? My father theorized that many of his "white" route customers were perpetually strapped for cash, as they were supporting expensive homes and all that goes along with them. He felt that many of his customers along his "blue" route lived below their means. As a result, they always seemed to have cash on hand with which to pay him when he collected.

The lesson in this story, according to my father, was there was a difference between *looking* rich and *being* rich, and that most people who looked rich weren't—they lived above their means and therefore usually had little money with which to be generous to others. By and large, my dad was right, though I learned that there are some people—although a small percentage—who are truly glitteringly rich. If you read *The Millionaire Mind* or have ever heard me speak about the rich, you will recall me mentioning a Halloween experience I had when I was 9 years old: Instead of trick-or-treating in our own blue-collar neighborhood, we ventured into Fieldston, one of the wealthiest neighborhoods in New York City. We were rewarded by treats of money from the likes of James Mason, the distinguished British actor, and bags of money from a home with an ill resident who had left coins for groups of children in the milk box. I proudly showed off our loot to my dad, making the counterargument that people who live in big beautiful homes are rich. He maintained that we got lucky and accidentally hit on a few of the cash-rich households that do exist.

Subsequent experiences and much study have shown me that, overall, my dad was right about those who look rich versus those who really are rich. More people look richer than they really are, and the really rich often don't look anything like what we think they should look like.

Meet the Aspirationals

From the age of 13 to 17, I caddied, carrying a lot of golf bags between early April and mid-September. This helped fund my passion for model airplanes and boats, but I received a lot more than money from caddying.

I learned a great deal about people. In fact, much of the knowledge I gained on the golf course provided a base for my lifelong career studying rich people—and those who only act rich.

As a caddy, I alternated between two distinctly different golf courses. One was a public course; the other was part of a private country club. The public course was not typical of most public courses that were open to anyone. It had a natural terrain that was both demanding and rather spectacular. Half of the holes bordered a large reservoir and horticultural institute forest. Judging golf courses is subjective, but in my view the public course was way above the norm, better even than many private country club courses.

Most of the golfers at the private course were of a different sort from those I worked for at the public course. Most of the private club members were lawyers, physicians, dentists, accountants, and corporate middle-level managers. In the minority were business owners and senior corporate executives. Nearly all private club goers drove prestige makes of cars. At the time, members had to employ and pay for the services of a caddy—even those who drove electric carts. Not all of the members liked that rule.

Things were different at the public course. Golfers there had the option of hiring a caddy or carrying their own bag. About half paid for a caddy. Many of those who did were self-employed types, ranging from craftsmen to owners of small- and medium-size blue-collar businesses such as plumbing firms, hardware stores, contracting, and the like. Some of my best clients were sales and marketing professionals. Few golfers at the public course drove luxury cars or wore top-of-the-line golf attire like those who played at the private club.

As a work environment, there were certain advantages as well as disadvantages associated with each golf course. The fee for a caddy was 25 percent higher at the private club, but it took less time for me to commute (by bicycle) to the public course. This was not the only advantage of caddying at the public course. In my four years caddying, during each loop around the course, each and every customer at the public course offered to buy me a hot dog and a Coke for lunch. Only about one in four players at the private club made such an offer. In addition, about two-thirds of my public course clients tipped. Most of the golfers at the private club never tipped their caddies, although those who did tipped very well.

During my first two years of caddying at the private club, the caddy master never assigned me to a big tipper. Early in my third season, I asked the caddy master why.

"Stanley," he said. "You are not a great caddy. Big tippers demand great caddies."

His comments were perplexing to me, since some of the caddies who regularly got the big tippers were anything *but* great. About halfway through my third season, I figured out what made caddies "great" in the caddy master's eyes. I ran up a sizable tab on the caddy master's IOU ledger for sandwiches, soft drinks, and other snacks. Once my tab exceeded those of all the "great caddies," the caddy master finally saw the light. He discovered that I was the best caddy in the county after all! All of a sudden I was assigned almost exclusively to the country club's small group of big tippers. He nearly wore me out with all the big tipper business he sent my way. Often I carried two bags for 36 holes in one day. Every time I finished a round, I would pay off about 10 percent of my tab. Then the next day that I showed up, I put at least that same dollar amount or more back on my tab. (It is important to maintain—or, even better, enhance—one's reputation as a great caddy.)

Just who were those extraordinarily generous people at the private course, the big tippers? How did they differ from those members who never tipped a caddy or even offered him a hot dog for lunch? Today I have a clearer understanding of both of these types of people.

Most of the big tippers were classic big spenders in the genre of Vanderbilt, Rockefeller, Gould, or any number of modern-day megastars such as Buffett, Soros, Madonna, P Diddy, and thousands of glittering rich names you've never heard of. At the top were very successful owners of privately held corporations. Some were senior corporate executives of public corporations. My best client was a physician and his wife. The couple owned several hospitals and a variety of other commercial real estate. They were always in good spirits, even though neither one could hit a ball very well. And they were certainly generous!

The glittering rich had the economic means required to generate considerable wealth and simultaneously support a high-consumption lifestyle. Paying club-related fees and buying lunches for caddies didn't put even a minor dent in their financial statements.

What about the other type of golfer I encountered at the private course? I believe that a lot of them were, in fashion and retail parlance, "aspirationals"—people who act rich, want to be rich, but actually aren't rich. Aspirationals have two "highs": high occupational status and a high-consumption lifestyle. They often try to imitate the big-spending, glittering rich, but it is nearly impossible to do it all—from home to car to clothing to drinking and dining with an income that is only a fraction of what the typical glittering rich generates. Much of the aspirational income goes toward consumption categories that supposedly denote high occupational status and prestige: homes, cars, clothing, designer-grade golf equipment, and, of course, country club memberships.

But what about those consumption items that are not badges or symbols of socioeconomic success and superiority (real or imagined)? Here is where aspirationals go ultrafrugal. So what if your caddy got soaking wet three times retrieving your balls out of the lake during your round of golf? So what if he gave you some pointers that helped you shoot an all-time low score? No one will know if you stiff the caddy. Tell him you are "just a bit short on cash today" and will "catch up with him next time." It takes a lot of money, relative to income and net worth, to be an aspirational. Perhaps that is why more than two-thirds of those who are country club members are not millionaires.

How very different the aspirationals I encountered were from the business owners I caddied for at the public course. The business owners always seemed to have a good amount of cash with them, often in rolled up wads. They could afford to be generous with their hired help. Most had no interest in emulating the consumption patterns of the big-spending, glittering rich. Unlike the aspirationals, they didn't feel the need to display a variety of expensive badges that are supposed to indicate socioeconomic superiority. They bought what they could afford within their value system of priorities and were happy to pay for it. If they used the services of a caddy, they paid the caddy. If they didn't want to pay a caddy, then they didn't hire one. They didn't pay to belong to a private club when the nearby public course was so much better.

With the knowledge that I have today about wealth, particularly in America, including what I learned from my caddy experiences, what do I conclude? Most people who act rich are not rich!

The Sobering Statistics

The financial crisis of 2008–2009 has certainly cost many people a great deal of money. A lot of wealth has evaporated, and all of a sudden wallets have slammed shut. Recent statistics indicate that people are saving like they haven't saved in decades. Neiman Marcus sales are plummeting, while Wal-Mart sales are growing somewhat. The *New York Times* publishes stories on trading down in clothing and make up with tips and leads. It's hip to be frugal. For the moment.

Time will tell if society and people have really changed or are simply taking a sick day, if you will. My research indicates that people—for generations—have become so accustomed to consuming that it is second nature, and I am fairly certain that they will resume their spendthrift ways once outward symptoms of the financial flu have passed. In other words, what we are experiencing is fear. Once the fear passes, it will be back to business as usual. In the United States, in particular, we have a long history of spending big and often frivolously. We like stories about people who make gobs of money and then spend it all—usually lavishly and with great aplomb—from the fictional Gatsby to the real-life antics of rappers draped in bling. To look at all the things we have—from iPhones to custom suits to new cars every year—it would seem as though we are rolling in dough, even in these tough times.

But are we really rich, or have we just been acting the part? The numbers tell a sobering story. More than $70 trillion in realized or reported income was generated by U.S. households between 1997 and 2006,[1] yet only 3.5 percent of these households were in the millionaire category (i.e., having investments valued at $1 million or more).

In 2007, about 2.2 million American seniors passed away. What did they do with the more than $2 trillion in income they earned during their lifetimes, given that only 2.6 percent left behind a gross estate (all assets included) of $1 million or more, and 75 percent of these estates were valued at under $2.5 million? What about the other 97.4 percent of decedents? If they did not save their income, invest it, or allocate it to things that appreciate or at least hold some of their value, where did the money go?

The answer: Beyond the basic necessities, an awful lot of it was spent on things, many things that now reside in landfills or thrift shops.

Ours is a culture of hyperconsumerism. Not only can and do we buy nearly anything (except for the truly outrageously expensive), but we seem to have come to believe that we can and should have it all and that who we are is dependent on the ability to live in the right neighborhoods, with appropriately sized homes filled with brand-name appliances, with prestige cars parked in the driveway with expensive golf bags and clubs in the trunk, and so on. And so we spend. We may be spending somewhat less after the 2008 financial crisis, but we are still spending. Savings may have increased to its highest levels in decades, but the reality is that that is not saying much, since the savings rate has been so abysmally low.

We seem to have become fairly good at generating an income, enjoying (for the moment) a very high standard of living. But it is fleeting because we have not accumulated wealth—for our retirement, for our children's educations, for emergencies. What kinds of trade-offs are we making? In America, the proportion of people who owned boats in 2005 exceeded the proportion who left an estate of $1 million or more in 2007 by a ratio of nearly 5 to 1. Even more pronounced is the ratio between the number of cell phone subscriptions and the number of households with $1 million or more in investments: nearly 60 to 1. The cold, harsh reality is that most people live well today, but they will pay for it tomorrow when their standard of living falls off the proverbial cliff due to a lack of resources to pay for retirement, healthcare, or even the cost of a trip to visit the grandkids.

The True Measure of Wealth

When I use the term "millionaire," I refer to those with investments of $1 million or more. "Investments" include such items as stocks, bonds, mutual funds, equity shares in private businesses, annuities, net cash value of life insurance, mortgages and credit notes held, gold and other precious metals, certificates of deposit (CDs), T-bills, savings bonds, money market funds, checking accounts, cash, and income-producing real estate. Basically, anything of value that is reasonably liquid.

This is not the traditional way of expressing a household's level of wealth. For many years, I defined net worth as the current value of all of one's household assets minus all of its liabilities. But things have changed. I now refer to this measure (assets less liabilities) as augmented net worth, or embellished net worth, or enhanced net worth, or even nominal net worth. Why the change? Embellished net worth includes, for example, the equity in one's home. Home values exploded between 1997 and 2007. As a result, so did the population of enhanced millionaires. What percent of American households had an augmented net worth of $1 million or more due to real estate appreciation? The answer is more than twice the percentage of those with investments of $1 million or more (8 percent versus 3.5 percent) did—but now they don't. So much of their augmented wealth was invisible. If your net worth was $1.5 million with 85 percent of that from your home, and the value of your home depreciated by 50 percent (which it has in many areas), then your wealth wasn't real.

Many people have become experts in exaggerating the value of their assets while underestimating their liabilities, and some assets can be prone to bubble inflation during certain times. In the late 1990s, we saw lots of dot-com millionaires with tremendous assets—at least on paper. Once that bubble burst, many of those millionaires exited the millionaire club. In the latter part of the most recent decade, real estate valuations exploded, only to come back to earth in 2008. Many real estate millionaires are no more. It is as if many people have been filling out loan applications where their lives depended on the bank's approval. It usually takes a certain degree of discipline, proactive planning, prioritizing, and investing to become a true millionaire. Conversely, many of those who reached the $1 million embellished level of wealth did so because of some temporary asset bubble, such as the value of their homes, got them there—for a moment. In both recent cases, the dot-com bubble and the real estate craze, many won the lottery but didn't even have the presence of mind to lock in their gains. In the case of housing, the majority of people who live in expensive homes (valued at $1 million or more) are not millionaires—they are (or were) "house rich." And many of them, as we've come to see all too painfully, are now house poor because their real estate debt exceeds the current value of their property.

My dad had it right.

As I have been writing and lecturing about for over 30 years, studying the ways and means of true millionaires is very enlightening. Think of the millionaire population as a continuum. At one end are the glittering rich. They generate extremely high incomes, have vast sums of wealth at their disposal, and spend accordingly on high-prestige cars, mansions, dinner every night at $300-plus per person restaurants, couture attire, and the like. No matter what they spend their money on, though, it's just a fraction of their overall net worth. In other words, even the glittering rich spend below their means. They are a very small minority, about 2 percent of U.S. millionaire households; no more than 80,000 in total. As of the first quarter of 2007, in order to qualify as glittering rich, one needed to generate an annual realized household income of over $2 million, have a net worth in excess of $20 million, and live in a home valued at over $2 million (at least $3 million in California). At the opposite end of the millionaire continuum are millionaire households that are extremely frugal and live in homes valued at under $300,000. These people became millionaires because of their frugality and their fastidious saving and investing habits. They are at ground zero in terms of their inventory of luxury products. Note that aspirationals are not found anywhere along this continuum; they are not millionaires.

So why are we talking about the glittering rich, and why do they even matter, as they make up such a small percentage of the population? They matter because they are rich, and they act rich—by driving top-of-the-line (usually European) makes of cars, by shopping at exclusive stores, by extravagantly vacationing internationally, often to exotic places, and by consuming the most expensive of everything, from watches to vodka to vintage wine. They really matter to us because, sadly, we have become a society that seeks to emulate their consumption lifestyle to the detriment of our financial health. We have been acting rich but we aren't rich—by any means.

But don't we deserve to enjoy the fruits of our labors? Most of us would like to be rich in order to spend like and act like glittering rich people, but we aren't taking steps to become financially secure or financially independent. Why? Because to do so would require a drastic change in our habits. We would have to plan, cut back, be prudent, maybe even shop at Wal-Mart, invest, and even downsize. We lack the discipline, the *guts* it takes to become rich.

Most people will never earn $10 million in their lifetime, let alone in any single year. In fact, most households are unlikely to ever earn even $200,000 or more annually. Currently only about 3 percent of American households are in that category. So what if you will never hit the top 3 percent mark? What if you are unlikely to become rich by playing extraordinary offense (i.e., generating an extraordinarily high realized income), as the glittering rich do? The only way you will become rich is to play extraordinary defense like those millionaires at the other end of the continuum: by living well below your means, by planning, saving, and investing. We need to stop acting rich, and you need to adopt the values and lifestyles of self-made millionaires. Why? To be happy, to achieve the most satisfaction you can get from life. But you say that having that special car will make you happy, that living in a certain home in a specific neighborhood will make you happy. I say: Not so fast. It turns out that what we say and what actually brings us happiness are a bit different.

For years, many of my clients insisted that I ask respondents to my surveys and focus groups about their goals. I tried to discourage them from doing this for one reason: The goals that people report do not discriminate very well between hyperconsuming high-income/low-net-worth types (the aspirationals) and millionaires/soon-to-be millionaires. Both groups will tell you that their goal is to be financially independent someday. But talk is cheap. In studying millionaires and those who merely act rich, I have determined that it is much more productive and insightful to ask people about their actual behaviors, habits, and real lifestyles than to ask them about their stated intentions and conjured goals.

So what if your real goal is to act (or continue acting) rich? I suppose I can help you. I will tell you what the glittering rich buy, then, when making brand choices, you can order off the appetizer menu since you cannot pay for the really expensive entrées. You certainly can at the very least display the brands of vodka consumed by the rich and shop in stores patronized by the "beautiful people."

The buying behaviors of the glittering rich, especially brand selection patterns, are completely opposite to those of the millionaires who may never in their lives have had an annual earned income of $100,000 or more. They invest regularly and wisely. Their entire consumption life- style is congruent with the types of home and neighborhoods in which they reside. Bottom line, it is far more attainable to become a millionaire through hard work and saving than it is likely to become a celebrity mil- lionaire, win the lottery, or inherit from a mysterious rich aunt.

However, in a perverse twist on the modern take of the rich, our society gives those who have achieved the greatest success by work and diligence short shrift. We are not interested in emulating the Toyota-driving, modestly attired, bling-less entrepreneur or sales professional. Instead, we take as our role models celebrities and athletes, masters of the universe. Rather than attempt to find their luck, we have come to think that if we *act* like them, look like them, drive the cars they drive, we are glitteringly rich. In the process of buying into the marketing hype, of getting sucked into the brand advertising, we have frittered away our wealth. It's not your fault, in a way, as some of the smartest people in the world seem to be working in marketing and advertising, and with the increased media coming at us every day from every angle—print, broadcast, online—it's difficult to resist the siren song of Grey Goose, Mercedes, Tag Heuer, Hermès, and all the other prestige products around us.

Poor Richard's Wine Cellar

In a study I conducted of high-net-worth/high-income households in 2005–2006, I uncovered the brand choices of 1,594 respondents, of whom 944 were millionaires. (Appendix A outlines the sample design, and Appendix B profiles these millionaires.) At one end of the millionaire consumption spectrum were respondents such as the fellow who complained that the questionnaire did not have enough space for him to list all five of the $10,000 and over watches he owned and the Ferraris he bought/sold/kept, and the decamillionaire who wanted extra credit for the numerous airplanes he owned ("instead of a yacht"). At the other end were wealthy individuals who were extremely frugal. A word of caution: The data indicates that the glittering rich not only have a very high propensity to purchase certain brands, they tend to buy more of just about everything, from prestige makes of cars to expensive watches to super-premium vodka to expensive suits. In order to emulate them, you might have to allocate more time shopping. The size of one's inventory is telling.

Store patronage habits are among the strongest measures that define glittering. And where do glitteringly rich people shop for their clothing and accessories? Responses to my national survey indicated that Saks Fifth Avenue and Neiman Marcus are the top two retail discriminators that distinguish the glittering from the others. In fact, the correlation between one's position on the glittering rich scale and shopping at Saks is even more substantial than one's choice of makes of automobiles. Stores that also rank high along the scale include Banana Republic, Brooks Brothers, Gucci, high-end independent specialty stores, Nordstrom, and Polo. So if you are not rich, you can fake it by displaying pictures of yourself walking out of Saks and Neiman Marcus overloaded with shopping bags, or by filling up the backseat of your leased prestige make of motor vehicle with shopping bags conspicuously filled with goods purchased at the stores listed above. Then drive around town and give rides to people you are trying to impress! No one will downgrade you because your car is leased; they probably don't know that 84 percent of glittering rich people purchase their cars versus 94 percent of millionaires in general.

It is not enough to drive just any make of vehicle. What are the makes and variety of makes of motor vehicles that scored highest on the glittering rich people scale? The upper-level (higher-price/true luxury) models of Mercedes-Benz and BMW ranked highest. In fairness, even among the glitteringly rich, there were not enough respondents who drove Ferraris, Rolls-Royces, or other very exotic makes to generate stable estimates of their positions on the scale. But keep something else in mind. For the glittering rich people segment, the number of cars owned begins at three and ends in double digits. The glittering rich almost by definition own at least one trophy vehicle—that is, a top-of-the-line BMW, Mercedes, Lexus, etc. Also, most have at least one SUV. Yet many of the SUVs are not in the luxury class. Full-size SUVs produced by Ford and General Motors as well as variety of Jeeps are extremely popular among the glittering rich. So if you currently drive an Explorer, Tahoe, or Wrangler, you may be acting rich.

Because the glittering rich entertain a lot, they purchase a great deal of both spirits and wines. There is a high correlation between one's position on the scale and the number of bottles of both spirits and wines in one's home inventory. Glittering rich people tend to collect wine and many have a well-stocked wine cellar. Plus the higher you are on the scale, the greater the price you paid for the wine served to guests.

If you cannot afford to own a fully stocked wine cellar, but you still want to play act the role of a glittering rich person, here is something you can do. Study wine and begin to give informal speeches about wine. No audience is too small. You may convince some, including yourself, that you are really rich and glitter like gold. Designate a room in your basement as a wine cellar. What if you do not have enough money to stock your wine cellar? Do what Jon-Jon, originally from the Gun-Hill Road section of the Bronx, a perpetually relocating corporate middle manager—did. He provided free wine storage to other aspirationals who did not have the necessary space. So technically Jon-Jon told the truth when he bragged about having a fully stocked wine cellar, even though not all the wine was his.

Glittering rich people keep a wide variety of spirits in their homes. But almost all of the brands they have are of the premium and super-premium type. What brand best discriminates glittering rich from the other types surveyed, that is, occupies the highest position on the glittering rich scale? Grey Goose vodka is the winner. In fact, its discriminant score exceeds those of many of the expensive brands of watches as well as prestige makes of motor vehicles. Absolut and Ketel One are high up on the scale.

What can happen when glitteringly rich people compete against each other in terms of conspicuous consumption? The battle is sometimes fought with bottles. Just how many bottles of premium and super-premium spirits and vintage wines can be put on display at a party hosted by glittering rich people? It is not clear, but in my database, it was Richard S. who had the greatest number of bottles on hand. He and his wife love to host parties for friends, neighbors, clients, and suppliers. Plus they frequently attended parties hosted by other glittering rich people. Richard was not always number one in this war waged with bottles, but he—an extraordinarily competitive multimillionaire—figured out a way to beat all his competition.

When Richard has a party at his home, there are cases upon cases of expensive brands of spirit displayed. The cases are positioned around his 30-meter swimming pool, stacked on a series of 4-foot-by-8-foot wooden plywood boards and supported by sawhorses covered with linen tablecloths. It is not unusual for the number of cases of spirits to exceed the number of guests being entertained.

Some might say that Richard's enormous display of bottles is overdoing it a bit, even for an exceedingly wealthy person. But there is more to Richard's story. For years Richard designated himself as the number-one customer of a neighborhood liquor store. Shortly after he learned that the proprietor was about to sell out, Richard essentially became his own best customer. He bought the store and kept all of its employees. Today, everything is about the same at the store except for one thing. There are a lot of cases moving back and forth between the store and Richard's home! Now Richard no longer has to buy all of those cases he displays. Most of them are just on loan from the store. But no matter. His conspicuous display of high-priced brands and vintages helps him qualify as being "beautiful." Perhaps this is the model for a new type of liquor stores; we need a "rent a bottle" outlet in every town.

Richard may be very successful, but he also has much in common with most of us. He has been conditioned by marketers. Like Richard, too many of us believe that premium and super-premium brands are badges that denote success and that those people who do purchase these brands are successful and, by extension, those who do not purchase those brands are not successful.

Yet from my surveys and studies, I know that this is not true.

It is all right for Richard to display pricey badges, even in grotesque quantities. He is a success, the real deal in terms of both income and wealth. Perhaps he should brag; he certainly can afford to do so. Yet there is a growing danger facing us: What happens when people are conditioned to believe that owning the badge is the achievement? Why work hard to succeed when "success" can be bought (most likely with a credit card)? You can act rich by displaying just the right selection of store-bought symbols.

A Compromise

I know what you may be thinking:

> Okay, okay, Dr. Stanley. I get your message. I understand that I can't be glittering. I don't have that kind of wealth. But isn't there some sort of minor league glittering division I can be in? I want to be somewhat wealthy and spend some. I want to at least sparkle a little. After all, I have a fairly high income. I work hard, so I want to live, I want to enjoy my money as well. There has to be a compromise. I don't need to live in a $10 million home. But I do want to live in a home valued in the high

six to low seven figures situated in an upper-middle-class neighborhood, drive luxury motor vehicles, wear expensive suits and accessories, shop at upscale stores, and serve my guests super-premium distilled beverages and vintage wines. I want these types of things. But I also want to be a millionaire even if only of the augmented variety. Is it possible to do so?

In a large part, it depends on your ability to generate income. And, even in the minor leagues, you will need a fairly high income to do both. Those who do both are among the least productive in terms of transforming their income into wealth. I refer to these types as income statement affluent, or IA for short. Yes, they are millionaires, at least of the augmented variety (if we include the value of their homes). But their net worth is, in a statistical sense, significantly lower than what is expected, given their high income. What might happen after you learn just how expensive their high-consumption lifestyle is to sustain? You might not want to be among the IA or even act like one. I hope you may want to follow the ways of those millionaires who are very productive in converting income into wealth: the balance sheet affluent (BA).

Transforming Income into Wealth

Emulate the behavior of BAs and you will likely become financially secure. But first understand how much you should be worth. In order to do so, I developed the Wealth Equation,[2] which I introduced initially in my first book, *Marketing to the Affluent* (1988):

> Simply stated, your net worth [augmented] should equal 10 percent of your age times your annual realized household income (0.10 × age × income = expected net worth). If your actual net worth is above this expected figure, I consider you affluent, given your age and income characteristics.

Interestingly, there is a wide variation, even among the affluent, in terms of what I call the wealth index (WX). Your WX is the ratio of your household's actual net worth (augmented) over its expected or predicted level as computed from the Wealth Equation.[3] The BAs have indices way above the norm. It is just the opposite for the IAs.

The BAs became wealthy by playing great defense via serious financial planning, wise investing, and being frugal. Most never generated high incomes, yet they became wealthy nonetheless. Their objective was to build wealth.

The focus of the IAs is on maximizing their realized incomes. They became wealthy by playing excellent offense. In other words, they generated high earned incomes. Most IAs fit the definition of minor league glittering rich people by earning just enough money to buy almost anything. Even though they hyperconsume and are lacking in budgeting or financial planning, they have become millionaires.

I computed a WX for each of my latest survey's 944 millionaire respondents. But the WX that I was particularly interested in determining was not their current WX. I wanted to know at what age and at what corresponding level of annual realized income they first crossed the millionaire (augmented) threshold. All 944 respondents reported what their age and annual income characteristics were when they hit the mark.

With this information, I computed a WX for each respondent. Then I ranked each respondent according to his WX. In turn, the 944 were divided into three groups or categories. The BA group contained those who ranked in the top 25 percent in terms of their WX. The threshold WX for those included in the BA group was 1.84. The median WX for those in this category was 2.49. In other words, the "typical" member of the BA group had an actual net worth that was 2.49 times the expected figure, given his age and income at the time he first reached the seven-figure wealth threshold.

The IA millionaires ranked in the bottom quartile along the WX continuum. The highest WX within this group was 0.880; the median WX was only 0.665. This means that the typical IA had an actual net worth that was only 66.5 percent of what was expected, given his age and income at the time of hitting the millionaire threshold. When he first became a millionaire (again augmented) 11 years prior, the typical BA respondent was 45 years of age and had an annual realized household income of $89,167. Given this age and income, his expected net worth was only $401,252. But it was actually 2.49 times greater than the expected amount. At the time he first reached the million-dollar plateau, the typical BA generated the equivalent of $11.20 of net worth for every $1.00 of his annual realized household income.

The median age of an IA member when he first reached the affluent threshold was 45 years 5 months while his median annual realized household income was $331,250. Thus the typical IA member needed $1.00 of income to generate the equivalent of $3.02 of net worth. Contrast this figure with the $11.20 of net worth accumulated for every $1.00 of income generated by the typical member of the BA club. It becomes clear that the BAs, those who played great defense, were much more efficient than the offense-minded IAs by a ratio of 3.7 to 1 ($11.20 versus $3.02).

Why We Buy

Why do so many people hyperspend? Prior to the economic reversals we have recently encountered, most people had similar sets of beliefs about the positive relationship between spending on products and happiness. But in reality, increased spending does not make one more satisfied with life overall. For many people, it actually has the opposite effect. But, conversely, who are those who are happy? Typically they are those who spend below their means while building wealth and ultimately becoming financially secure.

How is it that some people gravitate toward becoming BA types while others emulate the hyperconsuming lifestyles of the IA affluent? The extraordinarily "e-z" credit terms of the recent past, especially in the mortgage market, helped fuel our gluttonous ways, obviously. Yet even during the heyday of the "nothing down" era, some people never overspent or borrowed heavily. Some were millionaires, some were decamillionaires, and others were on their way to becoming wealthy. How did they remain immune to the marketing and social pressures to spend, spend, spend? We'll look at those answers throughout this book but I'll give you a clue: You may be living in the biggest reason of all.

The best and most creative marketers in the world have worked hard to convince many of us that spending heavily will bring us all sorts of joy—we'll be more popular and admired. They have also conditioned us into believing that "you are what you purchase" and "you are superior to others if you outspend, out display them." And, accordingly, "the products you own supposedly define you and your achievements in life." So, why not buy now? Why wait to become financially secure, a genuine socioeconomic success before you significantly upgrade your collection of consumer artifacts?

Nature and Nurture

Most of the BA types had a different socialization process when growing up than those in the IA group did. If you are like most of the high-net-worth and/or high-income producers I have surveyed (more than 9 out of 10, or 92 percent), you will be able to answer the following question with certainty:

In comparison with all the parents of students you attended middle/ high school with, where do you believe your parents ranked at that time in terms of their annual household income?

There is a significant inverse relationship between where the types of respondents thought their parents ranked in income and their WX. Those who thought that their parents produced, relatively speaking, lower income when they were young still bear the scars today. This does not mean that all their parents were poor. Some were middle-income producers. But, as one IA respondent put it, "I went to a high school with a lot of rich kids." In a way, the high-income-producing hyperconsumers of today are making up for the past. Now they think, "I'll do what the rich do; I will spend heavily on products that denote my current or future economic success."

To a considerable degree, it is the uniquely American upward socioeconomic mobility that fuels much of the hyperconsuming engine of the market for luxury goods, prestige products, upscale brands, expensive homes, and so on. In America, it is not at all unusual for children from modest means to become high-income-producing adults. Then they are fooled into thinking that all those with the means to do so hyperconsume. They are wrong. Most rich people become wealthy and stay that way because they are frugal and are investment, not consumption, oriented. Most of those who have high wealth indices said that they came from families that lived well below their means. Their parents purposely avoided living in homes situated in neighborhoods that would constantly remind them that:

> We have financial difficulty living in this environment . . . of making ends meet. Among our neighbors we are on the low end of the economic scale.

It is not the BA who likely encountered this type of environment while growing up. Instead, it is the IA. Plus, the IA types are significantly less likely than the BAs to say: "My parents taught me how to invest and manage money."

What happens when your children attend school and/or interact otherwise with kids who display an abundance of expensive consumer products? Your children are likely to ask you why you do not supply them with the same collection of products. Tell them essentially what the parents of the BA types told their children:

- Never judge the true quality, the caliber of a person, by what can be purchased.
- Often people who dress and drive as if they are rich are not. (Show your children the data given in this book.)
- Try Shakespeare if all else fails: "All that glitters is not gold."

For some, hyperspending is an attempt to somehow change their humble beginnings, in essence to change the past. But it is futile. One cannot change history. Look at increases in income first as opportunities to invest more and to become financially independent. If the need to spend on high-status products arises, one should wait to spend until after one is wealthy, not before. Otherwise one may never become financially secure.

It's Only Money

One of the most memorable focus group interviews I ever conducted was with eight highly compensated professionals. All were IA types with mid- to high-six-figure annual incomes. Four were physicians and the others were attorneys.

One respondent dismissed the notion of budgeting. But he did mention that his wife owned 187 pairs of shoes. Then he said approvingly that when she couldn't decide which color of shoe to buy, she bought three pairs. Then a surgeon, who earned over $400,000 annually, reported that he had three boats and five cars; but he had not gotten around to developing a pension plan. He said of his colleagues: "I don't know even one guy who hasn't been beaten to death in the financial markets. As a result, they don't have anything. At least I'm going to enjoy spending my money."

Later this same surgeon summed up his financial philosophy: "Money," he said with a wave of his hand, "is the most easily renewable resource." Even today, too many people spend as if money (their earned income) is the most easily renewable resource. Now a growing number are shocked to realize that they were mistaken. Highly compensated physicians, attorneys, and managers of public corporations tend to have low wealth indices; that is, they are highly concentrated in the IA segment. Managers of private corporations are not. They tend to be quite frugal and invest heavily in their own businesses.

What other occupational groups have significantly higher wealth indices than the norm? Two of the more revealing are engineers (discussed in detail in later chapters) and educators, such as teachers and professors. The financial lifestyles of educators, often the lowest-income-generating professions, actually have high wealth indices that epitomize the BA population in America. Thus, I think it is safe to say that the ways and means to secure wealth building apply to almost everyone who wants to become financially secure.

Indeed, educators as a group are very productive in terms of transforming their household income into wealth. In the survey undertaken as the basis for this book, for every educator who was in the IA category, there were three in the BA segment. This finding is consistent with the other studies I have conducted over the past 30 years.

Another piece of compelling data is illuminating as well: The estate data of recently deceased Americans from the Internal Revenue Service shows that of all people who died in 2004, fewer than 18 in 1,000 (1.76 percent) had a gross estate of at least $1.5 million; of those, about 1 in 12 (8.13 percent) of these wealthy decedents were once educators. Given the proportion of the working population, the expected concentration should have been only about 4.21 percent. In other words, educators are overrepresented by a multiple of nearly two times, given their overall representation in the working population. Many educators do not have the money or income needed to spend lavishly *and* become rich. Income is a correlate of wealth, but it is not wealth. While it is true that most teachers individually do not earn six-figure annual incomes, annual income is nowhere near a perfect predictor of wealth. Plus, most educators are part of a two-income household. In many ways, it is not how much one earns annually that counts: It is how one lives each year. It is how much one saves and invests annually that really matters. For most people, accumulating wealth is a long-distance marathon. It takes years and years of frugality and wise investing to accumulate wealth. If one does not earn a six- or seven-figure income today, one can still become wealthy tomorrow if one is financially disciplined and strongly motivated. Many educators possess these very characteristics.

Let's use Laura's mom, Dr. E., whom I profiled in an earlier work, as an example. Dr. E. has been a professor for more than 30 years, and she is still going strong. Says Laura:

> My mother is a classic Balance Sheet Affluent . . . never made much money (college professor—you should know about that—at a small women's college). But [she] always saved religiously, and is going to retire a multimillionaire (if she ever retires). Even now that she has the money, she refuses to spend it. Typical example is the Miata. She lusted after one for 10 years, but refused to buy such a frivolous car. All of that angst, over a $20,000 car, in a world of $50,000 SUVs! She finally gave in and got one six months ago—but only because she found a great deal on a used one.

In fact, Dr. E. is a millionaire today with a net worth in excess of $2.5 million. But, like most of the BAs I have surveyed, she never ever owned a home valued at $400,000 or more before she became rich. Is Professor E. just a rare occurrence within the world of the wealthy? Actually, her profile is pro forma among those millionaires who never earned a high income.

Obviously, something other than income accounts for the presence of so many educators within the millionaire category (alive or dead). I estimate that there are currently more than 350,000 millionaire educators, working or retired. Teachers tend to be a frugal group. They are savers and investors more than they are spenders. In fact, it is considered bad taste among most educators to overdress or to overspend on cars, homes, or so-called appearance-enhancing products and services. Plus, they are anything but credit prone. As an example, in a national survey, I recently profiled the high-income-producing population of two-career couples where at least one partner is an educator. Nearly 7 in 10 have no car loans, no boat loan, no home equity loans, no unpaid credit card balances. Less than half (48 percent) of the doctors, attorneys, and corporate executives with high incomes can say the same.

Most educators work in an environment with certain characteristics that are strong correlates of wealth accumulation. Pension planning, investment seminars, and tax-advantage supplemental investment plans are part of an educator's on-campus socialization process. Adopting a frugal consumption lifestyle and developing good financial and investing skills are all akin to catching a cold. What happens when you consistently come into contact with sick people? You get sick. Work with frugal people, and you may become frugal. Associate with colleagues who are astute investors, and you may become wealthy one day. Many educators become good investors because their jobs require them to research, study, and learn new material on a continuous basis. These processes are easily applied to making investment decisions.

Most BAs, as a group and not just educators, live in moderately priced homes located in nondescript neighborhoods. Few live in mansions or anywhere near homes valued at $1 million or more (excluding those who live in California). It is not hard to avoid emulating the consumption habits of the IAs if you do not live near any of them. And in relations to their neighbors, where do the BAs rank along the wealth (net worth) continuum? Nationwide, outside of the state of California, most rank in the top 5 percent within their respective neighborhoods.

Who are those other millionaire types who live in neighborhoods that contain wealthy educators? In terms of occupational categories, I find engineers, supermarket store managers, discount store managers, owners of small businesses (nonretail), mathematicians, regional planners, writers and chemists, just to name a few.

So who else has been acting rich? Given the consumption, it's more than just millionaires in the IA category. They are rich and can afford to act rich. The reality is that most people who act rich are nowhere near being wealthy. In fact, most of those who live in neighborhoods where the BAs reside are living above their means. The same applies to neighborhoods where the IAs can be found. Why is it that most of the neighbors of millionaires are not rich? They are living well beyond their means. They try to emulate the consumption habits of their rich neighbors. But their rich neighbors, especially those BAs, are able to live comfortably on 80 percent of their household's income. They earn more and accumulate more than most of their neighbors. They have no difficulty buying a new Toyota, for example, every four years. Their neighbors imitate them. They do the same. Yet they can barely make the car payments.

What does this all mean? If you want to become wealthy via the BA way, live in a neighborhood where your household is among the top income generators. For example, what if your household's total realized income is in, say, the high five figures? Then live in a neighborhood where the median market value of a home is less than $300,000. Do so, and the chances are that among your neighbors, your household will likely be in the top 20 percent along the income continuum. Then live and consume as though your household's income was only 80 percent of what it actually generates. Save and invest the rest. Now you are on your way to becoming wealthy.

What is a good rule if you are determined to become wealthy?

The market value of the home you purchase should be less than three times your household's total annual realized income.

It is okay to own a pricey home after you become a millionaire. But most IAs did not wait that long. Two-thirds of the IAs own/occupy primary homes that have a current market value of $1 million or more. Most BA types are not house rich. They became millionaires in part because they adhered to one of the golden rules of wealth building that I wrote about in *The Millionaire Next Door*.

If you're not yet wealthy but want to be someday, never purchase a home that requires a mortgage that is more than twice your household's annual realized income.

A Good Habit Is Hard to Break

What are some of the habitual differences that distinguish BAs from IAs? Here are a few things you'll come to learn throughout this book:

- BAs are more than three times as likely than IAs to say that their favorite brand of suit is JCPenney private label, Joseph A. Banks, Macy's, Menswear Outlet, or Sears private label. IAs favor Brooks Brothers, Hickey Freeman, Armani, Joseph Abboud, Nordstrom's private label, and Polo.
- BAs are significantly more likely than IAs to purchase apparel (not just suits) from Kohl's, Marshall's, Ross, Sears, Target, and Wal-Mart. IAs are three times more likely than BAs to patronize upscale apparel retailers such as Brooks Brothers, Neiman Marcus, Nordstrom's, and Saks Fifth Avenue.
- Most of BAs wear a watch that cost under $200. In contrast, most IAs wear an expensive prestige make of watch, such as Rolex,

Omega, Breitling, Cartier, and Tag Heuer. Also, most of IAs own multiples of these prestige brands.

- Does your liquor cabinet contain a variety of premium and super-premium brands of distilled beverages? If so, shake hands with a typical member of the IA group. You have something in common. BAs, however, are significantly more likely to purchase middle-of-the-road brands of spirits. More significantly, IAs have many more bottles (three times as many) in their home inventory.

- Over the past 10 years, what make of motor vehicle has been acquired more than any other by each group? IAs like Mercedes-Benz, ranked first, followed closely by Lexus, while the favorite among BAs was Ford followed by Toyota. What about the most popular make in terms of the most recently acquired motor vehicle? Lexus was number one among the IAs; Toyota ranked first among the BAs. Some millionaires, especially those who are most productive in converting income into wealth, drive vehicles well below their means.

Rendering Unto Caesar

How much more difficult do you think it would be for you to become wealthy and at the same time support your family plus one other? Think of the one other as the typical BA unit. In a way, that is exactly what the IAs do. The average IA paid more in income tax than the typical BA generated in income during a year: $95,847 versus $89,167. Overall, IAs pay nearly six times more in tax than the BAs. IAs pay the equivalent of about 10 percent of their wealth each year in tax. BAs pay less than 2 percent. The large tax burden associated with being an IA is reflected in their less-than-stellar wealth index.

This situation will worsen given federal and state tax increases that high-income earners now face. The road to becoming rich via the IA method is lined with income tax tolls and consumption-inspired road-blocks and detours. If you are determined to hyperspend like most of IAs, a high income is required to buy prestige consumer goods. So is paying high income taxes (to say nothing of sales taxes on the goods purchased).

Avoiding the Cereal Trap

We have all fallen trap to the brand game, the symbolism, and hype to greater or lesser degree. I admit that I have fallen for the pitch. At one time, my income increased more than fourfold in one year. During this time I went from working as an instructor while earning a doctorate to being an assistant professor. A year later we bought a home, a new car, and our first beagle. But that is not all; I also changed breakfast cereals! Ah, the influence of advertising that capitalizes on the needs of the socio economically mobile. I gave up Cheerios for a competing brand that touted health and nutrition. It was a cereal for sophisticated and discriminating adult consumers. Its brand name sounded like a secret chemical formula. It also cost more than Cheerios, but I was willing to pay extra for a brand, a badge that reflected my recent achievements and success.

This cereal tasted like cardboard, but I suffered with the brand for nearly a year. Then I noticed an article in *Consumer Reports* that dealt with the nutritional content of 44 popular brands of breakfast cereals. According to the study, Cheerios ranked second in the estimated nutritional quality among the brands of cereal tested. And where did my upscale brand rank? It was second from the bottom, in 43rd place.

What does this have to do with acting rich? People who are encountering upward socioeconomic mobility are often most vulnerable to advertising themes that imply: "All rich people, all successful folks buy our brand, 'Chemically enhanced Wheat Dust #127.' It costs more but it is worth it. Don't be the only high-income household in America that is without #127, the symbol of achievement."

If I, who study and analyze the rich, can fall into the symbol trap, is it any wonder that many others have as well, though sadly much more expensively? In a way, it's not your fault: The messages bombard you every day. They are nearly impossible to escape. If you live in an urban, metropolitan area (made worse if you live on either of the coasts), every day is a downpour of marketing, advertising, telegraphing, and now Twitter messages that tell you what success looks like and that practically demands that you act successful *now* because if you are not a success, you are a loser.

If you don't wear X or drink Y, then it almost seems as though the ads are telling you that you are a loser. Who doesn't want to be thought of as discriminating? Everyone wants to be seen as "special" and "deserving." It takes a strong will to beat back the messaging.

It is said that the first step in solving a problem is to identify and name it. Our problem, then, is acting rich. The second step is to understand it, and the third step is to craft a plan. I do not purport to give you specific financial guidance, but I will help you understand that much of what you believe about being successful is almost assuredly wrong. After reading this book and learning how rich people *really* spend their money (and not the glittering rich outliers), you will see the marketing hype for what it is: smoke and mirrors intended to do nothing more than part you from your money. The makers of Grey Goose may not care about your retirement; they care about selling you vodka. I will show you how to avoid falling into the acting rich trap, how to get out of it, and how to start living like a real millionaire—and not a figment of your or, more likely, some marketer's imagination.

Most important, by taking this journey through the numbers that uncover the real behaviors of the rich, you will learn that most rich people do not drive their balance sheets or wear their income statements. In essence, most understate their considerable achievements. Their satisfaction with life has much more to do with becoming a socioeconomic success than having an expensive home filled with upscale brands. Those who think that acting rich must be predicated on hyperconsumption are likely to end up on the short side of both the wealth and the happiness scales.

A study conducted by Ryan Howell, an assistant professor of psychology at San Francisco State University, and presented at the 2009 annual meeting of the Society for Personality and Social Psychology, showed that people are made happier by experiences than by things.[4] So, I suppose, if you are going to spend like you are rich, at least do it on social interactions that will actually make you happy, such as taking vacations or going to the theater. As an added bonus, Ryan's study indicated that cost is not important; just have a life experience—one that has the added benefit of enhancing the lives of loved ones and friends around you.

One of the things that set wealthy people apart from others is that they have a wide variety of interests and activities. In fact, there is a substantial correlation between the number of interests and activities that people are involved in and their level of financial wealth. Some wealthy people feel that owning a vacation home, for instance, would restrict them by obligating them to spend time at that property; if they didn't spend the time there, then the dollars spent on the property would be underutilized. Millionaires value their time. The allocation of their dollars flows accordingly, almost as second nature.

Life experiences, preferably positive ones, will not only enhance your bottom line but will also steer you clear of another problem: your children. The experiences we have as children, the experiences we give children, teach them a lesson they hold for life. Today's children get an average of 70 new toys a year.[5] We may inadvertently be providing the next generation with a foundation for permanent financial dependence and dissatisfaction with life.

The financial crisis of 2008–2009 (and for who knows how much longer) has forced many to stop and think about how they spend. But experience shows that once warmer economic winds blow (and they will come again), we will quickly revert to old ways. In fact, a case could be made that the spending diet has the potential to lead to a wicked binge spending spree later. In the late 1990s, spending was based on inflated stock portfolios. Once that bubble burst, we barely stopped to catch our breath and considered the reduction in our retirement savings before we enjoyed the ultimate net worth enhancer: inflated real estate values that many were quick to cash in to buy the lifestyles of the glittering rich.

2 | Everything You Think about Rich Is Wrong

My goal . . . you want to know about my number-one financial goal? It's to spend my last dollar the day I die. Nothing left over . . . otherwise I would have deprived myself.
          —Fortune 50 corporation senior executive

You can act rich or actually become rich. Few of us will ever be able to do both, and we certainly won't get rich by acting the part before we have the financial resources with which to pay for la dolce vita.

We live in a time when it has never been easier to act rich than to actually become rich, even with the devastation of the financial crisis. At the end of the day, not only are we bad actors because it is simply impossible for us to keep up with the glittering rich (if we buy one expensive, prestige car, they buy 20), but we are terribly misguided and ill informed about how millionaires really spend and what they actually buy. Instead of focusing on millionaires generally, we are enamored with the few glitteringly rich people, but we miss that even though they spend like crazy and often ostentatiously, their spending is nonetheless well within their means—in fact, below their means. The Jay Gould family famously dropped tens of millions of dollars here and there, rarely even accounting for loans of $3 million on their books; their wealth was so vast that it was hardly missed. And this at the turn of the twentieth century when $3 million was really something. Even today most people will never attain that kind of wealth.

While it would do us a world of good to emulate Horatio Alger or Benjamin Franklin or any number of modern-day millionaires (such as the owner of the hardware store down the street), we instead want what Britney or Madonna or Jay Z are photographed or filmed as having without actually having achieved their financial status. We understand why Damon Runyon, upon receiving his first paycheck as a New York newspaper reporter, dropped the entire load on the most extravagant shoe trunk imaginable, even though he had but a single pair of shoes and was in arrears to his landlord and friends.[1] Spending extravagantly is fun!

Amusing though the antics of celebrities may be, in following their prescription, we are but poseurs and will assuredly run into the poorhouse eventually, if the financial crisis hasn't already forced us there. In the early part of 2009, there was much outrage over this and that politician, bailout plan, and banker and insurance giant bonus-receiving employee. But at the end of the day, we should be outraged with ourselves for having bought into a myth: the myth that we can have the things the glittering rich have without having the financial resources; the myth that acting rich would somehow convey real wealth upon us.

In our hyperconsuming society, there exists a set of social expectations. In the United States, in particular (though one could make the case that the disease has spread throughout the western world, my surveys have been confined to the United States), people are judged by certain conspicuously displayed symbols, such as watches and motor vehicles. As we will see, certain occupations are prone to high incomes but low net worth. The people in these occupations—and society reinforces it—believe that with a certain position and income come certain accoutrements. Ironically, many of these occupations, such as doctors, take great pride in the status they have attained, but more often than not they are poorer than blue-collar–type millionaires. If these people looked at the hard data and the numbers on the balance sheets, they would see that they have status, they have expensive toys and tastes, and they have no money while their less elite, "tasteless" brethren with fewer or less expensive things have way more money.

The reality is that most millionaires are quite consistent when it comes to the price points for the items they purchase. The term "moderately priced" typically applies to how the majority of millionaires allocate their dollars. This applies across the wide spectrum of the things they own. But moderate spending on suits, cars, homes, and such will not get one noticed or much envied by strangers on the street. But neither notoriety nor envy will pay your mortgage, fund your children's college education, nor even support you when you are retired.

Just Because the Glossies Show It Doesn't Mean Millionaires Buy It

Let's look at how real millionaires spend their money and what they pay for goods and services.

Real millionaires pay about $16 (tip included) for a haircut at a traditional barbershop—no appointments taken, no coloring provided. Only 5.7 percent of millionaires surveyed nationally paid $1,000 or more for their most recently acquired suit. In fact, even among the very affluent, such as decamillionaires (those with a financial net worth of $10 million or more), the median price paid for a suit was only $482. No James Bond Brioni suits for today's millionaires. So who are they selling all those $2,000-plus suits to, exactly? Dress for success may be a valid aphorism for the office, but overspending in anticipation of future financial wealth will not make anyone rich.

But rich people buy expensive watches, right?

Trey is worth over $20 million. The watch he wears every day was purchased at a Wal-Mart store for $15. Why does he wear such an inexpensive watch? The answer is quite simple. Trey's industrial real estate properties do not care what he paid for his watch.

Jim H. of Texas has a net worth in excess of $30 million. Jim and his family, along with six dogs, live in a log home. The choice of a log home is understandable since Jim is a forest farmer. His watch of choice is "a $300 Swiss Army" brand. He wears it "everywhere," even when he is mowing down weeds and unwanted brush with his Kubota tractor, all the while listening to XM radio.

What do the folks at Jim's upscale health club think of him, given his inexpensive watch? Trick question. Jim is not a health club rat. He does not even have a personal trainer. Yet Jim is in excellent physical condition. He stays in shape and enhances his knowledge of trees by personally planting 10,000 trees each year. He hires people to plant the other 3.5 million.

Why would someone worth over $30 million wear an inexpensive watch? The price he paid for his watch has no influence on the growth of his trees.

Trey and Jim share something else in common. Both feel it is important to be recognized by their respective industry's trade associations as winners. Conversely, they understand it is meaningless to be recognized and envied by strangers for a watch. Their badges of honor and success are not about inciting watch envy in others. They are rich and don't need to flaunt it to everyone they come in contact with on a daily basis. However, they both admit that it is very satisfying being rich, and they relish their industry awards and recognition. Of the millionaires surveyed who do wear expensive watches, half received them as gifts.

But rich people, millionaires, enjoy good food and drink, right?

Rodney has not accomplished much in life as of yet; he is a retail clerk. Yet he has a strong need to be admired, and so he drinks expensive vodka ($60 a bottle). In his mind, it is well worth the price. Rodney is convinced that by associating himself with a super-premium brand, he will be perceived as a winner. After all, he believes that people who are very rich and/or extraordinarily successful buy only super-premium brands of distilled beverages.

But Rodney does not realize that he has been conditioned into developing a strong preference for a super-premium brand that has nothing to do with the reality of what millionaires drink.

Rodney should meet Carlton, who is worth in excess of $30 million. He is a member of a special group of rich people who pay about $17 for a 1.75-liter plastic bottle of their favorite scotch. The other categories of spirits he serves his guests are also in the low-price, nonpremium plastic bottle variety. Most millionaires do not spend a lot of money on spirits. They entertain frequently and consider themselves warm and gracious hosts, but their entertaining is about social bonding, not about the brand of vodka served.

But rich people drink expensive wine, right?

In the last 30 years, a small subculture has grown into an industry in the hundreds of billions worldwide. A good amount of the wine sold is not inexpensive, and it seems as though anyone who can't talk wine is a loser. How much you spent on that bottle of wine you served at your dinner party defines success and your entrée into an elite club. In addition to the time wasted learning about ridiculously priced wines and the time wasted spent listening to silly wine talk, it turns out that only 16.5 percent of millionaires even care much about wine. (Yes, the majority of them do drink and enjoy wine, though presumably as part of entertaining, interacting with others, and relaxing and less about the actual "brand" of wine consumed.) In fact, only 7.3 percent of the millionaires surveyed own a bottle of wine that retailed for more than $100. But nearly 4 in 10 have wine of the $10 or less variety. (Many wine aficiona-dos buy their wine on the cheap and then store and save it for when it will be best; they know that the expensive bottles typically are more about hype than anything else.)

But every successful person drives a great car, you say?

Many people believe that all truly rich, successful people drive prestige makes of cars. This is why so many aspirationals drive these types of cars. In their view, drivers of "common" makes of motor vehicles, such as Toyota, Honda, Chevrolet, Ford, and the like, are not people of high status, wealth, or the types of people who should be admired or emulated.

After housing, the auto myth may be the most pernicious of all about the rich. A bottle of Grey Goose will set you back $50 or $60, but the price of one of these expensive cars can be downright injurious to your financial health, aside from the fact that it depreciates drastically the minute the back tires leave the lot. It's just not true that the rich drive expensive cars. The median price paid for motor vehicles among mil-lionaires surveyed was $31,367. Truly rich people don't drive BMWs; they drive Toyotas. But nearly all of us believe otherwise. Witness this illuminating case:

Dear Dr. Stanley:

Our physician recently telephoned to tell us laughingly that he had received the "Millionaire Next Door" award.

When I questioned him, he explained that the hospital where he works hired a new security guard who refused to let him into the doctors' parking lot; the guard didn't believe he was one because of the car he drives, a Honda.

We very much enjoyed your book and wish you continued success.

Sincerely,
Mrs. J.A.M.

The physician in this case is a millionaire. In spite of his socioeconomic achievements, he does not express his success by driving an expensive prestige make of motor vehicle. Better yet, he can laugh over the parking lot incident. How many of us would be amused by being denied access to a place we are supposed to be, have in fact earned the right to be, because of the make of our car? Even parking lot attendants make assumptions about people, their profession, and their net worth based on car make and model. What would the security guard think if he knew that only one in four doctors in the high-income category has an investment portfolio worth $1 million or more? In general, high-income-producing but low-net-worth physicians have a propensity to acquire luxury items, such as expensive prestige makes of motor vehicles. But balance sheet affluent doctors drive Toyotas!

Would you change your thinking about cars if you knew that only about 7 percent of new passenger vehicles sold in the United States in 2006 were purchased by millionaires, but that one in three people who traded in their old car for a new one were upside down and owed more on the trade-in than its market value?

So rich people don't drink Grey Goose or buy expensive wine or European model cars. They must buy boats!

But they don't. The majority of millionaires in America (70 percent) have never ever owned a boat or a yacht, not even a raft. What about those with more than just $1 million? Two-thirds (66 percent) of the decamillionaires I surveyed have never owned a boat, yacht, sailboat, trawler, fishing vessel, or any other vehicle that floats.

How about those millionaires who actually purchased a boat sometime during their lifetime? Most bought one, sold it, and never bought another one. These people found little or no satisfaction from owning and operating a boat. But their satisfaction with life increased just after they unloaded their watercraft. So why did they ever purchase a boat in the first place? Many were favorably impressed with the seemingly high level of happiness demonstrated by the people they met at boat shows. Could it be that boat ownership is an impediment to building wealth? More than 93 percent of boating enthusiasts are not millionaires. Could it be that owning a boat and becoming a millionaire are mutually exclusive? Here is where the power of marketing and advertising shows itself fiercely. Significant dollars are spent on persuading people to buy boats—marketing that offers the promise of instant happiness. Boat advertisements depict all those happy people boating across the lake in their super-runabout. The ads practically scream "Happiness is but a boat purchase away." Turns out that boat owners may be less satisfied with life than most people.

So, millionaires must spend their money on vacation homes. Who else has been buying all that property?

Once again, the numbers belie the truth: Most millionaires do not own a vacation home.

I once considered buying a vacation home. At the time I was not close to being rich. Can you say "e-z" credit? It was tempting and I came close to taking the plunge, but about the same time, I was hired by a large trust organization to conduct a national study of multimillionaires. The results had a significant influence on my way of thinking. Most of the millionaires studied (those with a net worth of $5 million or more) did not own a second home. Faced with the facts, I thought that it might be better to "put a few bucks in the bank" before buying a second home. Twenty years later, I did buy a second home for $76,000, a small cabin (1,200 square feet of living space) on the top of a mountain overlooking the Appalachian Trail.

Much has changed in the past 25 years. There are a lot more millionaires, even with the economic downturns and market crashes. According to the National Association of Realtors, second homes accounted for 4 of 10 residential home sales in 2005. Who bought all these vacation homes? The newly minted millionaires? In fact, 64 percent of the millionaires surveyed never owned a vacation home, beach bungalow, or mountain cabin, not even a lean-to or tree hut in the woods.

If it is not the millionaire segment of our economy that drove the growth of the market for second homes, then what was it? Who bought these properties? According to the National Association of Realtors, the typical second home buyer was 52 years of age and had a median household income of $80,600. That is just a bit lower than the median household income ($81,700) of someone who purchased a new Harley-Davidson motorcycle in 2006.[2] But only 3 in 10 Harley-Davidson buyers graduated from college. Most home buyers attended college. Furthermore, I estimate that the median embellished net worth of those who purchased vacation homes in 2006 was approximately $380,000.

Could it be that some vacation-home buyers, who were not really wealthy, wished to emulate the behavior of those who were already wealthy? If so, they were emulating behavior that doesn't exist. Some second-home buyers may have enhanced their balance sheets this way. More often these buyers grossly underestimated the real cost (in terms of dollars and time) of buying, furnishing, maintaining, commuting to, renting, and possibly selling a second home. Time is money. Place a high price on your time; most millionaires do so. Like them, be less concerned with the prestige that may come with owning something, whether it is a vacation home or a watch.

Look at the statistics. What degree of prestige, if any, was bestowed on all those people who bought a vacation home in 2005? Most of these homes were not multimillion-dollar retreats. It may be more prestigious to hang around with people who recently purchased a Harley-Davidson motorcycle. In general, they generated higher incomes.

Should you buy a vacation home (particularly now that many properties are coming on the market cheap)? Buy if you and your family will love hanging out there and if you can afford to do so. Do not buy if you are looking to increase your prestige. At the end of the day, success cannot be purchased.

Edmund S. Phelps, the recipient of the 2006 Nobel Prize in economic science and professor at Columbia University, can't be bothered. In an interview he explained that "he and his wife, an interpreter fluent in four languages have lived for 32 years in a three-bedroom apartment. . . . They [don't] own . . . a country home, not wanting the bother of maintaining a second residence, [instead] Ms. Phelps said they like to travel."[3]

Success is winning the Nobel Prize or some other accomplishment. Success is not a second home.

The Money Pit

When we make home-buying choices, we look at several factors, mostly the carry costs of the home such as mortgage and taxes. It's basic math: Do I make enough money to pay the bills? Stupid loans aside, it has long been a fairly easy question to answer when buying a home. As the cost of borrowing dropped, we could move up so much more easily. New homes were especially enticing. Most people think of homes being a money pit in upkeep and repair or remodeling. But if we could buy a brand-new home, then we would avoid these problems.

What we don't realize is that the true cost of living in certain homes and neighborhoods is unseen but truly devastating. I believe the greatest detriment to building wealth is our home/neighborhood environment. If you live in a pricey home and neighborhood, you will act and buy like your neighbors. In other words, human beings have an innate tendency to act and be like those around them—to fit in—and even to compete (in a neighborly way, of course). The type of home we live in and where we choose to live often takes the greatest toll on our financial wealth, and from it, all other perils flow.

The more expensive homes, the more affluent neighborhoods are a vortex of sociological forces. As we will see throughout this book, the more affluent the neighborhood, the more its residents spend on almost every conceivable product and service. From cars to haircuts, and from wine to watches, those living in "prestige estates" spend more. We take consumption cues from our neighbors. If many of our neighbors have a much higher level of income and wealth than we do, we will have set ourselves up to lose the war before we have even begun to battle.

If the priority is to act rich, then move from a modest community to a high-consumption neighborhood. Here there will be enormous social pressure for you to spend, spend, and spend more on just about every category of consumer products and services.

Contrary to popular belief, however, most of the self-made millionaires I have studied have one thing in common: They were able to build wealth precisely because they never lived in a home or neighborhood environment where their domestic overhead made it difficult for them to build wealth. In essence, they ran their households like a productive business. It is not only about how much you make (or generate in sales). More important, it is how much you keep. And the "keep" component begins and ends at your home address.

Buying an expensive home is a great way to fool people into thinking that you are wealthy. And it is likely that you will not feel out of place. Many people who live in pricey homes situated in tony neighborhoods are not millionaires. If you want to actually become rich one day, then enhance your chances by living in a modest home—say, one valued at under $300,000.

Remember that there are just over 4 million millionaire households in the United States. There are over 54.5 million existing homes in America (or more than 70 percent of the total) that have a market value of under $300,000. Only about 2 percent of these homes are owned/occupied by millionaires (see Table 2.1). Nevertheless, there are more than 1.1 million

Table 2.1   Homeowners in America: High Income versus High Net Worth?

Value of Home	% of Households with		Homeowners with Investments of $1 million or more (%)/ Homeowners with incomes of $200,000 or more (%)
	Annual Income of $200,000 or more	Investments of $1 million or more	
Less than $300,000	0.99	2.09	2.11
$300,000–$449,999	5.19	6.20	1.20
$450,000–$599,999	11.45	10.11	0.88
$600,000–$999,999	23.16	15.10	0.65
$1,000,000 or more	41.41	27.09	0.65

millionaires (or 28.3 percent of the total) residing in homes and neighborhoods that would not likely be classified in the high-prestige category. Included in this population are more than 67,000 millionaires who currently reside in mobile homes. Of course, this translates into a small percentage of the approximately 8 million American households that occupy mobile homes.

But you say, "I don't want to emulate people who do not act rich. I want to act like the people who live in homes valued at $1 million or more." Then upgrade to a more expensive home and neighborhood. You will think that you are acting rich. Millionaires are more concentrated in homes valued at $1 million or more, but only about 27 percent of homes in this league are owned/occupied by millionaires, which equates to 13 times the concentration of millionaires who live in homes valued under $300,000. A substantial proportion of high-income producers live in expensive homes, but the truth is that most are not millionaires. Nearly three out of four of those living in expensive homes, in spite of their high realized incomes, are not really wealthy.

Statistically, it is much easier to become a millionaire if you live and consume like those who live in modest homes than in expensive ones. Other than those homeowners who live more or less within their means, there are two other categories of homeowners. Within every home market value category in America, there are some who live well below their means. Among them are those more than 1.1 million millionaires who live in homes valued under $300,000. Conversely, there are those who are only acting as though they can afford to live in the home that they "just had to buy." If you examined homes by value from the lowest to the highest, you would find that as the value of homes increases, so does the proportion of people who are living well above their means. Of course, this does not mean that all people who live in modest homes are living below their means. Nor does it suggest that all the people who live in modest homes are enjoying life. But it does suggest that there are a lot of people living well above their means who are likely not terribly satisfied with their lives.

Most millionaires do not live in homes that have a market value of $1 million or more. About 90 percent live in homes valued at under $1 million. But because high-income-producing households are more highly concentrated in expensive homes/neighborhoods than are millionaire homeowners, it will be more difficult, more expensive, and less probable for you to become wealthy if you live in a neighborhood that has a high concentration of high-market-value homes. As an example, look at the numbers for those who live in homes valued in the $1 million or more category. Four in 10 (41.41 percent) are high-income producers (i.e., having annual realized household income of $200,000 or more). Yet, in contrast, only 27.09 percent of those who reside in homes valued at this level are millionaires. The ratio of millionaires who own/occupy homes at this level in contrast to the percentage of high-income-producing households who own homes at this market value is .65. In other words, it takes the equivalent of 100 high-income-producing homeowners who live in pricey homes to produce just 65 millionaires. But the ratio of those who reside in homes in the less-than-$300,000 market value range is 2.11, meaning that it took the equivalent of only 100 high-income-generating homeowners to produce 211 millionaires.

In the United States, at least, wealthy households are much more highly diffused geographically than are high-income-producing households. There are nearly three times more millionaire households (1,138,070, or approximately 28.3 percent of the total, versus 403,211, or about 10 percent of the total) living in homes valued at $300,000 or less than there are millionaires living in homes valued at $1 million or more. The data strongly indicate that this ratio of "wealth-building productivity" is inversely related to the market value of one's own home as well as those of one's neighbors. Once the market value begins to move up beyond the $500,000 level, wealth-building productivity moves into the unproductive range (i.e., less than 1.00). Nationwide only about one in eight owner-occupied primary homes has a current value of $500,000 or more. Buying a more expensive home is likely to decrease the odds of becoming financially independent.

An article published in the *Wall Street Journal* supported my research findings. In it the author contrasts the efficacy of buying a $1 million home as opposed to a $400,000 home and investing the balance in mutual funds. What you would save by not supporting a $1 million home? The author contends that in the long run, the "small house/invest the rest" strategy is far superior to the "big house" strategy in terms of return on your money:

> [Y]our portfolio would be worth $2 million in today's dollars . . . almost twice what you would pocket with the "big house" strategy. With the "big house" strategy, not only would you face hefty mortgage payments. But . . . also . . . property taxes, maintenance costs, homeowner's insurance and utilities. However . . . you would live in a grander place but that just highlights what this is all about. Buying a bigger house

isn't an investment. Rather it is a lifestyle choice—and it comes with a brutally large price tag.[4]

And this assessment came during the real estate boom. If it was better to buy down-market when valuations were reaching epic proportions, wouldn't it be safe to say that it's even better to downsize now?

To enhance your chances of becoming financially independent, you should live in a home and neighborhood environment that has high wealth-building productivity characteristics. You need to be surrounded by neighbors who have lower incomes than your household generates.

Status Is as Status Does

Our net worth, whether we calculate it based on the size of our investment portfolio or our augmented net worth, is nonetheless only "worth" what we can liquidate relatively easily for cash. Real millionaires have investment portfolios and savings that provide them a cushion to weather asset bubbles and crashes. If the value of their stock portfolio decreases, they have significant bond holdings, for instance, or they own a valuable business. Even if we look at the augmented net worth of the millionaires in the $1 million to under $2.5 million net worth category, including the value of their homes, for instance, we find that the "home real estate" portion of the overall portfolio is only about 27 percent (see Table 2.2). In other words, it is just over a quarter of their entire net worth, not their entire net worth or the bulk of their net worth. In fact, the wealthier the person, the lower the value of their home as an overall percentage of net worth. Also keep in mind that typical millionaires have an outstanding mortgage balance of less than one-third of the market value of their home.

Living in a pricey neighborhood will cost you more than just a jumbo-size mortgage and is not, in fact, how most millionaires live. Why is it that most millionaires live in moderately priced homes situated in less-than-

Table 2.2   Homes of Millionaires in America: Average Value by Augmented Net Worth

Net Worth	Average Net Worth	Personal Residence/ Homes: Average Value	Value of a Home as a % of Net Worth	Net Worth to Home Value Ratio
$1,000,000–under $2,500,000	$1,493,804	$404,240	27.1	3.7
$2,500,000–under $5,000,000	$3,416,267	$620,779	18.2	5.5
$5,000,000–under $10,000,000	$6,859,864	$1,034,411	15.1	6.6
$10,000,000–under $20,000,000	$13,687,961	$1,818,699	13.3	7.5
$20,000,000 or more	$59,919,891	$2,735,436	4.6	21.9

Wealth Works database estimate for 2007.
Net worth (augmented) in estimates included the current value of all assets less liabilities.

prestigious neighborhoods? The majority report that their spouse (typically the wife) is more frugal than her frugal husband. In more than 80 percent of the cases, the husband in a millionaire household is the main breadwinner. Those respondents who are most productive in converting dollars of income into dollars of net worth often tell me, "I can't get my wife to spend money, no matter how hard I try." For these spouses, displaying a family's economic success through home and related products is not important.

Yet the status that society assigns to your occupation has much to do with the type of neighborhood in which you live. The higher your occupational status, the more likely you are to live in a neighborhood that contains high concentrations of expensive homes. Plus, a disproportionately large share of those with high occupational status reside in or near metropolitan areas. What is the predictable impact on your net worth if you live in an expensive home in an affluent neighborhood that is located within a high-cost-of-living metropolitan area? As discussed previously, these factors have a dampening effect on your ability to transform income into wealth.

As will be detailed later, within the high-income population, occupational status is negatively correlated with net worth. How can this be possible, given the fact that people with high occupational status tend to generate high incomes? The reality is that income is not wealth. Often high occupational status dictates high consumption. What if you live in or even near a geographically defined high-consumption environment? It is where most people with high occupational status live. In such environments, it is easy to deplete even substantial income through consumption. It costs a great deal to live among those clusters of people who have high incomes and high status, as you can see in Table 2.3. Call it high overhead.

You have a much better chance of becoming wealthy if you do not try to emulate the consumption habits of those with high occupational status. I have examined the wealth characteristics of 10 occupation groups (see Table 2.4). Consider two of the occupational groups: physicians and farmers. High-income-producing physicians are heavily concentrated in and around cities. They tend to live in fine homes situated in pricey neighborhoods, drive expensive motor vehicles, dress well, patronize expensive stores, and hyperconsume in a variety of other ways. Most farmers, irrespective of income level, live and work in rural areas. They do not demonstrate their socioeconomic status by living high on the consumption continuum. This applies to most farmers, even those who produce high incomes.

Approximately 4 in 10 physicians have an annual realized income of $200,000 or more. That equates to almost 13 times the percentage for the total household population in America. Yet in spite of this large percentage being in the high-income-producing group, only about 1 in 10 is a millionaire and has financial assets of $1 million or more. However, for every farmer with a high income, there are nearly 2 (1.9) having an investment portfolio worth at least $1 million. Overall, this figure grossly understates their total level of wealth since the calculations exclude equity holdings in

Table 2.3　Neighborhood Defined Consumption Lifestyles Where Millionaires Reside

Lifestyles and Consumption Habits (including Selected Brands)	Current Market Value (Median) of Homes by Neighborhoods		
	Group A	Group B	Group C
	$300,000–under $400,000	$1 million–under $1.2 million	$2 million–under $4 million
Opinions and Lifestyles (% Agreeing)			
Most good hosts I know serve expensive beverages, costly foods, etc.	34	51	68
I collect wine.	6	15	28
I am more frugal than my spouse.	29	44	47
Wine Orientation			
Typical price paid for a bottle of wine served to friends/neighbors in home (median).	$10.60	$14.77	$18.87
Number of bottles of wine currently in home inventory	6	18	37
Brands of Spirits Currently in Home Inventory (%)			
Vodka			
Absolut	25	32	37
Grey Goose	13	24	45
Smirnoff	27	23	28
Scotch			
Johnnie Walker Black	9	16	21
Chivas Regal	13	23	26
Dewar's	16	20	31
Glenlivet	10	15	23
Bourbon/Whiskey			
Jim Beam	14	11	10
Jack Daniel's	29	38	41
Maker's Mark	10	12	14

Table 2.3 Neighborhood Defined Consumption Lifestyles Where Millionaires Reside (*Continued*)

Lifestyles and Consumption Habits (including Selected Brands)	Current Market Value (Median) of Homes by Neighborhoods		
	Group A $300,000–under $400,000	**Group B** $1 million–under $1.2 million	**Group C** $2 million–under $4 million
Watches			
Brand Worn (%)			
Rolex	10	17	19
Seiko	32	15	12
Timex	18	12	7
% who paid over $1,000	12	29	44
Retail Patronage Habits			
Apparel Purchases Made in Past Year (%)			
Banana Republic	4	17	18
Brooks Brothers	7	19	32
JCPenney	36	10	6
Kohl's	34	18	9
Macy's	21	38	28
Neiman Marcus	2	13	23
Nordstrom	14	45	48
Polo Ralph Lauren	7	11	22
Saks Fifth Avenue	3	15	27
Sears	26	6	10
Wal-Mart	23	11	7
% who paid over $1,000 for most recent suit purchase	1	7	44
Price paid by men for most recent haircut (median $)	$13.50	$19.48	$23.25

(*Continued*)

Table 2.3   Neighborhood Defined Consumption Lifestyles Where Millionaires Reside (*Continued*)

Lifestyles and Consumption Habits (including Selected Brands)	Current Market Value (Median) of Homes by Neighborhoods		
	Group A	Group B	Group C
	$300,000–under $400,000	$1 million–under $1.2 million	$2 million–under $4 million
Motor Vehicle Acquisition Habits			
Make of Most Recent Acquisition (%)			
BMW	3	11	13
Chevrolet	9	5	7
Ford	12	6	6
Honda	7	6	3
Jaguar	2	6	13
Lexus	6	13	12
Mercedes-Benz	3	8	20
Porsche	1	1	13
Toyota	14	9	8
Volkswagen	4	11	10
Volvo	4	13	14
Number of miles on vehicle most recently traded in/sold/ discarded (median)	77,500	74,200	49,857
Number of years, months retained motor vehicle most recently traded in/sold/ discarded (median)	4 years, 7 months	4 years	3 years, 9 months
Purchase price of most recently acquired motor vehicle (median $)	$25,500	$31,625	$43,167

Table 2.4 Wealth-Producing Characteristics of Selected Occupations: High Income versus High Net Worth

Occupational Group	Millionaires		High-Income Producers		Millionaires (%)/High-Income Producers (%)		How many high income producers does it take to produce the equivalent of 100 millionaires?
	%	Rank	%	Rank	Ratio (× 100)	Rank	
Physicians and surgeons	10.01	4	38.30	1	26.1	182	383
Attorneys	8.85	5	24.33	5	36.4	173	275
Farmers and ranchers	4.76	40	2.53	134	188.2	8	53
Managers (middle level)	4.45	47	8.27	28	53.8	137	186
Managers: Farms and ranches	4.93	33	3.40	98	145.0	17	69
Funeral directors	6.10	21	4.36	73	140.0	21	72
Authors and writers	7.96	9	7.49	37	106.3	42	94
Mining and geological engineers	4.51	44	1.49	184	302.4	1	33
Chiropractors	4.90	35	14.37	10	34.1	177	293
Desktop publishers	3.29	81	1.54	178	214.3	6	47

farmland, homes, livestock, and equipment. It takes only 53 high-income generating farmers to produce 100 who are millionaires. But it takes 383 high-income-generating physicians to produce just 100 millionaires.

Many farmers are rich because they adhere to the basic rule for building wealth: Whatever your income is, live below your means. This is very difficult to do when you live in a high-occupational-status, hyperconsuming neighborhood that begets even more expenses. Move to Affluent Estates, live next to doctors, join country clubs. You will be mingling with hyperconsumers, but you won't likely be mixing it up with actual millionaires. If you want to hang out with truly wealthy people, then attend trade shows and conferences put on for farmers, scrap metal dealers, dry cleaners, engineers, and the like. Isn't it ironic that those who have the so-called highest status afforded by society, who live in the toniest neighborhoods, and who drive the nicest cars are ultimately not the richest?

Farmers are among the most productive occupational groups in terms of transforming income into wealth. But what occupational group is the most productive among the top 200 high-income-producing occupational categories in America? Mining engineers.

Mining and geological engineers rank 184th in terms of producing high incomes, yet overall they rank 44th in wealth accumulation. It takes only 33 high-income-producing mining and geological engineers to produce 100 millionaires. They rank number one in this regard among the top 200 high-income-producing occupational groups. Engineers in general are a frugal group. They have a higher-than-average propensity than others in their income/age cohort to accumulate wealth. They are less likely to favor expensive status-denoting products and brands than others. For many of them, substance, design, and endurance are more important factors in selecting a product, even a home, than showy style and status connotations.

Why is it that the mining engineer, in particular, is so successful? Consumption lifestyles are a function of temptation, imitation, and conformity. Hyperspending is highly influenced and actually endorsed by status-seeking neighbors. But most mining engineers live in small towns. Many work in and around mines. A home that sells for over $1 million in metropolitan New York or Los Angeles, for example, goes for under $300,000 in Mineville. If you live in Mineville, it is difficult to shop at, say, Brooks Brothers or a BMW dealer when the nearest ones are hundreds of miles away. And the same is true about all the other upscale retail stores, from Saks Fifth Avenue to Gucci.

When Johnny the mining engineer goes to work, he most likely is not wearing an $800 Brooks Brothers suit or expensive Cole Haan shoes with tassels. Imagine if you were a hyperconsuming doctor, Dr. Clark. What if you and Johnny changed places for a day or two? What would your neighbors think when they see Johnny's dust-laden Ford F-150 truck in your driveway? How would your colleagues react when you show up at a hospital staff meeting wearing steel-tipped boots and well-worn Carhartt overalls? Would the hospital parking lot guard wave you through?

You know the answer. Essentially you are where you live, which is defined in part by the status characteristics of your occupation. For those with high status, each component of food, clothing, and shelter costs much more in that social system. Perhaps you have managerial skill and experience that could be transferred to another industry. Have you ever thought of one day becoming a farm manager? Look at the numbers. It takes 69 high-income managers of farms to produce 100 millionaires. Plus, there are some really big benefits of living and working in rural America. The air quality there is a lot better than in most urban areas. Or you might want to become a funeral director. They are a productive group. Plus they are not highly concentrated in upscale environments.

Two other occupational groups are noteworthy: attorneys and corporate middle managers. Note that nationally the middle manager group ranks 28th and attorneys 5th out of the top 200 high-income occupations in terms of the percentage of its members who have annual realized incomes of $200,000 or more. Middle managers do rank 47th and attorneys 5th in terms of the percent with $1 million or more in investments. But now compute the ratio of these two percentages (the percent of millionaires over the percent of high income producers). The resulting ratios of

53.8 percent and 36.4 percent, respectively, are telling indeed. They indicate that it takes the equivalent of 100 high-income-producing middle managers and attorneys to produce approximately 54 and 36 millionaires. In other words, members of these two occupational cohorts are not very productive in accumulating wealth—especially given their income characteristics. Let's look at it another way: It takes 186 high-income-producing middle managers and 275 attorneys to produce the equivalent of just 100 millionaires.

Why are these high-status groups so bad at accumulating wealth? There are many reasons. Most live in or near high-cost-of-living metropolitan areas. They tend to live in expensive homes situated in or near exclusive neighborhoods. And so they spend accordingly, with little left over for saving and investing.

The most productive accumulators of wealth spend far less than they can afford on homes, cars, clothing, taxes, vacations, food, beverages, and entertainment. As many millionaires see it, living in a pricey neighborhood is a bad idea. Why live in a million-dollar neighborhood when one filled with $300,000 or $400,000 homes will serve the purpose? Real and actual millionaires understand that when you live in a luxury house, you are also buying a luxury lifestyle. Included in this lifestyle are the social pressures to redecorate frequently, join the country club, and send your children to private schools. Your property taxes continue to skyrocket, along with the cost of utilities and insurance. Plus the prices of nearby services tend to be higher, from grocery stores to dry cleaners.

Last but not least is the assumption that bloodlines have something to do with how wealth is expressed, that basically the wealthiest are *Mayflower*-type descendants. In reality, no one ancestry group dominates the population of households living in homes valued at $1 million or more. In fact, the concentration ratio—the percentage of a particular group living in homes of $1 million or more—is highest among the more recent immigrant groups, such as Iranians, Iraqis, Taiwanese, and so on (see Table 2.5). What the data seem to suggest is that new immigrant groups rise quickly in the United States

Table 2.5 Top 20 Ancestry Groups Who Own/Occupy Homes* Valued at \$1 Million or More: Total Number versus Concentration

Rank of Ancestry Group/Ethnic Origin of Head of Household	Total Number Living in Homes Valued at \$1 Million or More	Rank of Ancestry Group with the Higher Concentrations Living in \$1 Million Homes	Concentration Ratio: Percent of Group Living in Homes Valued at \$1 Million or More
1 English	167,963	1 South African	21.6
2 German	161,983	2 Iranian	14.7
3 Irish	143,701	3 Iraqi	11.3
4 Italian	97,096	4 Israeli	11.0
5 Russian	52,789	5 Taiwanese	10.5
6 Polish	42,082	6 Russian	9.0
7 Scottish	36,385	7 Indonesian	7.9
8 Chinese	28,866	8 Sri Lankan	7.5
9 French	25,197	9 Palestinian	7.0
10 African	22,167	10 Chinese	7.0
11 Norwegian	20,097	11 Australian	6.8
12 Swedish	19,664	12 Asian Indian	6.6
13 Asian Indian	15,967	13 Armenian	6.3
14 Dutch	14,682	14 Japanese	5.8
15 Mexican	14,545	15 Austrian	5.4
16 Japanese	13,061	16 Afghan	5.4
17 Iranian	10,290	17 Korean	5.3
18 Hungarian	10,258	18 Pakistani	5.2
19 Greek	10,249	19 Maltese	5.0
20 Austrian	9,489	20 Egyptian	4.9

*Refers to owner-occupied/primary residences. Only 2.8 percent of those of English ancestry own/occupy homes valued at \$1 million or more.

while more established groups fall in wealth. Could it be that as we "achieve" more, we become more spendthrift on status objects that erode wealth?

The data show that many of our assumptions about wealth—who has it, what they spend it on, how they live—are downright wrong. We have confused status and prestige with wealth. The glittering rich spend below their means, and the merely wealthy spend below their means. The hyper-consumers, particularly high-income individuals, have little wealth and spend on those things they assume their flush counterparts spend on. We try to emulate the consumption patterns of the glittering rich, not realizing that we can never pass muster and will only erode our own wealth by doing so.

We need to stop acting rich and start living like real millionaires.

Do the Shoes Make the Man?

Know first who you are; then adorn yourself accordingly.

—Euripides

Imagine for a moment that you are a valet, parking cars at an exclusive country club. It is lunchtime, and you have never been so busy. Today there is a luncheon meeting of women in business. As you run back to your station after parking that lovely BMW 5 Series, you notice a stunning woman flash past in a top-of-the-line Jag convertible. You put on a burst of speed and beat out the other attendants to open the door for the lovely Ms. Anna After.

As Anna emerges, you cannot help but notice the fine quality of clothing and accessories she is wearing. You know a lot about the pricey stuff from your days in the stockroom of an exclusive women's clothing store.

You estimate that the Chanel suit Anna is wearing cost $3,000. It is her favorite label. She owns more Chanel than any other brand. Then there are her watch and handbag, a Louis Vuitton, the real thing. The watch is a Cartier. What you don't know is that she received this $10,000 timepiece as a gift from her husband in recognition of the couple's business becoming a major success. From the tip of Manolo Blahnik shoes to her perfectly coiffed hair, there is no question but that Anna glitters.

Of course Anna shines. Her hair is perfect. It should be, since her most recent haircut cost $230. Note that only about 1 percent of the millionaire women surveyed spent this much (see Table 3.1). This figure is more than 5 times what the typical millionaire woman allocated for a haircut and more than 14 times more than the typical male millionaire most recently spent.

As you sigh in appreciation (and maybe a little envy) of Anna, another car, a Mercedes-Benz E class, pulls up. The driver, Ms. Barbara Before, is just as glittering as Anna After. She is also wearing an expensive suit, a Rolex watch, Manolo Blahnik shoes, and carries a Gucci handbag, the real thing. Barbara seems as confident in herself as Anna is. Her athletic pace and posture, even her greeting, seem to denote an air of high status and

Table 3.1   Price Paid by Millionaires for Their Most Recent Haircut

Price (including tip) Paid		% Who Paid	
Female Millionaires	Male Millionaires	Less than This Amount	More than This Amount
$ 14.85	$ 9.34	10	90
23.69	11.88	25	75
44.58	16.00	50	50
69.38	24.83	75	25
115.00	34.75	90	10
146.50	39.85	95	5
236.25	86.67	99	1

much success. You'll park her car too. Both Anna and Barbara should be good tippers.

After the luncheon is over, you retrieve both ladies' vehicles. Anna tips you $10; Barbara gives you $1. You are confused, convinced that both of these women are wealthy, probably very wealthy, but one was generous and the other cheap. Go figure. Most people in your shoes would have come to the same conclusion. And everyone would be half right.

In terms of actual wealth, Anna After and Barbara Before are at opposite ends of the net worth scale, but impressions, being what they are, lead us to false conclusions.

Anna After and her husband are decamillionaires, members of the glittering rich millionaire demographic; Barbara Before is very near ground zero financially. But if Barbara is in upside-down land (i.e., negative net worth), what explains all the high-price, high-status artifacts? Barbara Before acquired her very expensive clothing, accessories, and automobiles prior to—before and in anticipation of—becoming wealthy. Barbara consumes aspirationally; she aspires to be rich but is not, although spends as if she is. Barbara is in her late 30s, and her economic reality is stark. She has led her life convinced that she would make it big in modeling or films. Her early optimism was enhanced by people who told her, "Barbara, you are beautiful. You have supermodel potential written all over you . . . movies . . . lead roles in your immediate future." Her career, such as it is, has been all about just getting the right break, just a matter of being discovered.

Barbara did some modeling, but she never made much doing it. She also was once a cheerleader for a professional sports team. When she first made it onto the cheerleading squad, Barbara believed that she was within inches of making it big. But it didn't happen. She has made some money training others to cheer and to dance, and then she became a personal trainer and coach for young talent. Work provided a steady source of income, but there has been an upper limit on how much she has been able to earn training others.

What about all those expensive clothes, Jimmy Choo shoes, and Gucci accessories that Barbara has in her big-enough-to-park-an-SUV closet? What about her car, her hair? Within the millionaire population surveyed, those with Barbara's patronage habits have incomes in the mid-six figures and above. Many, like Anna After, are decamillionaires. But Barbara is neither a high-income earner nor a decamillionaire. In fact, Barbara lives in a rather dull condo and she's thinking of downsizing. Her furnishings look like early American junk shop.

What is Barbara doing dressing, and driving, and paying for decamillionaire habits? Like many others of her ilk, Barbara has bought into the myth that simply looking the part would get her the gig. She then made the mistake of focusing her energies on acquiring badges of wealth instead of working hard to build a career or business, in the expectation that of course she'd be living in a mansion one day. Time has exposed both delusions.

But to the parking lot attendant, Barbara looked to be in the money, a success, even though she actually does not have two cents to her name. Is this success? Having parking lot attendants you will likely never see again think that you are a success?

Anna After, however, ranks in the top 99.9 percent in wealth. Only 1 in 1,000 households is in Anna's league. There are more cases of malaria contracted each year in America than there are households in the 1 in 1,000 category. Anna's position of wealth is like making a perfect score on the SATs. Barbara's financial SAT score equivalent would place her in the bottom 20 percent.

Now, what if those who had a perfect score were all given special badges to wear? The badges would prominently indicate extraordinary performance on the SAT. Some people could buy such a badge at a pawnshop and pretend that they are very, very smart, but it wouldn't make them smart. This is analogous to Barbara's display of rich accessories. Only Barbara's clothing and accessories and related symbols are indicative of those like Anna, who really do score in the 99.9 percentile on the wealth test.

Unfortunately, Barbara believes that she was somebody like Anna After *before* she actually achieved Anna's level of success. Did the delusion help her? No. Not only did it put a huge dent in her net worth, but it may very well have lessened her chances for success by focusing her energies and time on the wrong things. There are people who are so devoted to their craft—art or acting or athletics, what have you—that they will pursue these dreams no matter how unlikely they are to ever achieve financial success. These are a small percentage of people. Others, like Barbara, focus on achieving a highly unlikely dream without doing the work necessary to get to success. They go through life expecting to hit the lottery any moment.

There are 715,506 professional entertainers in America. The average annual net income for the entire population of entertainers is only $5,686; only 61 percent have a positive net income. Only 6 in 10 even generate enough money to pay their expenses. How much does the professional athlete net? It is nowhere near what the press tells us that superstars earn. The average is $6,098. There are many, many more semiprofessionals and minor leaguers than there are major league superstars. For these reasons alone, all high school students should be required to complete a course in probability theory. If Barbara had completed such a course, she might have never bet on becoming rich via the entertainment route and she may have reconsidered buying Jimmy Choo shoes.

Barbara's case is not all that unusual. Even though she certainly is better looking than most and her outfits are very expensive, her dilemma is a common one facing many people. They too had talent and potential. They also believed that they would become financially successful one day. And they also felt that acquiring high-priced "things" was the ticket to Happyville. But today, like Barbara, they are not happy. These people are hyperconsumers, aspirationals. Very few of them become financially successful. As I have said many, many times:

If you spend in anticipation of becoming rich, you are
unlikely ever to become truly wealthy.

People like Barbara Before have confused the advertising message with real life. People do not become successful because they wear $800 shoes. It is just the opposite. The "before" types believe that those who became wealthy in one generation did so because they wanted to dress rich, drive rich, re-create rich, and so on. They are wrong. Most millionaires are motivated by their need to gain financial independence. For most, consumption is a nice side benefit to becoming wealthy. It is not the most compelling reason why these people became financially successful. When asked, they will tell you that given the choice, they would readily unload their consumer goodies before ever giving up their independence.

What happens to the Barbara Before types when reality finally hits? It is as devastating to their egos and self-esteem as to their net worth, and it is nearly impossible (but not entirely) to recover from. To add insult to injury, people in this situation panic and fear that their entire future, especially their lifestyle, is at serious risk. Then they make really big mistakes born out of vulnerability that we'll talk about later.

What Barbara should do immediately is to hire a financial planner and credit counselor to work out a debt reduction strategy and then a wealth accumulation program. She should not despair; all is not lost. Barbara is still young, and most of her productive years are ahead of her. And with her professional cheerleading experience, Barbara could start a business that is extremely profitable, such as choreographing for cheerleading squads.

Barbara Before would do well to pay close attention to what Anna did, not what she wears. But Anna's case is not typical of millionaire success stories. Most millionaires do not become rich until they are in their late 40s. Anna and her husband hit it very big financially while they were much younger than the norm. Today they spend heavily on clothes, cars, jewelry, and entertaining. My research suggests that part of Anna's high-consumption lifestyle is a function of how she was raised. Her father was frugal, to a fault. *Webster's Dictionary* must have been describing her father when it defined "miser" as "a greedy, stingy person who hoards money for its own sake . . . a miserable wretch." He had plenty of income to spend, but he insisted on his family living like impoverished monks and nuns. Although he had the means to purchase and maintain a nice home in a decent neighborhood with high-quality schools, he chose to live in the lower end of Bluecollarville. His daughter, Anna, rebelled against her father's perverse economic ways as soon as she and her husband became very wealthy. In this regard, she is like those self-made millionaire Beta women whom I profiled in *Millionaire Women Next Door* (2004). Their parents did not nurture their children.

Today, as economically successful adults, the daughters of these types—Anna After included—tend to overcompensate for the early void in their lives. They do so by nurturing themselves. They tend to purchase conspicuously displayed badges of success such as expensive clothes, cars, homes, and the like. What if you run into Anna the next time you are shopping at Gucci's? Please ask her to put my name on her guest list. Of all the people I have studied, it is Anna who serves the most expensive foods and beverages to her many guests.

Anna drives a Jaguar, while her husband recently purchased a Porsche. The couple also has a Range Rover. Today, they live in a million-dollar-plus home surrounded by others in the same price range.

Given Anna After's consumption lifestyle, some might think that I do not respect her. After all, I have always advocated that people should live well below their means. However, given her level of wealth, Anna does live below her means. Unlike Barbara Before, Anna waited until after she was rich to upgrade her consumption habits. Eleven years ago, Anna and her husband purchased their first home for $150,000. This purchase was made before they became successful, while they were making lifestyle sacrifices and working hard building a business.

It was only *after* making millions that the couple traded up to their million-dollar-plus home. Some might say that Anna, even with her "after" orientation, is foolish, even selfish to spend so much money on herself. But Anna, and those like her, tend to be a generous bunch. How much of Anna's household income does she contribute annually to charitable causes? It is a lot more than the average for all households in America, which is only about 2 percent. Anna gives 10 percent—and that is 10 percent of a sizable income! It is hard to be critical of Anna's consumption lifestyle given the fact that she gives so much to noble causes. Anna doesn't brag about her giving, because, like most people who give to noble causes, she receives more satisfaction from the act of giving than from recognition of her generosity.

What impresses you more about Anna? Her Jag or her charitable contributions? Be honest. Like most others, you would likely be more awed by the sight of her behind the wheel of her car than by seeing her name on a roster of top givers to XYZ charity. And in that we come back to the power of marketing. We all have bought into the image over substance; looking beautiful is more important than actually being beautiful.

Walk a Mile in Real Millionaire Shoes

Very few millionaires, whether they are men or women, ever spend $800 for a pair of shoes. Anna After is an exception. Those who become millionaires when they are in their 20s and 30s are prone to be hyperspenders. These fast-track, highly successful glittering rich are those whom Barbara

Before imitates. She believes that if she looks and dresses like them, she will become them.

What Barbara Before should know is that most millionaires do not reach the millionaire threshold until they are near 50 years of age. Most became millionaires, in large part, because they led a frugal lifestyle. By the time they reached the millionaire category, they were set in their ways, so even after becoming wealthy, they typically remain frugal.

The typical millionaire woman never paid more than $140 (median price) for a pair of shoes for herself or anyone else. That is less than 20 percent of what Barbara Before paid for her favorite brand of shoes, and she has a dozen or more pairs of Manolo Blahniks, yet she is not a millionaire. Millionaire women usually wear "good-quality" brands of shoes but not overly expensive ones.

The top five most preferred brands[1] of shoes worn by millionaire women in descending order are:

1. Nine West
2. Stuart Weitzman
3. Easy Spirit
4. Cole Haan
5. A two-way tie between Enzo Angiolini and Ferragamo

More than 25 different brands were designated as "the most preferred brand" by at least one respondent. Shoe preferences of millionaire men were much more varied than for women. More than 60 preferred brands were reported at least once. Yet just 5 brands accounted for over half of those preferred by millionaire men. The brands most preferred by men were in general pricier than those most preferred by women, reinforcing the findings that millionaire women are more frugal than men. But this does not mean that men spend frivolously on shoes. Most wear high-quality brands. Interestingly, only

1 of the 944 millionaires surveyed indicated that his favorite brand was "custom made."

Men have a stronger preference for shoe brand than for brand of suits. Fully 78 percent reported a preferred brand of shoe. In contrast, only 62 percent preferred a particular brand of suit. What were the top five most preferred brands of shoes worn by millionaire men?

1. **Allen Edmonds** (12.2 percent). This brand is particularly popular among senior corporate executives of public corporations. More millionaire respondents in this occupational category indicated Allen Edmonds as their preferred brand. However, the brand is fairly popular among millionaires from a variety of other occupation groups. Why would so many frugal millionaires spend several hundred dollars for a pair of shoes? They believe that the product is worth the price. In general, Allen Edmonds never goes out of style and can be refurbished over and over again. As an advertisement for this brand in the *New York Times* stated rather simply: "Not all high return investments involve stocks" (April 21, 2006, p. A2).

2. **Cole Haan** (11.8 percent). More self-employed millionaire respondents preferred the Cole Haan brand than any of the other brands studied. This brand is also very popular among highly compensated millionaire marketing/sales professionals as well as among senior corporate executives of private corporations. Comfort, quality of material, and timeless styling are just some of the many hallmarks of this brand. The Cole Haan and Allen Edmonds brands are the favored among that elite group of millionaires who have annual realized incomes of $1 million or more as well as among decamillionaires.

3. **Johnson & Murphy** (11.2 percent). This brand ranked just behind Cole Haan among millionaire respondents who were self-employed business owners. This brand was tied for first place with Cole Haan

among millionaire marketing/sales professionals. It was number one among the millionaire lawyers surveyed. Johnson & Murphy epitomizes the conservative and traditional style of dress among wealthy men.

4. **Florsheim** (10.8 percent). Florsheim was the number-one brand of shoe among those millionaire respondents in midlevel management positions. It was also popular among engineers, architects, and professors. This brand was also number one overall among those millionaires who have annual incomes under $100,000. These people have a proven ability to convert a higher portion of the dollars they earn into wealth. They are, in many ways, "the Millionaires Next Door."

5. **Rockport** (7.5 percent). If you are in need of a comfortable, reasonably priced shoe that gives great support and longevity, Rockport may be your choice. It is likely that the balance sheet affluent physician who helped deliver your children was wearing Rockport. It was the number-one brand of shoes among the doctors and dentists surveyed.

Millionaires tend to wear those brands of shoes that are generally in the higher price range. Most millionaires, especially multimillionaires, are somewhat insensitive to variations in the first cost or initial price/purchase price of shoes. They are much more quality sensitive and thus tend to focus on the variations in life cycle cost among competing brands. High-quality shoes can last 10, even 20 years if treated properly. Most millionaires are not slaves to fashion.

What did I find in my earlier study of multimillionaires (those with an average augmented net worth of nearly $10 million)?

Are the affluent in America the ultimate consumers of goods, buying today and discarding tomorrow? Perhaps the thought of recycling, or specifically resoling, shoes is abhorrent to them. The findings from my national survey of millionaires contradict that hypothesis: 70 percent of the millionaires surveyed have their shoes resoled. This number is something of an underestimate because about 20 percent are retired millionaires who normally give up wearing their "dress uniform," which includes footwear that tends to be resoled.[2]

Millionaires tell it like it is. You are cheating yourself if you buy cheap shoes. Or, as one respondent stated:

CHEAP SHOES WEAR YOU; YOU DON'T WEAR THEM![3]

Similar rules apply when selecting shoes or building a home. If you are going to cut costs or compromise, do not do it on shoes (the foundation). Poorly constructed shoes, like cheap foundations, will adversely affect all that goes on top of them. So, while the shoes do not make you successful, it is wise to invest in quality furnishings, just as you would want a sturdy foundation for your home. Do you want to be unhappy? Wear cheap, poorly constructed shoes and you may get your wish. Most male millionaires especially have a strong preference for high-grade, high-quality brands of shoes. But their preference for certain brands has less to do with status than the actual performance characteristics of the shoes.

Dressing for Success

Millionaires were asked to report the names of the stores from which they made a purchase within the past year for such items as suits, shirts, blouses, ties, scarves, coats, and dress or work shoes. From the results, it appears that millionaires tend to be cherry pickers when it comes to buying various items of consumer goods, including clothing and accessories. Cherry pickers are those who tend to shop at a variety of retailers. Each of these sources/stores carries products, often a narrowly defined line or lines, which have the best mix of quality, price, convenience, and value overall. Often millionaires will buy their shoes at one store, their suits at another, and their underwear and jeans somewhere else. The top 10 stores patronized by the millionaire men include:

1. Nordstrom (38.6%)
2. Macy's (27.3%)
3. Kohl's (21.7%)
4. Target (21.6%)
5. Costco (21.3%)
6. Dillard's (20.9%)
7. Brooks Brothers (19.3%)
8. Gap (15.9%)
9. Wal-Mart (15.5%)
10. T.J. Maxx (14.7%)

Millionaire women shop for clothing more than do millionaire men. Accordingly, many millionaire women are also cherry pickers. The top 10 stores they patronize include:

1. Ann Taylor (47.5%)
2. Nordstrom (44.6%)
3. Macy's (43.6%)
4. Target (39.6%)
5. T.J. Maxx (33.7%)
6. Talbots (32.7%)
7. Gap (28.7%)
8. Costco (27.7%)
9. Lord & Taylor (25.7%)
10. Saks Fifth Avenue (24.8%)

What stores score highest on the glittering rich scale? Remember that the glittering rich distinguish themselves from others in terms of the uniqueness of the clothing and accessories they display. The stores that scored highest included: Saks Fifth Avenue, Neiman Marcus, Brooks Brothers, Gucci, Nordstrom, and Polo. Upper-level independent clothing stores, as a general category, also scored high among the glittering rich. Like Anna After, only a minority of millionaires shop exclusively at so-called prestige retail boutiques. Most wealthy people became millionaires without patronizing these types of retailers. After becoming wealthy, and generally when they are in their mid-40s to mid-50s, these people never changed their retail patronage habits. This is something that hyperconsuming types like Barbara fail to see.

Many of the key findings discussed in *The Millionaire Next Door* shocked readers. One statistic, in particular, stood out from all the others.

> . . . the typical American millionaire reported that he (she) never spent more than $399 for a suit of clothing for himself or for anyone else. Fifty percent or more . . . paid $399 or less for the most expensive suit they ever purchased. (p. 31)

Note that 92 percent of the millionaires surveyed for *The Millionaire Next Door* were men. What if more women were surveyed? Some might conclude that if they had been, then the "most spent for a suit" figure might be significantly higher. Yet this is not the case at all. Again, self-made millionaire women are more frugal than men.

There is a problem associated with the "most ever spent on a suit" measure. What if these affluent respondents purchased what they feel is an expensive suit only on rare occasions? Some may have purchased their "most expensive suit" for a special occasion or as a gift for a son or daughter. If this is the case, then the median "most spent" dollar figures reported may actually be higher than the amount these millionaires usually spend on a suit.

To test this hypothesis, millionaire respondents in my latest national survey were asked a somewhat different question. Respondents were asked how much they spent for the suit they *most recently* purchased (actual sales price). The typical millionaire in this survey spent $299.50 (median) for the suit he most recently purchased. In other words, 50 percent paid this amount or less for the suit they most recently purchased. Are you looking for the ideal graduation gift for your son or daughter? Let me suggest a traditional-styled suit in the high $400 range. Yes, the median for decamillionaires (those with a net worth of $10 million or more) was only $482! Only about one in four decamillionaires paid $908 or more. These are the glittering rich.

Millionaires are indeed a frugal bunch when it comes to allocating their financial resources for clothing. Do you wish to emulate the typical millionaire and not the glittering rich and their poor, aspirational imitators? If you do, keep something in mind when shopping for your next suit: Buy a conservative style of suit. Do not overspend. If you want to act like a glittering rich person, be prepared to spend a minimum of two to three times more than the typical millionaire pays.

What was I thinking as the numbers rolled in from my latest survey? I was somewhat surprised at how frugal the respondents were in the prices they paid for suits. But it had been a while since I bought a suit, and I was not all that comfortable with my knowledge of current market offerings. I wanted to know what type of suit sells for $299.50, the median price paid most recently. I began reading newspaper advertisements and strolling through stores that sell suits.

One Sunday afternoon, on my way back from the mountains, I took a short detour. I popped into a Brooks Brothers outlet store and a Ralph Lauren Polo Factory store. Neither looked anything like a factory. Both stores were filled with first-class merchandise and fixtures. Given these facts, I had a suspicion that I would not find any suits in the $299.50 or less range. I was wrong. The Brooks Brothers outlet had several fine suits

on sale in that price range. And just past the threshold of the men's department in the Polo Factory store, there was a sign stating: Lauren men's
suits . . . jackets $189 . . . trousers (matching) $89. What kind of a suit can
you get for $278? The answer is: a pretty good one. The suits bearing the
label "Lauren-Polo" were made of 100 percent virgin worsted wool. They
were well made, stylish, and nicely tailored. And yet they were just $278.
This was not a special price or a once-a-year sale price. Two weeks later,
our son bought one of the men's Lauren suits for just $225 during a special
sale. The comparable suits for women were selling that day for even less.

Later that day I opened the Sunday newspaper that contained several
advertisements for suits. I was particularly interested in the JCPenney flyer.
Penney's has a long history of marketing well-made suits, especially its
own private label ones, at reasonable prices. Even its everyday prices seem
to be in the "good value" range. But what about when it is "sale" time? Its
advertisement for women's wear read as follows:

> Suits for her from collections for Le Suit, Worthington, Sag Harbor . . .
> Originally $180–$200 . . . entire stock [now] $79.99

Again, these are good-quality suits that are nicely tailored. But what
about the men's suits featured in the same flyer?

> Stafford Executive Suits, 100 percent worsted wool. Regularly $395
> [now] $299

What if you do not wish to emulate most millionaire discount shoppers and instead wish to buy a suit at full retail price? You can buy a
Chaps brand suit for $275 (full retail) at Kohl's. That is a "decent suit at a
good price."[4]

Nearly 4 in 10 millionaires (38 percent) did not have a strong enough
brand preference for suits to designate any particular "off-the-rack" brand

as being their favorite. Sixty-two percent did have a clear preference. Overall, a total of 77 different brands received at least one vote from this sample of millionaires. Among the men in this population with a strong preference, the top five brands, in rank order, are as follows:

1. **Hart Schaffner & Marx** (11.5 percent). This mid-priced line is considered by many to be among the best value in men's suits. It is a particular favorite among the very frugal millionaires next-door type of affluent consumers. It is the number-one suit among millionaires who are senior officers of private corporations and highly compensated marketing/sales professionals. It is also the favorite among those respondents who earn seven-figure annual incomes.

2. **Brooks Brothers** (10.7 percent). President Lincoln wore a Brooks Brothers suit. He was a traditional type of fellow. Those who seek a high-quality product and excellent service, and who have are short on time often patronize Brooks Brothers. They are more sensitive to minimizing the time needed to shop and less sensitive to variations in price of competing brands of suits. This brand is number one among decamillionaires as well as highly compensated attorneys and multimillionaires who are business owners.

3. **Jos. A. Banks** (6.1 percent). This make of suit is a particular favorite among corporate middle managers and directors. It especially fits the needs of these managers who seek a traditional look.

4. **Hickey Freeman** (5.3 percent). Within the higher-price range, this brand is considered by many to be among the top-quality suits of traditional design. The number-one buyers of this brand are highly compensated senior executives of public corporations.

5. Tie between **Men's Wearhouse Private Label** and **Nordstrom's Private Label** (3.7 percent).

The Cinderella Syndrome

The brand of suit that millionaires wear has little to do with their level of overall satisfaction in life. The same is true in regard to the high-income population (including both millionaires and nonmillionaires) in general. Who are those in the very satisfied to satisfied with life range? Ninety percent of those who indicated that Brooks Brothers was their favorite brand of suit are happy versus 86 percent of the Jos. A. Banks's patrons and 83 percent of the Men's Wearhouse patrons. These differences are only nominally, not statistically, different, and are explained mostly by income differences. There is a correlation between satisfaction in life and income. Six in 10 Brooks Brothers' customers surveyed were in the $200,000 and over income bracket as compared to 52 percent of the Jos. A. Banks's customers and 33 percent of the Men's Wearhouse customers.

What happened when I first presented these numbers to an audience? I was asked about millionaires who prefer custom-made suits. We seem to be under the assumption that wealthy people have their suits custom made. Actually, only 4.6 percent of the millionaires surveyed purchase custom attire. Most important, they are not any more satisfied with life than those who buy suits off the rack.

Could there be another reason why the large majority of millionaires buy off the rack as opposed to being custom fitted? My surveys have found that the typical male millionaire is a perfect suit size 42 regular. He is 5' 10" tall (median) and weighs 183 pounds (median). The typical female millionaire is 5' 5" tall and weighs 138 pounds.

The estimated market share and rank of brands of suits preferred by women millionaires are as follows:

1. Jones New York (13.2%)
2. Talbots (11.3%)
3. Ann Taylor (9.1%)

4. Tie between Dana Buchanan and Kasper (7.6%)

5. St. John (5.7%).

Most of the best data on millionaire buying behavior is available for male millionaires because there are more of them. Thus it is much easier and more reliable to profile the characteristics of males by brand preference. Nonetheless, and in contradiction to popular opinion, it turns out that millionaire women pay less for their suits than do men.

The habits of these affluent buyers of suits are so interesting because their choice of brands and prices paid understates the level of both income and wealth. For example, even those who wear the very expensive Hickey Freeman and Oxford brands can very easily afford to do so. These buyers have among the highest levels of both income and net worth. To spend four figures on a suit does not put a big dent in a seven-figure income or an eight-figure level of wealth. The dent is even smaller for those multi-millionaires who wear the midpriced Hart Schaffner & Marx label. About a week after I told my friend, Roland, this, he sent me the e-mail shown on page 78.

It is not just income and wealth that accounts for one's choice of brand. Within the same income/net worth cohort, what occupational group is most likely to purchase expensive suits? The answer is those with very high occupational status, such as senior corporate executives. Who is least likely to purchase these types of suits? The answer is business owners—those whom society does not rank high in occupational status.

A suit is a uniform, a wrapper, a cover on a book. Most millionaires do not judge a book or a person by the cover, the suit, the wrapping on the box. Yet far too often people who are not affluent attempt to emulate successful people by "overdressing." Overdressing will not make one a success, and it will not favorably impress those who are truly wealthy. Do you want to stand out from the crowd? Do it with your achievements and not by wearing a clown suit, even if it is what the fashionistas are wearing.

Dear Tom,

Here is the story behind the infamous suit purchase at Macy's for your book.

We went to Macy's at North Point and stopped at the men's clothing department.
A clerk named Sandy asked if she could help. I replied I was just looking around. She
said there was a great deal she had on some clearance suits and what was my size.
I said 46 long and she then pulled out a grayish glen plaid Hart Schaffner & Marx suit.
I tried it on and the only alteration needed was cuffing the pants. The regular price was
$695, on sale for $347.50. But the good news didn't stop there! She then said there
was a special coupon she had which would take another 20% off, and if I reactivated
a Macy's charge, then another additional 20% would be deducted off the total. Bottom
line, the suit ended up costing me $222.40 before sales tax!

My next question to Sandy was: Do you have any other Hart Schaffner & Marx suits at
that price? She said no, but she did have a Nautica blue wool in my size. Original price
$495, my price thanks to Sandy, $158.40!

If this was a MasterCard commercial, my comment on buying two quality suits including alterations for a total price of $433.46, priceless!

Regards,
Roland

By various definitions, most of the millionaires profiled are successful. Most believe what Shakespeare wrote:

To gild the gold, to paint the lily
Is but ridiculous excess

What about people who are not gold or lilies? The fluid nature of our socioeconomic system allows people to transform themselves into gold in one generation. Most millionaires did exactly that. They do not need to gild, to paint their achievements. Yet most people with good, even great incomes go in another direction. It is easier to finance the purchase of products that supposedly define high status, call it painting one's image, than it is to truly achieve. Follow the dictates of the latest advertising and glamour images, and you too can look like a winner—even if you are not a success.

The Glittering Ones

There is a small population of people who will pay big bucks for their suits (and cars and everything else). Paying $5,000 or $6,000 for a suit has much to do with vanity. The concept of vanity relates to certain forms of consumer behavior. *Webster's* defines vanity as follows:

> Excessive pride in one's appearance; qualities, abilities, achievements; the character or quality of being vain; conceit . . . lack of real value; hollowness; something worthless, trivial, or pointless.

Just imagine if you had a list of every high-income producer and/or millionaire who is at or near the top of the vanity scale. If you did, you could become wealthy selling it to every major marketer who sells high-priced display artifacts. Yet no complete list exists. But there are many determined marketers who take it upon themselves to identify these types of people. As I wrote in *Marketing to the Affluent* in 1988 (some things never change), marketers of super-expensive luxury goods have to seek out their market since it rarely comes to them. Some clever marketers and salespeople seek out their vain prospects by identifying those whose pictures appear frequently in the media. And then they take their wares to them and sell them using vanity.

For instance, of the 445 Rolls-Royces sold in the United States in 2005, about one-third of the buyers were celebrities, such as sports figures and entertainers.[5] This is an interesting statistic when you consider that based on the high-income-producing celebrity population, they should account for just 4 percent of Rolls-Royce customers. Of the nearly 140 million income producers in the United States, only about 354,000 generate an annual realized income of $1 million or more, and the majority of those are business owners. No more than 4 percent of these high-income producers are celebrities. These facts bring home two important points:

1. Most millionaires do not spend lavishly on luxury items.
2. The people who do spend extravagantly on prestige items are celebrities, a terrifically small proportion of the overall population and a tiny percentage of even the millionaire population—and they spend disproportionately on these items (which may explain why we read so often about celebrities going broke).

In reality, ego products and brands are not common among the affluent population. They did not get rich buying such items, and they don't stay rich by indulging. When they do indulge, it is because the prices of these items are well within their means or because they are celebrity vanity purchasers.

Dressing like a Real Millionaire

If you want to become financially independent and stay that way, you should not try to accomplish this goal by emulating the consumption habits of vain celebrities or the high-consumption glittering rich. Some do attain financial independence by demanding and receiving the extremely high incomes that are congruent with extraordinarily rare God-given talent. In a way, they are freaks, anomalies in our economy. But for too many, their own extraordinary success is not enough to satisfy them. They are compelled to paint their lily, to gild their gold. They focus on the packaging and not on their real selves.

Conversely, most millionaires get so much satisfaction from becoming successful that they do not need to wear suits from "the middle of the four-figure collection." Rare is the millionaire in the $5,000 suit—1 in 900. Rather, real millionaires purchase quality clothing at bargain prices. They do not dress for success but dress for work, with the focus being on the work. Their attire is practical, long lasting, and not dictated by fashionista dictates or marketing messages.

Brother, Do You Have the Time?

Your time is limited, so don't waste it living someone else's life.

—Steve Jobs

Are you tired of being ignored and unrecognized by store clerks? You do not have to be any longer. You just need the right badges, the appropriate brands, symbols of wealth, superiority, and hyperconsumption. But what badges? And whose opinions should you rely on when selecting these symbols that are supposedly designed to generate attention?

According to an article in *BusinessWeek*, all you need is the right watch. After wearing expensive watches (several priced at over $20,000) and then assessing the reactions from people with whom he came in contact, the article's author noted:

> ...a surefire way to get noticed...a huge hit...a seriously big deal...Men came over to say they really liked it...women loved it...[at] the counter for a coffee...waved with my left hand...people flocked to the watch.[1]

What if during his field research at the coffee counter in Manhattan this same watch tester wore the brand of watch most popular among millionaires? With a Seiko on his wrist, it is possible that he would still be standing in line for coffee, unserved and unnoticed.

Some are amateurs at judging the socioeconomic status and buying habits of people from their badges. Others make a living doing it. Take, for example, those who are skilled at selling very expensive watches. In general, people who wear expensive clothing tend to buy expensive accessories, such as high-priced watches. The most productive sales professionals capitalize on this relationship by sizing up prospective buyers as they enter a store. The woman wearing a Marc Jacobs dress and Gucci shoes will be approached immediately; the kid in ripped Levi's and Chuck Taylor's will be ignored.

What if the store is filled with prospective buyers? To whom should the sales clerk allocate his time and effort? Target those who show the tells, those loaded with expensive badges. The others are likely to be "tire kickers" or recreational lookers, not serious prospects. Successful marketing is all about targeting and allocating resources in ways that will generate the greatest number of sales.

You don't have to have much wealth in order to purchase expensive clothes and accessories. Buy now, pay later is our mantra. Those who sell these items do not care if you have a high or low net worth. If you dress the part and can write a check or have enough credit, you qualify as a prospective buyer.

What happened the first time I visited one of the most exclusive watch retailers in America? I was teaching at a university and wore a Seiko. It was lunchtime; I was in the Fifth Avenue district of New York; it was a workday. It was a very crowded store. I spent about 10 minutes studying the merchandise. The clerks ignored me. But they did not ignore those who were overdressed, overaccessorized, overcoiffed, and overmanicured.

I was not at all insulted by the actions of the clerks. My expertise is in marketing, so I was actually impressed with the marketing intellect of the sales personnel working in the store that day. There was near-zero probability that I would buy an expensive watch that day or any other day, though I likely would have purchased an inexpensive waterproof watch if one was demonstrated to me.

No doubt the clerks picked up my aura that day. It was not at all indicative of a hot prospect for a $10,000 watch purchase. Plus, even a rookie clerk could have seen that I was not glittering rich or even an aspirational. What was it that gave me away? Was it the inexpensive $15 haircut from, as I call it, John the Butcher's barbershop? Perhaps it was my suit, a designer label that my Uncle Harvey picked out for me from the rack in his "Harvey's" WSF fashion boutique. WSF stands for water, smoke, and/or potential fire damage. Nobody, including other salvage merchants, under-priced Harvey's offerings. It was my kind of store. Maybe it was my dull Alden shoes. Great shoes but a bit tight that day, as I recall. They probably shrunk a half size given the heat from the fire and the fire department's water cannon treatment.

Did the clerks have x-ray vision? How else did they know that my button-down oxford shirt had a small burn mark in the back, below the waistline? Harvey sold it to me for $4.00, a great deal. There were even better bargains if you do not mind burn marks above the waist. Harvey always recommended that buyers of these shirts "always keep their jackets on." Maybe it was my underwear—also not a designer label. But my JCPenney top-of-the-line, 100 percent cotton underwear has always served me well. Since I didn't ask, I couldn't say with complete accuracy what clues these clerks used to categorize me correctly as a looker and not a buyer.

Why was I even in a high-priced watch store if I was not interested in buying a $10,000 watch? I did it more to gather information about waterproof (also called water-resistant) watches. I fish a lot and often get wet when wading in a trout stream. My Seiko was not waterproof, and necessitated me placing it in a waterproof pouch when I went fishing. Eventually I did purchase a water-resistant watch, a Timex for under $50, at a Wal-Mart store.

I happened to visit the exclusive watch retailer a second time some weeks later. I dressed pretty much the same, but this time the experience was completely different.

I had barely crossed the threshold when I was immediately greeted by a short version of George Hamilton, who looked me straight in the eyes and uttered those wonderful words with great eloquence: "BONJOUR!" I was startled by his salutation. I thought for a moment that he might have been addressing someone else. I glanced over my shoulder, but there was no one behind me. Indeed, he was talking to me. Bon jour indeed.

How did I rate this immediate recognition on my second visit yet after being ignored on my first visit? Could it be that the greeter, Andre, was a novice in the world of selling? No, in fact he was a veteran salesman.

Andre asked me if I was interested in a particular watch. I told him that I was "just looking," but that did not deter this sales commando. As I began walking slowly past the showcases he shadowed me, all the while asking, probing, and seeking a reaction. No matter what turn, what speed I took, he was on me like white on rice. In his mind, I was a big fish who just needed to be reeled in. As much as I tried to discourage him, I was unable to shake Andre, so I finally told him that I enjoyed fishing and was interested in waterproof watches.

With that the floodgate opened. The first watch he showed me seemed to get him more excited than it did me. "It's water resistant to 2,000 meters . . . it's eight . . . "

I thought to myself, "Who fishes at a depth of 2,000 meters? Whales don't fish at 2,000 meters." I just wanted something that would work at less than five meters that didn't cost more than several months mortgage. How, I thought, could I tell this guy that there was zero likelihood of me buying an $800 watch and an even lower chance of me paying $8,000? With that I knew I had to get out of "affluent watch world."

I told Andre that I had to leave to deliver a speech and then catch a flight to Atlanta. Even this did not discourage him. He responded with "Let's keep in touch. May I have your name and address?"

I decided that it was time to fully light up this fellow's after burner. I said, "Yes, of course, Andre, I am Dr.—." With that he interrupted me, "I thought when you first entered that you might be a physician!"

How could it be that two weeks prior I had been given the cold-shoulder treatment but on this day I got the "bonjour," the close order drill, the "let's communicate" and "I knew you were a physician" reaction? What categorized me as a hot prospect on my second visit but not on the first? Walking down the street to my presentation, it finally dawned on me. I was holding in my hand a tell that signaled to Andre that I was a big fish. Earlier that morning I had had breakfast with a good friend in the apparel business who sent me off to a little known prestigious designer outlet where I could buy my wife a very nice scarf for less than $20. I heeded my friend's suggestion and headed for the Gucci outlet (which I understand is no longer in operation). I never would have found it without the instructions from my friend. It was off a side street, down a hallway, and up a small elevator. I proceeded there and purchased a scarf for only $19.95, and the clerk gift wrapped it for free. What a bargain! Then she asked if I would like a bag. "Yes," I responded. "Give me the biggest bag you have. . . . I have some more shopping to do this morning, and it would be great to put everything in one bag."

The bag she handed me was the biggest shopping bag I had ever seen. It was large enough to carry our golden retriever. And I soon filled it with birthday gifts for my children and two loaves of New York rye bread. I kept the gift-wrapped Gucci scarf on top so it would not crush the wrapping.

By the time I entered the exclusive store that sells very expensive watches, the bag was nearly filled. Actually, the bag crossed the store's threshold before I did. It must have been the first thing anyone noticed about me. It was the Gucci bag that triggered Andre's quick and aggressive response. He must have assumed that I was a Gucci guy, a fellow who just spent thousands of dollars on Gucci accessories. Andre knew, and my own empirical data confirms, that those who spend heavily on so-called status/expensive accessories at Gucci are likely to have a high propensity to buy expensive watches. According to my surveys of millionaires, about 80 percent of those who are Gucci patrons wear expensive prestige brands of watches, such as Breitling, Cartier, Movado, Omega, Rolex, and Tag Heuer.

In assessing my buying potential, Andre discounted my dull suit, mundane haircut, and lack of accessories. The Gucci bag trumped everything else. It would likely not have mattered to Andre if I were a grammar school dropout, convicted felon, wife beater, drug dealer, Phi Beta Kappa, or Nobel Prize winner. These qualities are not readily displayed, and even if they were, they likely would not have made a big impression on Andre. He judged prospects based on their conspicuous symbols of expensive status artifacts. All Andre cares about is whether his customers are likely to spend money with him or not.

Do you want better service, better responses from retail clerks, especially from those employed in the fashion arena? If so, keep a Gucci bag or one from another upscale retailer with you when you shop. Sales clerks will trip over themselves to be helpful; strangers will glance your way in appreciation and awe of your fashion sense. You may go home and kick the dog, pay your bills late, and serve your children TV dinners, but people you don't know will think highly of you.

Should those who judge others via brand habits be our most important audience? Many of the millionaires I have surveyed and interviewed question the motives and even the common sense of those who look like overbranded, overaccessorized hyperconsumers.

What if you find yourself needing to impress a real millionaire (as opposed to a salesperson who just wants your money)? Do it with your intellect and your substantive achievements. Besides, the millionaire owner of a company you are applying to might not think too much of your priorities if your watch costs more than his.

Will Buying One of Your $10,000 Watches Make Me Happy?

Ask any sales clerk if an expensive watch will bring happiness and be prepared to take out your credit card and dump that boring Timex or Seiko. But can the variation in happiness across the high-income-producing population be explained by the rate of adoption of status brands? The answer is no in general and certainly no in terms of choice of brands of watches. For millionaires surveyed who wear the following watches, their average level of satisfaction with life overall, measured on a five-point scale (five being the highest), was

Rolex: 4.26
Seiko: 4.20
Timex: 4.23

The differences are not statistically significant, and certainly not worth the price differential between a Rolex and a Timex. Those who wear a Seiko or Timex are just as happy statistically with their lives overall as those who wear a Rolex. In a nominal sense, those who wear Rolexes are ever so slightly happier. But these differences can be explained by the fact that those who wear Rolex watches have higher incomes overall than those who wear either Seiko or Timex. Of those surveyed, nearly two-thirds (63 percent) of the Rolex wearers have annual realized household incomes of $200,000 or more. Only 34 percent of the Seiko wearers and 32 percent of the Timex wearers are in this high-income bracket.

Watches, no matter how much they cost, are better at telling time than making a person happy. But if you want to enhance your changes of being unhappy, it is easy to do. Just keep buying expensive badges you can barely afford. And be prepared to buy them again and again.

More than 25 years ago, I conducted my first focus group interview with multimillionaires. What stood out from that interview and the many subsequent ones I undertook? It was not just what the respondents said. What was really illuminating was the clothing and the accessories that they wore. Often part of my job as a moderator/host was to offer to hang up their suit jackets. This gave me a chance to check the labels. What have I found over the past 25 years from both observation and empirical surveys? As we have already learned, most millionaires do not wear expensive suits. My research indicates that most millionaires do not wear expensive watches either. Over the years, I have observed that among focus group participants, the most popular watch is Seiko. It is a fine timepiece; yet it is moderately priced. Has Seiko been dethroned by Breitling, Patek Philippe, Rolex, or Tag Heuer? Certainly by now the dull Seiko must have moved down in popularity among America's socioeconomic winners. We are told by the fashion media that our taste for luxury goods is just so much more sophisticated now. We are much more hip to the notions that "if you have it, flaunt it."

So much for logic, promotional hype, and news headlines. Many truly successful people never bought into the hype. According to my most recent national survey of millionaires, Seiko remains in first place

Table 4.1 Top 10 Brands of Watches Worn by Millionaires

Brand of Watch	Market Share Overall (% Rank)		Percent Who Received a Watch as Gift 42% (% Rank)		Market Share: Watch Purchased by User 58% (% Rank)	
Seiko	19.5	(1)	52.5	(2)	16.2	(1)
Rolex	15.4	(2)	46.4	(7)	14.5	(3)
Timex	10.8	(3)	17.1	(10)	15.8	(2)
Omega	5.7	(4)	50.0	(4)	5.0	(4)
Tag Heuer	4.3	(5)	51.4	(3)	3.7	(6)
Movado	4.2	(6)	47.1	(5)	3.9	(5)
Bulova	2.1	(7)	58.8	(1)	1.5	(9)
Cartier	1.9	(8)	46.7	(6)	1.7	(8)
Breitling	1.7	(9)	35.7	(9)	2.0	(7)
Pulsar	1.2	(10)	40.0	(8)	1.3	(10)

among America's affluent (see Table 4.1). Nearly one in five millionaires (19.5 percent) wears a Seiko. Do you want people to think that you are a millionaire? Then wear the number-one watch brand worn by millionaires: Seiko. Show it to all of your friends and associates. Tell them that you own the "millionaire watch." What if you cannot afford to buy a $200 or $300 Seiko? What about the third most popular watch brand among millionaires? Go for the $100 Timex. Yes, Timex, the watch designed to tell time, not to define a high level of socioeconomic success in an ultimately fruitless effort. Nearly one in nine of the millionaires surveyed wears a Timex.

What brand of watch is number two in terms of overall market share among millionaires? Given the otherwise displayed frugality of millionaires, it does seem a bit surprising that 15.4 percent wear a Rolex watch. Not surprisingly, nearly one-half (46.4 percent) of those surveyed who wear a Rolex received it as a gift. In contrast, only 17.1 percent of the Timex wearers received their watch as a gift. Overall, 42 percent of millionaires wear a watch that was given to them as a gift. What if you consider the market share of brands among only those millionaires who paid for their own watches? Among that group, Timex is the number-two brand and Rolex drops to third place. Seiko remains number one. What can be said about millionaires and their choice of watches? When they spend their own money on watches, they don't splurge on expensive vanity purchases.

What brand of watch is number one among decamillionaires and those who are members of the glittering rich segment? Rolex. About one in four wears this brand of watch. This may explain why, in my estimation, Rolex is probably the most imitated watch today. And the knock-offs are especially popular among the aspirational clan. But "looking like" does not mean that it is a genuine Rolex or that, in fact, a real millionaire, let alone a glittering millionaire, is wearing it.

Perhaps consistent with the number of expensive watches (and other baubles) purchased by low-net-worth but high-income producers, it shouldn't be surprising that one of the top 10 most profitable small businesses is pawn brokering. Could it be that the hyperspending and borrowing to the maximum during the high-water mark of our income-earning years has led to this unpleasant result? When our home equity is maxed out (or the valuation decreases) and our consumer debt is at an all-time high so that banks and credit card companies will not give us one more dollar, when we may have lost our jobs, we will have those expensive watches to pawn.

When we act rich instead of like real millionaires, we have no breathing room for any unforeseen event or economic downturn. Should that happen, someone else is likely to profit at our expense. One pawnbroker I interviewed reported that his best client in 2008 was a "professional man," a marketer of partnerships who hocked his Rolex four times in one year. Each time he borrowed $4,000 ("to cover living expenses") while his capital was tied up. He paid 25 percent interest per month, or the equivalent of 300 percent interest per year, to maintain that watch.

A Study in Contrasts

Imagine interviewing two millionaires. Both are wearing Rolex watches. Yet their orientation toward such status-defining artifacts could not be more different. The first respondent complains about the screening process. It asked what brand of watch the respondent wore. He, in turn, edited the screen instrument, writing in under the Rolex brand: "I have three of these plus I own . . . others . . . including . . . " He also owns multiple Ferrari and Lexus motor vehicles. For this reason I refer to him as Mr. Multipliski, or Mr. M for short. Not many people have the vast collection of status artifacts that Mr. M owns. And few could match the pride he exudes about having them in his collection. Mr. M ranks very high on the glittering rich scale.

What about the other millionaire? He too is wearing a Rolex, but he is not comfortable about it. In fact, he seems a bit embarrassed about it. As we will get to in a moment, he lets you know that he feels obligated to wear it. This millionaire, Mr. Nitty, Mr. N, is an extremely frugal type of millionaire next door. He is a full-fledged member of the anything-but-glittering or aspirational segments. He is wealthy because he and his wife played great defense; that is, they both lived well below their means and they invested wisely, mainly in rental properties. Yet the couple's earned annual income is just under $100,000 a year. Much of the Nittys' income is in another form: unrealized income from the appreciation of the value of their rental properties.

In sharp contrast, Mr. M has a seven-figure realized annual income. He became wealthy because he played tremendous offense. Mr. M is not at all frugal. He does not have to be since he is so very good at generating a very high income.

How do these two characters view the world of so-called prestige/ high-status artifacts? Mr. N comes from a long line of frugal people of the Scottish variety. He was taught that people who wear expensive watches, drive high-priced motor vehicles, and live in large, expensive homes have little or no wealth. According to Mr. N, people such as these wear, drive, and mortgage all of their income. Mr. N does not respect these people, and he never wants anyone to think that he is part of this crowd. Thus he is uncomfortable about wearing the Rolex.

Mr. M's views about the relationship between wealth and status brands could not be more different from Mr. N's. Mr. M believes that those who do not wear expensive jewelry (Rolex included), drive high-status motor vehicles, and live in expensive homes have little or no wealth. To him it is quite simple. Those who have it—wealth—show it; those who are not wealthy do not show it. Of course, in his own mind, Mr. M, a glittering rich person, is living proof that you can have wealth and, at the same time, own multiple Rolex watches, Ferraris, and multimillion-dollar homes. But what Mr. M does not know is that only about 1 in 1,000 households in the United States are in his income bracket. Yet he is under the impression, given the number of people he sees wearing Rolexes and driving expensive cars, that there are many more. Mr. M, for all his ability to generate significant income, has mistaken the marketing message for reality.

For Mr. N and Mr. M, there are no gray areas concerning wealth and conspicuous consumption. Mr. N strongly believes that wealth and status brands are substitutes. One is either wealthy (with a high net worth) or looks wealthy (with lots of status badges and artifacts) but has no wealth. Mr. M feels that they are complements. In reality, both men are wrong. It is true that most people cannot own or even lease or rent multiple expensive products and become wealthy at the same time. Most of us just do not generate high enough incomes to do so.

There is more to this story than variations in income. Mr. M and Mr. N come from two distinctly different backgrounds. And both are worth detailing to better understand why Mr. M owns multiple Rolex watches while Mr. N only wears his to work.

Understanding Mr. Multipliski

During the time that I was reviewing Mr. M's case study, I was interviewed by Richard Warner, a reporter for the local PBS station. Prior to being interviewed he asked me an interesting question, one with implications for the topic at hand.

MR. WARNER: I recently interviewed two billionaires. The one who made his fortune in retailing told me that he wears a $100 watch, inexpensive $300 suits, and has never owned a boat, let alone a yacht. The other fellow, who founded an insurance company, wears very expensive custom-made suits and has a drawer full of $10,000 watches. Plus he owns a yacht that costs over $10 million. How would you explain these differences?

DR. STANLEY: The fellow who wears inexpensive suits likely came from a middle-class background. His parents were not rich but they were, as often said, comfortable. He was never embarrassed about the socioeconomic position of his parents or the artifacts they owned. Even though he is a billionaire today, he never feels the need to express his success via clothes, vehicles, watercraft, and such. His achievements are often recognized by all those charitable causes he supports and by articles that profile him in the press.

MR. WARNER: What about the other fellow?

DR. STANLEY: He probably came from an economically poor family. Poverty might have hung over his head all the while he was growing up. He often felt embarrassed and humiliated about lacking even the most basic things. Plus it is likely that his parents provided him anything but a loving, nurturing environment. Today he wants everyone to know that he no longer lives on Hungry Street. He buys himself the gifts he never received as a youngster. How did I do?

MR. WARNER: You nailed it!

Mr. Warner was likely too generous in judging the accuracy of my assessment of the two billionaires. After analyzing a lot more data, I found that it is not perfectly accurate to say that all kids born into poverty who make it big financially automatically become hyperspenders.

Because there are so very few billionaires in the United States, especially those who tasted poverty as kids, it is difficult to determine statistically the origin of hyperspending among those who have such a proclivity. Yet I have learned something from my interviews with multimillionaires who came from economic ground zero. Even though I cannot yet prove it statistically, it seems that those who travel the longest distance along the wealth scale in one generation hyperspend on status symbols. They are the buyers of multiple of multiples like Mr. Multipliski. Sadly, many share something else in common: Their parents were anything but nurturing.

For some, an expensive status brand such as Rolex is a real symbol of extraordinary achievement, and Mr. M fits that description. He is worth more than $100 million. He is not shy about communicating his financial achievements. Mr. M has a very strong need to do so. In part, he seeks to separate himself from his dirt-poor working-class family background.

Overall, there is a statistically significant relationship between the amount one pays for a watch and one's level of income and wealth. But for those surveyed who have annual realized incomes of $100,000 or more, income explains only about 6 percent of the variation in the price paid for watches. Wealth or net worth explains an even smaller proportion.

Expensive status symbols are too often used by those who want a badge of success, an economic medal of honor, without really achieving. Perhaps Mr. M understands this fact. That is why he was so precise in telling me about the multiple badges of success that he has acquired. Yes, Mr. M is a bit unusual. But once we examine his background, we better understand his motives. But before I discuss his early socialization process, it may be useful to reflect upon something else. Mr. M's more current activities, especially his brand purchase patterns, are especially interesting as well as unusual.

Mr. M patronizes only three stores when purchasing his clothing and accessories: Neiman Marcus, Nordstrom, and Polo. Most of his suits are custom made or custom ordered. His favorite brand of shoes is Cole Haan.

Mr. M lives in a neighborhood where the average home sells for $10 million. His home is worth more than twice that amount. What types and brands of alcoholic beverages are in Mr. M's home inventory? Absolut, Grey Goose, Ketel One, Johnnie Walker Black, Chivas Regal, Jim Beam, Jack Daniel's, Maker's Mark. Only 1 in 1,000 millionaires whom I have studied during my entire career had more than 2,000 bottles of wine in their collections. Mr. M is among them. Also, not one of the bottles he owns cost him under $50.

Under what brand category does Mr. M's consumption behavior really stand out? He is clearly a "car guy." When you ask him if he owns a Ferrari, he will tell you the same thing he stated about his collection of Rolex watches:

"I don't own *a* Ferrari. I own *three!*"

His most recent purchase was a $330,000 Ferrari F 430 for which he paid cash. He never ever leases. Over 10 years, he has purchased other brands of automobiles including Lexus, Porsche, and Toyota. Perhaps he has made these purchases for no other reason than to fill up the 10-car garage attached to his home.

Most rich people have never owned a boat. But Mr. M is no ordinary millionaire. He most recently paid over $3 million for his. It goes nicely with the $40,000 Rolex he just acquired. On his way home from making this purchase, he had his hair cut for $100 plus a $20 tip. Mr. M spent more than seven times what the typical male millionaire pays for a haircut.

Expensive haircuts, a $20 million home, a drawer full of expensive watches, multiple Ferraris, custom clothes, and 2,000 bottles of vintage wine are symbols of more than success. This pattern of spending on the part of Mr. M denotes a background common among certain types of very wealthy people. They are usually from families that were at or very near economic ground zero. Mr. M's father was an unskilled factory worker who never even came close to earning $25,000 annually. Neither his mother nor his father attended college.

Mr. M attended a high school that had few "rich kids." Yet even among this predominantly working-class student body, he felt that his family was at the bottom of the income spectrum. Plus Mr. M revealed that he was embarrassed to have his classmates over to his home because it was so decrepit.

Mr. M shares something else with those who have an almost pathological need to display their success. Their families and their lifestyles typically were dysfunctional. There was little or no love and much disharmony. Their parents' orientation toward the children ran from total indifference and neglect to abuse. Moving from poverty to multimillionaire status in one generation is not easy.

Mr. M and others with similar backgrounds need more than money to mask the scars formed during their salad days. Even success in business will not fully eradicate the ghosts of their unpleasant pasts. People like Mr. M need to surround themselves with certain visual cues or status symbols that constantly reinforce the motto that "Today I am somebody." When Mr. M looks at his $40,000 Rolex, it tells him more than the time.

Mr. M's case reminds me of one that I highlighted in an earlier work. Faith's story was most inspiring. She, like Mr. M, came from an economically poor family. Her mother and father took turns beating her when she was a teenager. As a result, Faith left home when she was a sophomore in high school. Yet this high school dropout overcame, persevered, and eventually succeeded in life.

Like Mr. M, she wears a Rolex watch and drives an expensive car to show the world that she "is somebody." But the long-term goal of financial independence was always more important than owning status brands— brands she can clearly afford, given her seven figure income. Faith bought her badges after she became rich, not before. She and her husband live in a home valued at about $400,000. They could afford a much more expensive home. But Faith believes that it is better to put "big bucks" into structures that generate income, such as her chains of fast food restaurants.

Mr. M and Faith have something else in common. They do not spend a lot of time recounting the painful times from their past; they focus on the future. They use their time and emotional energy to enhance their careers as business owners.

Do you spend time dwelling on painful experiences from your formative years? According to Mr. M, if you do, you will likely never become a success. What if your parents were uncaring, dysfunctional, or abusive? Did they refuse to give you a dime for college tuition? Today, 10, 20, even 30 years later, are you still angry at them? Mr. M suggests that you forget about it. History can never be changed. Use your emotional energy nurturing your need to succeed. Just don't fall into the trap of thinking that buying expensive brands before you succeed will make you like the glittering people in the ads and heal the wounds of your past. To do so will only make you financially weaker and much less satisfied with your life.

In a letter that Faith sent me, she outlined her creed of life and success. Of all the many letters that I have received, hers was among the most illuminating. Faith wrote:

> Do not accept your future as when you were young. Every statistic was against me! I should be on welfare. I should be [in prison] part of the state correctional system! Don't use [the past] as your excuse. It's so easy just to say, "I was born poor . . . I had bad abusive parents . . . So you could not go to school. You say . . . I'll never get ahead because I started out too low on the food chain. If you do, you will lose . . . You are a quitter . . . You don't even want to try. If you are determined that no one will stop you . . . Never accept less of yourself. Never!

> Nothing is impossible if you believe in yourself. Use this value [of yourself] like an anchor. You will make mistakes . . . get over it . . . Otherwise you will waste time and energy.
>
> You are the loom that weaves the tapestry.

People like Faith and Mr. M deserve to reward themselves for their achievements. Having a large inventory of expensive artifacts is a way of spitting in the face of early experiences with poverty, neglect, and often abuse. Knowing this, perhaps we should be less critical of the rags-to-riches kids who are today's hyperconsuming glittering rich. They made it the hard way without the proverbial silver spoon in their mouth or even loving parents. These Mr. M types have every right to brag by buying badges.

Buying and Selling Badges

Mr. M didn't just magically become a business owner. His first full-time job was in sales. He took an instant liking to selling—the career that rewards performance irrespective of upbringing or pedigree. He paid 100 percent of his college education by selling automobiles. He was so good at it that an enlightened dealer made him an equity/junior partner in his business. He now owns multiple dealerships including several of the largest and most profitable ones.

Experience in selling is something that Mr. M shares with many other self-made millionaires who wear Rolex watches. Fully one in four millionaire Rolex wearers indicated that his first full-time job was in sales. Today more than half of them are business owners or senior executives of public corporations. Most of these millionaires will tell you that they are "still selling."

Success in selling requires courage and tenacity. Those who started out in sales and succeeded at it remain extremely competitive. People in sales start every day at zero. You are only as good as your next sale. Success in sales is about more than excelling; it's about excelling over and over.

Society does not ascribe high status to those in the sales profession or to those who are business owners. There are more than 35 million sales professionals and more than 21 million business owners in the United States. Only a small percentage of these people ever become multimillionaires like Mr. M. Those who do often feel the need to distinguish themselves from their less successful sales professional and business owner siblings. Like Mr. M, they often purchase their own success badges and recognition trophies in the form of expensive watches, suits, cars, home, and the like. Note that there is a very high correlation between one's level of net worth (wealth) and one's self-designated compulsion to succeed. Take those multimillionaires who wear Rolex watches as an example. Those who say that they have "a nearly uncontrollable urge to succeed" outnumber those who do not by a ratio of three to one.

Often multimillionaires, especially those with Mr. M's background, need to compete in business and win. They also need to compete and win the battle of displaying their successes. One of the problems associated with the sales profession is "lack of inventory." Sales, unlike manufacturing tangible products, cannot be inventoried. Those involved with selling must sell today and continue selling tomorrow and the next day and the next day, or they will have zero inventory in terms of production. This is one reason why recognition in the form of an expensive watch or even an impressive plaque provides some lasting measure of past performance. It is a way to stand above competitors.

To understand the need for recognition among top achievers with strong sales orientations, consider the case of Mrs. Jackie S. I first met Jackie at a top sales producer recognition dinner where I was the keynote speaker.

How important was it for Jackie to receive her performance award that night? The sterling silver plate given her cost only about $400 but, to

Jackie, it was worth much, much more. It was a symbol and public recognition among her peers of her splendid achievements. Not until several weeks after the dinner did I realize just how important the silver plate award was to Jackie. During my interview with her, she told me something I will never forget.

> Tom, you probably noticed the pillows I had behind my back when we were seated for the recognition dinner. . . . The night before the dinner, I backed into a lit candelabra which burned my back. It was painful. It was just as painful the next day when I flew down to Florida for the dinner. But there was no way that I was going to miss out on receiving my award . . . no way.

Like Jackie, the need for recognition of his many achievements is also part of Mr. M's personality. That is why he felt compelled to tell me his story. In spite of all his extraordinary achievements, Mr. M feels that he has never received adequate recognition. His is a modern-day Abe Lincoln story. But too often people do not want to hear about Abe Lincoln. They want to read about those who inherited their wealth or celebrities. It is almost as if we create a mythology around wealth that suggests that it is an accident of birth or environment and not the product of hard work. In this way, perhaps, we justify our own lack of wealth.

Contradictory Mr. Nitty

Prior to our interview, Mr. N was prescreened. According to his profile, he was on all counts the prototypical, frugal millionaire-next-door type. Yet not five minutes into the interview, he stated: "You may have noticed that I'm wearing a Rolex watch."

Could it be, I wondered, that Mr. N had suddenly changed his reported orientation from frugal, fastidious saver to something else? But he told my screener emphatically that he was the ultimate millionaire next door. He even quoted extensively from my previous book. Mr. N also revealed that the profile fits his parents to a T. He stated that he was frugal, his wife was frugal, and his parents were frugal. His grandparents were frugal, his dogs were frugal.

Had he recently hooked up with a "bad crowd," a group of hyperconsumers who lusted for luxury goods? Or had Mr. N won the $100 million lottery? If either of these were true, why was he still driving a pickup truck, still religiously following NASCAR, still occupying a modestly decorated office, still wearing a work uniform, and still living in an ordinary $250,000 home in small-town rural America?

The only thing that had changed since Mr. N was screened was his watch. Previously, he wore an inexpensive ($35) battery-operated watch bearing the logo of his favorite NASCAR driver, Tony Stewart. But now he was "Sir Nitty," as I jokingly called him at the end of the interview, wearing the oyster of oysters, the Rolex watch fit for kings.

Mr. N explained the circumstances under which he became a Rolex owner. He seemed uncomfortable, perhaps even embarrassed, about wearing such an expensive watch. Several times and in a variety of different ways he pointed out emphatically: "I did not buy the watch . . . it was a gift . . . received it from my employer, the owner . . . in recognition for ten years of meritorious service . . . that is what the commendation said.

Mr. N loves his job and is "very well treated" by his employer. He is the parts manager at a truck dealership. And yes, he very much appreciates the recognition he received at the organization's annual awards dinner. Nonetheless, Mr. N is not comfortable wearing an expensive watch. It does not fit his consumption lifestyle, so he only wears it at work to show respect for his employer. When Mr. N is not at work, he wears his inexpensive watch. The Rolex is never with him when he goes to NASCAR races and church or when he hunts, fishes, and just plain hangs out.

Mr. N is not alone. More than 4 in 10 millionaires who wear a watch that retails for $1,000 or more received it as a gift. Whether for business or personal reasons, many millionaires' pricey watches were acquired via *OPM*; that is, with other people's money. Just because someone is wearing a Rolex doesn't mean that they intend to show you their status badge, or that they are actually rich, or even that they bought it themselves.

In the context of business, you can call it what you may: a gift, a reward, a badge, a commendation, a token of appreciation. An expensive watch can be and often is an excellent way to reward folks like "Sir Nitty." Whenever he checks the time he is reminded of the ceremony in which his employer stood up in front of an audience and said, "Well done, Donald Nitty."

Might there be other tells that would indicate to us that Mr. N did not buy the Rolex he wears? Recall the motor vehicle he drives. Mr. N's pickup truck is telling. There is an inverse correlation between the price of one's watch and of pickup truck ownership. But there is more. In contrast to pickup truck ownership, consider the following scenario: You see seven different makes of motor vehicles pass you on the highway. Each is driven by a millionaire. According to my surveys, which driver is most likely to be wearing a Rolex that he/she bought for himself/herself? Would you bet it was the driver inside the Porsche, the Mercedes-Benz, the BMW, the Audi, the Jaguar, the Lexus, or the Cadillac? If you predicted that it is the driver in the Porsche, you guessed correctly. All of these makes of cars, listed in descending order, are favorites (in a statistically significant sense) among millionaires who wear a self-bought Rolex. Thus it seems that high-priced foreign makes of motor vehicles, especially from Europe, are favorites among those who wear the high-price European import called Rolex. Mr. N has never owned a Porsche or any other import. Nor has he ever had the slightest interest in owning one. But he does enjoy NASCAR and high-performance American makes of motor vehicles.

Are there any other differences that distinguish the millionaires who wear the self-bought Rolex? They do have significantly more wealth than those who received their watch as a gift. Also they are found in higher concentrations among very high–income-producing millionaire physicians and senior corporate executives. But, based on my surveys, one other occupational category has the highest concentration of self-bought Rolex wearers: Highly compensated millionaire attorneys are three times more likely to be in the self-bought category than those who received their Rolex as a gift. Could it be that too few people have a lot of interest in buying an expensive gift of this type for highly compensated millionaire attorneys? It is unclear. But what is clear is that many attorneys in this group feel that they deserve to be given one, even if it means that they gift themselves.

Mr. Nitty's boss is not the only millionaire who gives expensive watches to others. The CEO of an investment management firm also does the same. He wears a Seiko watch, but he gives "$5,000 watches" to his top sales professionals in recognition of their productivity (perhaps understanding that successful sales people need badges of commendation and display). Also, a top sales professional in the automobile industry, Beverly B., sold 369 luxury motor vehicles one year. Shortly thereafter, this top sales professional gave her mother a Rolex watch. Yet Beverly B. has never bought herself an expensive watch or any other prestige labels.

For the CEO, building a top investment management company is the real badge of achievement. But what about Beverly B.? Recognition as a top producer in the form of a plaque and formal presentation from her employer are her badges denoting real superiority. She described her mother in glowing terms as:

> The kindest, most unselfish person I ever met. [She] often said [she would] like to have a nice watch someday. . . . She came up so poor . . . as a single mom made so many sacrifices for us . . . the watch made her so happy.

Glittering Rich in Texas

Jim (who we first talked about in Chapter 2) is self-employed. Last year this triple-decamillionaire generated an income of over $3 million. Interestingly, his consumption behavior is much more like Mr. N's than the hyperconsuming Mr. M's. Jim lives in a midsize Texas town situated in the heart of timber country. His log home sits adjacent to one of the timber tracts he and his business partner own.

How much did Jim pay for his watch? Given his wealth, he could well afford to buy a $40,000 Rolex. Would you bet that this Texan imitates his neighbors, those who live in homes valued at a fraction of the ones in Mr. M's neighborhood or Mr. M.? Here is a hint. According to my national surveys of the affluent, the market value of a home is a stronger predictor of the price paid for a watch than both income and net worth.

Given this relationship, you might not be surprised to learn that Jim paid just $300 for his Swiss Army watch. His choice of watch is congruent with his consumption lifestyle overall and that of most of his Texas neighbors. Most recently, Jim paid $12 for a haircut, $140 for a suit ("Dillard's, on sale"), and $2,500 for a fishing boat. He usually pays around $15 for a dinner entrée at his favorite restaurant. In the past 10 years, he has purchased only Chevrolets and GMC motor vehicles. Most recently, he allocated $32,000 for a Chevrolet Silverado pickup truck.

Jim's partner has many of the same hyperconsumption habits as does Mr. M. Jim made it clear that his partner lives in a high-consumption environment—not anywhere near the Texas timber country.

Jim is better at telling his story than anyone else, so in his own words here are some highlights:

I greatly enjoyed your book, *The Millionaire Mind*. I too believe that most conservative millionaires differ from high-consumption millionaires (HCM). My partner is a HCM but still has a very high net worth. . . . His luxuries include: . . . three homes . . . valued at $9 or

$10 million . . . jet plane . . . a family lifestyle of $100,000 a month minimum living expense. . . . Our timber and apartment housing business is on a 50%/50% basis. We have only three employees . . . our annual sales of timber and timberland alone average $8 million. . . . Don't even have a secretary but I love what I do. . . .

Yes, I'm different . . . I enjoy also being the manager of one of our timber ranches, 5,000 acres . . . mow a lot on my Kubota tractor while listening to XM radio. . . . plant 3.5 million trees a year. I personally hand plant 10,000 trees for knowledge and exercise.

Jim understands what factors account for tree growth and correspondingly his net worth. The trees talk to Jim. They often tell him: "Jim, we don't care how much you spent for your watch . . . has nothing to do with our rate of growth. . . . But, in general, Jim, pricey watches may be detrimental to enhancing your wealth."

Jim needs a watch in order to know what time it is. He does not need one to imitate or impress his wealthy neighbors (if he had any). Jim's neighbors and his six dogs—"mostly strays I picked up on my timberland"—don't care much about status.

Do you think that the strays that Jim rescued would prefer that their savior wore a $40,000 watch and drove a Range Rover? They care that Jim took them in, housed them, cared for them, fed them, even loved them. Could it be that dogs have more common sense than a lot of us?

Jim does borrow money, but never for personal consumption:

Have debt . . . but always have $20 million worth more of trees than debt not counting land value . . . lock in rates for three to five years minimum.

Jim's bankers are not impressed by people who "wear their wealth." Rather, they admire and are very much impressed with Jim's balance sheets and income statements. These are meaningful badges of success.

Jim is not all work and no play. He detailed several of the activities he enjoys:

> We take care and greatly enjoy our three grandkids. Attend three movies a week with my wife. Regularly attend church and Bible study classes. Eat out . . . Mexican and drink margaritas at least twice a week.

Jim is like most of the truly successful, high-net-worth people I have interviewed over the years. They receive great satisfaction from activities that mostly involve social interaction with family and friends. Often these activities are not at all costly but account for much of the high degree of satisfaction that Jim and his cohorts get out of life.

> I usually act as a mentor and teacher to college graduates who want to start a business. . . . I love being involved with young, bright minds.

Many young adults (and even older adults) might not be particularly interested in having frugal Jim, the man who wears a $300 watch, serve as their role model. Our society has confused the consumption of certain elite brands with true success. Young people want to emulate the outsized lifestyles of movie stars, professional athletes, and other glittering rich people because they think that real success is product and brand defined. Given the choice, we seem to have come to a place where people would prefer to look rich than be truly well off. Perhaps the financial crisis of 2008 will give pause to the idea of rich for consumption's sake and case studies like Jim's will come to be required class reading.

A Change in Content

I often required my students to interview a successful business owner and then write a profile of the respondent. Those who were able to find and then solicit interviews with low-profile decamillionaires like Jim were given extra credit. Several of my students were eventually offered jobs by some of these extraordinary business owners.

Some students reported having difficulty finding the "Jim" types because they looked in the wrong places. The Jim types are rarely profiled in the popular press. The business owners who become media darlings are often better at getting good press than accumulating wealth. Instead, the number-one type of periodical read by low-profile, successful business owners like Jim is a trade journal, such as *Timber Grower, Loggin' Times*, and *Forest Farmer.*

Imagine you are a student and call Jim to ask for an interview. He asks how you found him and why you are interested in interviewing him. Your answer will make his day: "I just read the article about you in *Timber Grower*, where you were named Forest Farmer of the Year . . . a legend. That is why I want to write up your profile for my college class."

Chances are very high that Jim will agree to be interviewed. He may even come and lecture to your class. If he does, you and your classmates will learn more from him about the ways and means of succeeding in business than from a dozen courses.

There is one topic you may wish to include in the profile you develop. It relates to advertising. Many readers of trade journals, like Jim, are very wealthy. Given this fact, why is it that marketers of expensive watches, luxury cars, and related status artifacts rarely advertise in trade journals? Jim knows the answer. Readers of trade journals are more interested in learning about products, services, and methods that will enhance the productivity of their businesses and ultimately their income and wealth. They are much less interested in reading about how to look successful via store-bought badges.

Different Strokes for Different Folks

I interviewed two double-decamillionaires who are especially interest-ing. Fred wears a Patek Philippe watch that cost $17,000. Trey wears a $15 "bought it at Wal-Mart" watch. Why would someone worth over $20 million

wear such an inexpensive watch? And what factors could explain Fred's decision to buy a very expensive timepiece?

As we have seen (and will see again), there is a high correlation between
the price of one's watch and one's overall consumption lifestyle. Even though
these two respondents have the same level of accumulated wealth, they are
different people. Fred is positioned high on the glittering rich scale in terms
of consumption; Trey is not. Fred's annual realized income was just over
$2 million. Trey's was just over $400,000. While both are similar in terms of
wealth, the important difference is their respective return on net worth, or
RON. Fred's RON is 10.3 percent (income divided by net worth). Trey's
RON is only 2.1 percent. In other words, Fred generates the equivalent of
10.3 percent of his wealth in terms of his annual realized income. Trey's is
only about one-fifth of Fred's. Given his lower RON, it might seem that Trey
is not as astute an investor as Fred, but, in reality, he is very good at accumulating wealth. Trey's investment strategy is to minimize his realized/taxable
income while at the same time maximizing his unrealized income/appreciation
of his investments. Trey is deliberately cash poor but investment rich. You
cannot spend cash if you do not generate a lot of it.

I have found that during the period from 1980 to 2004, two occupational groups had especially low RONs (often in the 1.0 to 3.0 percent
range): millionaire farmers and those who own real estate investment companies. Trey is in the latter category. Trey's RON of 2.1 percent is not at all
unusual for either group. But Fred is in a different line of work. He is a senior
vice president and director (bonds/corporate debt) at a Wall Street investment
banking firm.

Now consider the economic productivity (net worth divided by income)
of Fred versus Trey. For every $9.70 of wealth accumulated by Fred, it requires
$1 of income. Trey generates $49 of wealth for every $1 in income. Trey is
much more productive.

Fred began earning a high realized annual income, joining the top 3 percent of income producers, before he was 30. Trey first hit the 3 percent level

when he was in his early 40s. Recall that those who earn big incomes early are among the most prone to spend heavily on expensive products with prestige names. But it is not just about income earned at a particular age; where and how you earn that big income also accounts for variations in consumption habits.

Fred works in New York City. He lives in a $4.5 million home in fashionable northern Westchester County, New York. The highest concentration of glittering rich people in America lives in the tristate metropolitan area of New York. Understandably, this area also contains the highest concentration of aspirationals. Not only are we what we eat, we are also products of where we live.

When at work on Wall Street, Fred is surrounded by a multitude of other glittering rich people and myriad retail stores that sell prestige brands. Fred believes that he actually lives well below his means, especially when compared with his colleagues. Unlike Trey, Fred judges his means in terms of his very high income. Trey looks more at his balance sheet as a base for making such judgments. Nor does Trey socialize with glittering people or their aspirational poor cousins. Trey lives in the South, one of the areas that holds the lowest concentration of glittering rich and aspirationals.

Trey lives in a home valued at $1.1 million, or the equivalent of just 5 percent of his wealth. His home is one of the most expensive ones in his neighborhood. Nonetheless, he still lives below his means. Fred lives high on the consumption continuum. But given his seven-figure income and eight-figure net worth, his $4.5 million home and related lifestyle are not likely to bankrupt Fred.

Who Do You Wannabe?

Imagine for a few moments that you are teaching a business course at a university. In one of your classes, you introduce a new component to the curriculum called "Who Do You Wannabe?" Imagine that both Fred and

Trey are part of this program. They will appear together and present their respective histories to your class. But first, you will introduce Fred and Trey to your students.

> Students, today we are honored to have with us two very special speakers. Fred and Trey are both self-made millionaires. Each is worth over $20 million. Based on what you hear today you are to write an essay. The topic is "Who Do You Wannabe." If you want to be like Fred someday, tell me why. But if you want to be like Trey, enlighten me. Only one essay is required. So will it be Fred or Trey for you? Ah, but there is a bonus. Not only will you receive extra credit for your essay, but the student who writes the best "wannabe Fred" essay will win a summer internship with him. The winner of the "wannabe Trey" essay will become his summer intern. As an intern, you will receive a salary. And all of your expenses will be paid by our sponsors. Of course, you may not have a lot of expenses since both winners will be staying with their respective sponsors and their families.
>
> Before introducing Fred and Trey, I will mention a few things about the two outstanding gentlemen. I hope this will not sound like a beauty contest.
>
> Fred is known by many of his friends as "fast-track Fred." He graduated Phi Beta Kappa at the age of 21 from a top-20 undergraduate program. Two years later he received a MBA in finance from a prestigious Ivy League university. Following his graduation, Fred was employed by a large, international management consulting firm. During his five-year tenure with this firm, he developed strategic plans for a large investment banking firm. Subsequently, at the age of 28, he was hired by this firm as a vice president. Today he holds the rank of senior vice president and head of one of the firm's major divisions. His current annual realized income is just over $2 million while his household's net worth is approximately $20 million. He first became

a millionaire at 32. Today Fred is wearing his $17,000 Patek Philippe watch and a $1,600 custom suit. The suits that he owns that are not custom made were purchased at Neiman Marcus, Saks Fifth Avenue, and Polo. He gets his hair cut once a week; it costs him $50 plus a tip. Fred's favorite shoe brand is Alden. Today he is wearing a $500 pair of Alden shell cordovan tassel moccasins.

For you car enthusiasts in class today, you may appreciate Fred's affinity for cars. In the past 10 years, Fred has purchased six BMWs, two Mercedes, one Jeep Cherokee, and one Jeep Wrangler Sahara model. His most recent acquisition was a 7 Series BMW that cost $88,000. Fred and his wife often entertain and have a fully stocked bar. He has an affinity for super-premium vodkas. Plus Fred has a wine cellar that contains over 600 bottles of vintage wine.

Trey says that he graduated from college in the top of his class. That is, the top 60th percentile or the bottom 40th percent. You can tell Trey has a sense of humor. He started his career after college as a management trainee for a large retail store. Eventually he started his own small retail operation. After years of struggling, he came to realize that the objective of a small retailer was to help his landlord become wealthy. At that time he made the transition into owning and operating his own real estate investment company, which he runs today. He first became a millionaire at the age of 43. He is currently married. He and his wife live in a home valued at $1.1 million in a neighborhood where the homes generally sell for less than that. Trey owns a vacation home that is about an hour's drive from his suburban home in Charlotte, North Carolina. He originally paid $80,000 for the home; he estimates that it is now worth $170,000. Trey is wearing his favorite watch, which he got at Wal-Mart for $15. Trey buys almost all of his clothes and accessories at JCPenney's. The suit he is wearing today is a 100 percent worsted wool Penney's suit that he paid $240 for on sale. His favorite brand of shoes is Bass.

Trey currently drives a six-year-old Ford Excursion that he originally paid $33,000 for. He only buys Ford Motor Company products.
He feels comfortable in doing so, especially when he drives down to
his favorite barbershop to get his $12 (tip included) haircut.

Not one "wannabe Trey" essay will be written. Each and every student will write about "fast-track Fred," the fellow with the $17,000 watch
and all that goes with it. But the reality of it is that not many people will
ever graduate from a top Ivy League university or qualify for entrance to
Wharton or be hired at such a young age as a highly compensated executive. Sure, students would prefer hanging around with Fred, the glittering guy, as opposed to Trey, the low-profile, JCPenney's customer. Yet most
people would significantly increase their odds of becoming wealthy if they
emulated Trey.

Wall Street may care about academic pedigrees and image, but real
estate, timber, plumbing, and any number of other endeavors are blind. Wall
Streeters may care about the price tag of the watch around your wrist, but
the vast majority of business and economic activity doesn't. More often
the scrap metal dealer, the bottler, the timberland owner have more wealth
and are more productive than Wall Streeters, and these millionaires usually
wear Seikos, not Rolexes.

Keeping Up with Your Spirits

I spent a lot of my money on booze, birds, and fast cars; the rest I just squandered.

—George Best

My mentor, the distinguished professor of marketing Dr. Bill Darden, often told his graduate students:

Get ready to compete in the marketplace with some real talent. The really brilliant ones in America don't work for the State Department. Not even in medical science labs. The great minds are working in marketing, designing ways of . . . convincing us that one brand of a hemorrhoid remedy is superior to another . . . that one wash detergent will produce whiter whites—thus assuring Mom will continue to be loved and admired by her husband and kids.

He was quite serious when saying this.

If Bill were still with us today and we could ask him to evaluate the marketing efforts associated with the liquor industry, he would likely tell us that, clearly, some of the best of the very best minds in America are at work marketing liquor. How else can one explain it? You take a colorless commodity, call it alcohol, flavor it, perhaps color it, age it, and convince people to pay over $100 for a bottle of something that could otherwise be had for $10. This is genius.

Bill told us something else. If you want to understand people and their brand selection habits, study the outliers, not the average consumers. One category of outlier is composed of people with money who live well below their means. Why are they insensitive to all the marketing propaganda and advertising themes that tell them to spend and spend? Why do they buy the lower-priced, uninteresting brands of alcoholic beverages when they can easily afford to purchase carloads of bottles of super-premium brands?

The other type of outlier are those individuals who, in spite of being of modest means, have a strong affinity for super-premium brands of liquor. Why? They think that drinking X brand will enhance their satisfaction with life. Aside from the fact that if one drinks to excess, drunk is as drunk does, the research data show that it is impossible for us to alter our level of satisfaction with life by selecting one brand of liquor over another. The price paid for a bottle of alcohol just doesn't have much influence on happiness. Yet the marketers of distilled beverages have spent billions of dollars convincing some of us that satisfaction is just a top-shelf purchase away, inside a beautifully designed bottle. For many of us, it doesn't matter how many times we fail to increase our satisfaction with life via an expensive bottle of liquor, we keep on believing and buying. The marketing genius that goes into selling premium goods may be at its zenith in the bottled spirits business.

Carlton of Crawford

Carlton buys, drinks, and serves low-priced spirits. He doesn't spend a lot on wine either. All of his purchases are in the $8 to $10 range. He likes red wines, Cabernet Sauvignon, and Merlot. He buys his wine at supermarkets and warehouse stores.

It appears that Carlton is price sensitive in regard to his beverage purchases. What might you conclude knowing that there is a statistically significant but not substantial correlation between what one pays for alcoholic beverages and one's income and wealth? Should we conclude that Carlton is a man of modest means?

To the contrary, Carlton is a triple-decamillionaire, with a net worth in excess of $30 million, and he has an annual realized income of approximately $1.5 million. Given his economic characteristics, you may be wondering why he doesn't purchase the premium grades of alcoholic beverages.

Carlton is living proof that neither measures of income nor wealth is fully able to account for the variations in prices paid for alcoholic beverages. Could it be that Carlton is some freak among the affluent population? In reality, Carlton may be different, but he is certainly not a freak. He is, in simple terms, "the decamillionaire next door." His frugal consumption lifestyle is much different from that of Fred (from Chapter 4) and Anna After (from Chapter 3), who have money and are compelled to flaunt it. Unlike Carlton and his ilk, Anna and her cohorts have been influenced by what the marketers of pricey brands of spirits tout in their promotional messages. We all know some of these themes by heart since we've been bombarded with them thousands of times. Yet the hundreds, perhaps thousands, of themes associated with each brand have a common element. All claim that "our brand is different . . . ours is superior" designed for people who are "superior" and "discriminating"—or who at minimum consider themselves as such. Carlton just isn't one of those who have been influenced by the advertising glitz.

Carlton's brand preferences regarding spirits (his favorite is scotch) place him in that special category of millionaire who only buys spirits in plastic bottles—that is, the Plastic Bottle Affluent. You would be mistaken if you thought that only those with modest means consume lower-priced spirits that come in these containers.

There are several possible explanations for Carlton's unusual brand preferences. First, Carlton thinks for himself. He is insensitive to the variations in the so-called quality among brands of distilled beverages that are touted in advertisements. These messages insist that Brand A is superior because it is consumed by more of the beautiful, successful, and sophisticated people of the world than any other brand. Have you ever seen ugly, poorly dressed models with missing teeth in advertisements for any brand of alcoholic beverage? Of course not; it is all about conditioning via association. But these messages have had no influence on Carlton even when they emphasized superiority via everything from the aging process to better water, premium ingredients, specially selected oak barrels, and so on.

Carlton believes that all scotch is great scotch. Otherwise it would not be called scotch. He feels the same way about red wines from California. Given Carlton's thinking, it is easy to understand why he avoids the premium brands. He prefers the Crawford's brand of scotch—not one of the more familiar brands nationally advertised. I had never even heard of it until he mentioned it. In fact, it took me several passes through a variety of liquor stores to locate it. Finally I found it on the bottom shelf in the scotch section. It seems that there is a direct correlation between the prices charged for various brands and the distance they are placed from the bottom shelf. So, unless you look below your normal focus point, you might miss seeing the Crawford's label. Yet some of the key informants (enlightened liquor store proprietors and sales clerks) I interviewed told me that Crawford's is "a lot of scotch for the money." You can buy a 1.75-liter bottle of Crawford's for $16.97 in Georgia. That is a lot less than the price of Chivas Regal ($59.97) or Johnnie Walker Black Label ($66.99).

Would you worry about offending your guests if you served Crawford's and other "bottom-shelf" brands of spirits to them? Perhaps they might conclude that you do not respect them and do not care much for their friendship. Some might think that you are not a very good host.

Carlton, however, does not worry about any of those things. He self-designates himself as being "an excellent host." He is of the strong opinion that entertaining is more about the human side, the enjoyable interaction with friends, than it is about serving top-shelf brands of spirits.

Carlton's choice of a bottom-shelf brand of scotch is an important clue in understanding his entire lifestyle. In spite of generating a seven-figure annual income, Carlton is not a big spender. This applies to everything from the wristwatch he wears (Seiko) to the car he drives (Toyota Avalon, one of the most popular makes among millionaires). Why didn't he buy the less expensive Camry? He is too tall for a Camry. The Avalon has much more headroom.

Why does the very wealthy Carlton drive a $28,000 Toyota Avalon? Carlton, like many millionaires, is value sensitive. To him the Toyota Avalon is, dollar for dollar, the best value available on the market; ditto the Seiko watch. Carlton has little need to tell others via his motor vehicle or his timepiece that he is a huge success. He has never owned a boat of any type or a vacation home or any other category of second home.

If you had Carlton's wealth and income, how would you live? Would you feel the need to trade up to fit in with your rich neighbors?

But what if most of your neighbors were not rich? Carlton doesn't live in Affluent Estates, gated off from the rest of us; he lives among regular people and so doesn't feel out of place driving a Toyota or serving bottom-shelf scotch. The typical selling price of a home in Carlton's neighborhood is in the mid-$300,000s, and his home is worth about 25 percent more than the norm for his neighborhood. There are no glittering people in Carlton's neighborhood. In fact, none of his friends, his fellow church members, or his buddies in the trade associations he belongs to can be classified as glittering. Yet Carlton does know a lot of rich people like him, and he fraternizes with them frequently every year at industry trade meetings. Often the concentration of millionaires within these groups is significantly higher than it is in so-called high-status neighborhoods. Most working decamillionaires (76 percent) attended at least one trade association meeting in the past year. Carlton's customers do not care where he lives. They deal with Carlton's company because it provides them with the products and intellectual property that they need. Carlton's offerings enhance the productivity of their operations. His consumption lifestyle—whether he drinks bottom- or top-shelf brands—is meaningless to his many industrial customers.

Carlton's neighbors and friends also have no clue about his financial position. In fact, only a few people outside of his family know the truth. His accountant knows, and so do his financial asset managers. The minister of his church has some inkling, because Carlton is a major benefactor.

Carlton is frugal when it comes to spending on products but he is generous when it comes to supporting noble causes. He is what some call a "10 percenter," donating at least 10 percent of his sizable income every year. What is typical throughout America? Decamillionaires next door are often the number-one contributors to their respective houses of worship. For most of these types, giving provides them with more satisfaction than displaying wealth through status symbols.

Why is Carlton so generous on one hand and so frugal on the other? Why does someone with such an extraordinary ability to accumulate wealth live among the ordinary? Several components of his background account for these behaviors.

When Carlton was a boy, his parents were missionaries. These adopters of the frugal lifestyle instilled in him many of the values that he adheres to today. They were masters of allocating resources and taking leadership roles, living by the waste not, want not creed. Their son wastes little and has few frivolous wants. Money did not change Carlton. But it was not only his parents who influenced him.

Carlton majored in chemical engineering in college. He graduated with a C average. Like many "good C students," Carlton eventually started his own business in the specialty chemical industry. His success in specialty chemicals accounts for much of his wealth.

As a chemical engineer, Carlton looks at products differently than most consumers. He is more prone to look at the chemical/physical properties of products. How does he respond to those marketers who claim that their brand of scotch is superior and well worth the higher price? He is not persuaded. Could it be that he believes that the chemical composition of various brands of scotch are pretty much the same? He judges most products the same way. It is one reason that Carlton uses the price dimension when selecting brands. He is like an industrial buyer who purchases ingredients that are essentially commodities. Thus, even the most brilliant marketers have a difficult time convincing Carlton to buy their magic.

In contrast, many people who have achieved economic success have been persuaded by marketers that they aren't truly successful unless they reveal it via hyperconsumption of prestige brands. Success equals wearing or drinking certain badges that show the success. Successful people look like those beautiful people in the ads and they buy and drink Grey Goose vodka. Crawford's scotch, however, is what people who aren't successful *have* to buy because they have no other option. But the other side of the story is that not everyone who drinks from pricey bottles is rich or even close to being successful. Worse, most will never become wealthy. They are merely acting rich on the basis of received marketing wisdom.

Whether they are wealthy or not wealthy, a major objective of many people who live in upscale neighborhoods is to demonstrate upper-middle-class membership. Perhaps these people all completed a course in class consciousness in which their instructor told them that society would rank them as upper middle class if they (1) had high-status occupational positions (corporate managers, professionals, or doctors), (2) owned a large home, (3) lived in a prestigious neighborhood, and (4) had income from inherited sources.[1]

As I wrote in *Marketing to the Affluent*:

> Proprietors of small businesses (such as Carlton), the segment I esti-mate to contain the largest number of American millionaires, are ranked fifth or third from the bottom on a seven-point scale of status characteristics. On the other hand, one can be very upper middle class and have a level of net worth nowhere near seven figures. . . . It is my belief that the number of households in America that are interested in looking wealthy is far greater than the number that are interested in being wealthy.[2]

Carlton has no such class aspirations, and he is not alone. People like Carlton do not buy expensive display badges in stores or from builders of luxury homes. I have repeatedly and consistently found that about half of the economically successful people in the United States do not live in either upper- class or upper-middle-class neighborhoods. Consumption lifestyles and income characteristics of households are more closely related to neighborhood "quality" than is actual wealth. In a way, America is a nation filled with people who are in constant need of renaming their own successes via the purchase of status artifacts. Yet many of those who pur-chase status symbols are not genuinely successful.

This is not to say that Carlton is so modest that he requires no recog-nition for his achievements at all. He does want his success acknowledged, but the merit badges he would like, and his audience, is specific. Carlton doesn't care what the sales clerk at the liquor store thinks about his scotch purchase. Rather, he places value on what his customers and his peers think. His customers vote for Carlton with their money. His peers vote for him in industry awards. He is not shy about showing off the plaques on his office wall. These industry-related recognitions cannot be purchased in any store no matter how exclusive it may be. Recognition by industry-specific affiliation groups is the true symbol, the badge of achievement in the marketplace. We won't ever read about Carlton in *People, GQ, Us Weekly*, or even *Architectural Digest*. He doesn't do or buy the sorts of status items that interest the mass media. In fact, Carlton enjoys his low-profile existence—though he does not object to having his picture appear on the cover of trade journals. Success is not the ability to go into a bar, high priced or otherwise, and order expensive scotch, and Carlton knows this.

Is Your Goose Cooked?

When asked, Carlton thought that Grey Goose was a bird! Clearly, he is not into vodka. Yet there are more than 300 brands of vodka on the market today. Given the saturation and highly competitive nature of the business, why would any company be foolish enough to purchase one of these brands, Grey Goose, for $2 billion? It was not a fool who did so. It was an astute decision on the part of the buyer, Bacardi Ltd.[3] In terms of growth and profit margin, the Grey Goose label is the jewel in the vodka industry's crown. This brilliantly conceived and positioned brand has encountered explosive sales growth (about 50 percent annually) over five years. Plus it is priced at a super-premium level.[4] Second in sales growth is Ketel One, with only a 15 percent increase.

There is another reason why the Grey Goose brand is so valuable: It is extremely popular among a certain segment of the affluent population.

People with money who enjoy demonstrating this fact—the glittering rich—have a high propensity to purchase Grey Goose. And whom do people wish to emulate? Whom do they reference when making brand-related purchasing decisions? Those who glitter, of course.

In my analysis, part of the increasing success of Grey Goose can be attributed to the brand's strong image among the aspirationals—those who wish to act rich. Ironically, it is not the wealthy who make the bulk of sales of certain brands but the aspirationals, the acting-rich actors, who account for a disproportionately large share of the profits generated within certain industries. This is why so many marketers target this segment. Marketers of spirits, especially vodka, are among the most aggressive in this regard. And they should be. According to the book *Trading Up* by Michael J. Silverstein and Neil Fiske, "The premium and super premium segments [of the vodka market] combine for a total of 30 percent of the category volume . . . and an astounding 70 percent of the category [vodka] profits."[5]

Why are so many members of the "need to look rich" population so willing to pay four or even five times more for a super-premium vodka? Silverstein and Fiske found that consumers of super-premium vodka often perceive it as a signaling device, a way of expressing a certain superior individual style. They note:

> Consumers distinguish themselves and make a statement about their sophistication, taste and hipness . . . calling for a Belvedere martini is sophisticated and hip . . . paying $15 for a Belvedere martini is an attainable bit of exclusivity.[6]

Do you believe that paying $60 for a bottle of vodka or $15 for a vodka martini will make you a member of an exclusive group? Of course, $15 is, in the scope of things, a fairly low initiation fee. And it is faster and less arduous and risky than building a business.

It is perverse to think that it is more exclusive to be in the elite martini club than to be among the financially independent. Yes, it takes more time, effort, and discipline to become financially independent than to drink a martini. While you are busy building a business or serving Crawford's scotch at your backyard barbecue you will be building a substantial nest egg, you won't get noticed as a superior person with discerning tastes. The good news is that you won't be alone.

What advice do I have for the aspirationals, those who seek to emulate the rich? They should seek out brands that "discriminate," that are most popular among the glittering rich and the least popular among the millionaires next door. Based on my survey results, I recommend Grey Goose vodka as the best bet. Note that 46 percent of millionaires who live in homes valued at $2 million or more purchase Grey Goose versus only 13 percent of those millionaires who live in homes in the $300,000 to under $400,000 category. Buying vodka is cheaper than buying a BMW or even a Rolex watch.

What makes Grey Goose an especially powerful symbol of the economic elite? It had the highest discriminant score, 4.6 times greater than the threshold for statistical significance. Other brands that scored high include Ketel One (3.7); Absolut (3.6); Johnnie Walker Black (3.5); Jack Daniel's (3.4); Belvedere (3.1); Glenlivet (2.9); Chivas Regal (2.8); Stolichnaya (2.7); Maker's Mark (2.7), and Dewar's (2.6). Keep in mind that it is not only particular brands that are favored by the glittering rich but also the variety of brands inventoried and the number of bottles on hand.

What if you cannot afford to fill your home with all these glittering brands? You are an aspirational. Perhaps you do not even own a home. Not to worry. Do your entertaining in bars and restaurants. This is what millions of aspirational people do on a regular basis. When you do, be sure to order a brand that glitters.

Rodney's Spirits

Rodney is a liquor store clerk. He is not rich, but he has more than a strong preference for Grey Goose vodka. He is a Grey Goose zealot. It is the only brand of spirits that he consumes.

How does Rodney explain his devotion to Grey Goose? He claims that "it's the taste . . . nothing else comes close." After he made this statement I asked him if he had reviewed the results of the taste test of brands of vodka conducted by the *New York Times*.[7] I mentioned that Grey Goose did not even make the top 10 in the list. Immediately after I said these words, I noticed that the veins at Rodney's temples begin to bulge.

Rodney told me that he has reviewed "all the results of all the taste tests" involving brands of vodka, including both those with as well as without beverage sponsors. Not one had any influence on his very strong preference for Grey Goose. Again he reiterated: "it's the taste . . . the Goose is far, far superior."

My opinion about the taste factor is very different from Rodney's. In my estimation, Rodney's sensitivity to the variations in taste among vodkas is heavily influenced by certain social psychological needs and advertising. He has a strong need, almost a compulsion, to affiliate himself with and try to emulate a variety of behaviors of a particular segment of the affluent population he perceives as rich and glittering. These are people with very high incomes, often in the seven figures and beyond, who live in expensive homes situated in exclusive neighborhoods. As the numbers tell us, Grey Goose is extremely popular among this group. Not only is it popular among the affluent population in general; the correlation between the preference for Grey Goose and income is highly significant in statistical terms. In fact, among those surveyed, this relationship is as strong as the one between income and the number of Mercedes-Benz automobiles acquired over 10 years.

Rodney is an excellent code breaker, and he has accurately decoded many of the consumption elements, the language, of the high-status brands among the glittering segment. But his code-breaking skills extend far beyond brands of beverages. Rodney has had thousands of opportunities to observe the consumption related behaviors of the rich. You see, Rodney is the senior-most sales clerk employed by one of the largest liquor/wine retail stores (supermarket size) on the East Coast. The store is located near several exclusive residential areas that rank in the top 50 in terms of both annual household income as well as market value of homes. Given the store's strategic location, it is no wonder that Rodney's customers include senior corporate executives, senior partners of major law firms, professional athletes, successful business owners, and very-high-income-producing physicians.

Rodney also has some influence on the brands his employer purchases and the manner and extent to which they are displayed in the store. Not surprisingly, sales representatives from a variety of liquor wholesalers often try to influence his personal brand preference. Relentlessly they cite taste tests and market data that support the theme of their messages. Understandably, Rodney has become tired of the constant marketing banter from these sales professionals. This is another reason why Rodney did not appreciate my reciting the *New York Times*' taste test results to him. But it was not a sales representative who convinced Rodney to purchase his first bottle of Grey Goose per se (though the marketers clearly played a role). Rodney's reference group persuaded him to prefer Grey Goose: It was the behavior habits of those who glitter that did it. Like most extraordinary sales professionals, Rodney is very observant, analytical, and curious. He noticed that customers who regularly purchased Grey Goose appeared to be more upscale, more affluent, more of the beautiful variety than most of the otherwise high-income patrons of the store. From their motor vehicles to their clothing, these people seemed to be on a higher consumption plane and more prone to purchase and display a variety of status brands. While most people purchase by the bottle, the glittering rich are much more prone to buy by the case.

Rodney's observations about the customers who purchase Grey Goose appear to be fairly accurate, according to an analysis of my survey data. Indeed, the higher a person's position on the glittering rich scale, the more likely he or she is to purchase Grey Goose vodka. Accordingly, these Grey Goose customers have a significantly higher propensity to purchase high-status brands across a wide variety of consumer goods, and they patronize high-status retail stores.

Rodney did not follow his customers while they were shopping for cars or for clothes and accessories, but he did notice the store-sponsored credit cards they carried when they opened their wallets at the checkout counter. Plus Rodney had many opportunities to observe the makes of motor vehicles his customers drove when loading up their vehicles with spirits and wines. Here his research findings and mine are in sync.

Grey Goose purchasers are significantly more likely than the others surveyed to:

- Purchase their clothes and accessories from Saks Fifth Avenue, Nordstrom, Neiman Marcus, Polo, Brooks Brothers, and the Banana Republic.
- Drive prestige makes of cars, such as Lexus, Jaguar, BMW, Mercedes-Benz, Land Rover, Porsche, and Rolls-Royce/Bentley.
- Wear expensive watches, such as Rolex, Breitling, Omega, Patek Philippe, and Tag Heuer.
- Serve their guests more expensive wine and maintain a significantly larger inventory of wine in their homes.
- Spend more on their dinner entrées when dining at restaurants.
- Purchase and inventory more bottles of spirits (i.e., Glenlivet, Johnnie Walker Black Label, Dewar's, Chivas Regal, Jack Daniel's, Maker's Mark, and Wild Turkey). It was clear to Rodney that the Grey Goose brand was number one among the glittering rich.

Rodney uses Grey Goose as a way to bolster his self-esteem. He needs to believe that his favorite brand of vodka tastes substantially better to him than all others. Rodney has convinced himself that extremely rich people have superior taste, which is why so many of them prefer Grey Goose. Thus Rodney's preference for "the Goose," as he often calls it, helps him connect and even feel like part of this clan.

But could it be that Rodney's need to associate with glitteringly rich has biased his taste buds? I am fairly certain that most of the people who buy Grey Goose do so because it is a way for hosts to tell their guests that they are well liked, appreciated, and respected and to demonstrate that they are excellent hosts and possess sophisticated taste. Serving Grey Goose helps them satisfy this need.

Rodney claims that "it is an acquired taste." Yes it is, Rodney. His taste preference became stronger each time he put yet another case of Grey Goose in the back of a customer's 7-Series BMW. But choice of brand of vodka is only one element of Rodney's consumption lifestyle. His brand choices for clothing and accessories have also been influenced by his customers. What is the first thing you likely will notice about Rodney? He dresses like a model for Polo sportswear. Thus you may have a difficult time distinguishing Rodney from his customers. He seems to have constructed an illusion that qualifies him as an auxiliary member of the glittering rich club. It is Rodney who is defined in Texas parlance as among those with "Big Hats, No Cattle."

It is unlikely that Rodney will ever become a full-fledged high-earning glittering rich person. Instead of ordering the entire dinner, Rodney orders off the appetizer menu. And as long as he can hang out with those who glitter in the proverbial hyperconsumption restaurant, he feels important and that he has achieved. Eating off the appetizer menu is what many of us do. We buy select prestige brands, symbols from within product categories that we can barely afford, and we feel these badges bring us success. But we know that's an illusion. We are not richer or more successful for having dropped $60 on a bottle of Grey Goose.

I don't mean to suggest that one live like a miser; the occasional guilty pleasure is perfectly acceptable. If you work hard and save accordingly, you should enjoy a treat from time to time. The problem is that people have come to enjoy the guilty pleasure every day to the exclusion of working for a financially independent future.

Rodney is an outstanding sales clerk. He is very customer-oriented as well as knowledgeable about the products carried in the liquor store. He thinks of himself more as a beverage expert and consultant than as a common clerk. Thinking this way bolsters his belief that he is connecting with and even becoming part of his clientele. His job does not pay big bucks, but the fringe benefits give him the opportunity to interact with the people he admires. Even better, he is a spirit consultant, the mentor of distilled beverages, and the glittering rich are his pupils. Is it not a fringe benefit for a kid from a blue-collar neighborhood who never attended a college to be an advisor to the affluent? In Rodney's way of thinking, it certainly is ego enhancing.

Rodney would do better if he would stop acting rich and start thinking about becoming a real millionaire. There is a correlation between the consumption of prestige brands and having the income to qualify for membership in the glittering category. Rodney is such a gifted sales professional that he even has persuaded himself into believing that prestige brands underlie success, instead of the other way around.

How was Rodney conditioned into having such strong preferences for certain prestige brands? First, like many, Rodney was trained to admire, even to have affection for the glittering rich. In countless news articles, TV programs, and movies, those who have money and spend it are not only featured, they are constantly placed in a favorable light, typically featured in the context of consumption. It is all about their multimillion-dollar homes, fleets of expensive motor vehicles, custom clothes hanging in countless closets, swimming pools, yachts, and on and on. Yet often missing in these feature stories are revelations about the extraordinary work ethic or downright good luck of these high-income producers. The media has convinced people to admire the consumption behavior of high-income-producing celebrities. Young people believe that consumption is good and hyperconsumption for prestige brands is even better. This is straight out of the handbook *How to Act Rich instead of Being Rich.*

Marketers use this admiration for big spenders as a weapon in promoting prestige products. What happens when one's favorite role model constantly is associated with a certain brand of product? The affection one has for the role model rubs off on the brand. One soon begins to love the brands that the role model directly or otherwise endorses.

This is what happened to Rodney. He has much admiration for his hyperconsuming, high-income-producing customers. Over time he has repeatedly seen the glittering rich purchase Grey Goose vodka. As a result of this association, the affection that Rodney has for his favorite customer segment has, in his mind, imprinted on Grey Goose. It is not really the taste of vodka that underlies Rodney's very strong brand preference. His emotional feelings for the big-spending rich have conditioned him by association to love and desire the brands that they display.

In a way, Rodney's case is one of classical conditioning à la Dr. Pavlov, although his conditioning/training took place in a liquor store and not in a laboratory. You may recall that Pavlov was able to train dogs to respond (salivate) to the sound of a bell. Dogs are not predisposed to do so. Just like Rodney, who prior to interacting with glittering rich people did not salivate over a certain brand as he does today. Pavlov was able to condition the dogs by constantly presenting meat along with the bell sounding. Eventually the dogs became conditioned to salivating to the sounding of the bell, even when the meat was not present.

In a way, the glittering rich took the place of the meat in Pavlov's experiments. Both elements have the effect of generating strong emotional responses. It is no wonder that the veins in Rodney's temples bulged when I mentioned negative things about the brand he loves.

The advertisers of prestige brands often capitalize on their knowledge of classical conditioning methods. They know what turns customers on as well as off. That is why you will never see an advertisement featuring a drunkard lying on a sidewalk clutching a bottle of Grey Goose or any other prestige brand.

What you do see are countless advertisements in which "beautiful people" are depicted enjoying this brand of expensive liquor or that make of prestige motor vehicle. But this poses an interesting question. If all of these brands of products are so superior in taste (as Rodney claims) or so unique or so much better in terms of their physical properties, then why are billions of dollars spent on advertising them? And it is not just the volume of advertising alone. Advertisers often feel compelled to use classical conditioning methods. In such cases, the real stimuli, such as the pitch by the "beautiful people," have nothing to do with the physical properties of the product offered. At the end of the day, people like Rodney are not buying a product brand. They are purchasing a promise, a ticket to the land of rich.

The other key to classical conditioning is that most people who are being conditioned in this manner do not realize that it is happening. In this case, it is hard to build up immunity to an unknown attitude change mechanism. This is what happened to Rodney. He will never realize why he has such strong preferences for brands that carry the umbrella label of "for really rich people." Does Rodney's physical makeup really include an extraordinary set of quality sensors? Most likely it does not. Rodney's perception of quality continues to be defined by the buying habits of his customers, the glittering rich.

I hope that someday Rodney will realize that satisfaction with life overall and control of it are complements. Of course, it is hard to be in control when one's life is controlled by spending and acting wealthy instead of achieving real wealth. Rodney has little interest in "saving for a rainy day." To do so would require giving up part of his aspirational costume and ultimately his auxiliary membership status.

In trying to act rich by imitating big-spending rich people, who is Rodney really impressing? Certainly it is not the rich! In reality, he impresses only himself and some of his friends who enjoy impersonating the glitteringly rich. If it weren't sad, it would actually be pretty funny. The Grey Goose buyer statistics clearly show that most buyers are trying to impress other actors who are trying to impress other actors who are trying to impress yet other actors. It is like being at an Elvis impersonator contest. It is hard to pick the winner from the hundred wannabes who look most like Elvis. At present, Rodney enjoys his life. Being single, he only has one mouth to feed and one act to support. Plus, at age 35, he has no difficulty connecting with many others in his age cohort who love to acting rich. But a big part of his satisfaction is based on his job. What if one day Rodney's boss decides that his job should be eliminated, that is cheaper to hire part-time help and/or a son-in-law? Rodney's illusion will evaporate. Unlike his customers who are in control of their economic destinies, Rodney in large part is at the mercy of his employer. Without his job, where he rubs elbows with the glittering rich every day, Rodney's socioeconomic dream world may come to an end.

Isn't it ironic that Rodney, the retail clerk, pays significantly more for his favorite brands of liquor than does Carlton, the triple-plus-decamillionaire? Carlton has a net worth that is more than 1,000 times that of Rodney. Rodney pays approximately $1 per ounce for the 1.75-liter bottle of Grey Goose that he purchases frequently. Carlton, on average, pays approximately 28 cents per ounce for his favorite spirit, Crawford's scotch, in the 1.75-liter plastic bottle. This means that Rodney spends about three and one-half times more per ounce for spirits than does Carlton.

But there is something that Rodney does not really understand about the rich in America, especially the glittering rich type. Often they personally pay a lot less for their bottle of Grey Goose than Rodney does. The majority of big-spending rich receive some form of entertainment and/or business development allowance as part of their compensation package. The glitteringly rich population is filled with senior corporate executives, for example, who often must entertain in their homes for business purposes. The same is true of the top partners in major law and accounting firms and a variety of other high-income producers. Therefore, it may appear that some of the people who patronize Rodney's store are insensitive to the variations in the price they pay for top brands of liquor. They can afford to be because they are not spending their money. Rodney and others like him need to realize that in many cases, they are spending more for their premium and super-premium brands of spirits than those who are truly affluent. In fact, Rodney may want to trade down when it comes to brand selection. He should employ a pro rata system. He assumes that the typical glittering person buys brands of spirits that sell for, say, $1 an ounce. Then he assumes that their income typically is about 65 times greater than his (or that his is equivalent to just 1.5 percent of theirs). This would indicate that he should allocate about 1.5 percent of what they pay for vodka. This translates into 1.5 cents an ounce. But even the least expensive brand of vodka retails for 15 cents per ounce.

What if you are unwilling to give up consuming vodka? As a compromise, you might agree to trade down in terms of your brand selection. Then perhaps you may wish to emulate Jerry, a millionaire plumbing contractor. He is a special type of millionaire, called HTB affluent. This means he has chest hairs sticking out of the top and bottom of his shirt! The only distilled spirit he consumes is vodka, and the only brand that he purchases is McCormick—which retails for $9.99 for a 1.75-liter bottle, or about one-sixth the price of Grey Goose.

When Jerry told me about McCormick, I wondered why I had never seen or heard of it before. Even if you look for it at my neighborhood liquor store, you might miss it, as it is not even on the very bottom shelf in the vodka section. It is in what is euphemistically referred to as the "party section" of the store. It is McCormick land, way in the back on the floor level near the fire exit. Yet Jerry, the tenacious frugal of frugal millionaires, first rooted this brand out years ago. His choice of vodka tells much about him. In terms of the other brands of products he buys, he is about as far removed from the glittering rich segment as one could imagine. Yet he is a millionaire.

Money is very democratic. It does not downgrade you because of your brand selection habits, something Rodney has so far failed to grasp. What if Jerry or Carlton stopped by Rodney's store one day? Rodney would never suspect that these customers are wealthy. Rodney believes that all rich people spend big on prestige brands. And in his mind, those who do not flaunt it must not have it.

Negative Correlates

Earlier I noted that there was a significant correlation between the purchase of certain prestige makes of cars and the consumption of Grey Goose vodka. But there are also several negative relationships that are of interest. For example, what popular make of motor vehicle is among the least likely to be driven by those who consume Grey Goose vodka? It is the make driven by Carlton, the triple-decamillionaire: Toyota—the common, reliable, homey, nondescript, and unfashionable Toyota. But Carlton does not need prestige brands to define who he is or to enhance his self-esteem.

Imagine if Carlton was a customer of Rodney's. How would Rodney likely react to him? Rodney perhaps would notice that Carlton drives a Toyota, wears a Seiko watch, and buys scotch that comes in a plastic bottle. Rodney would think that Carlton is a loser and anything but wealthy.

Given the choice, I suspect that Rodney would prefer merely to look like the glittering rich than to be rich if it meant suffering with Carlton's brand selection habits. But like many people, Rodney (via his consumption habits) whistles past the financial graveyard, instead of saving for true independence or a rainy economic period.

It is not too late for Rodney to change. He may wish to open his own liquor store one day. In spite of having little to invest, Rodney has some leverage upon which to capitalize. He has expertise in operating this type of business. Plus he knows many very wealthy people. One or more of them may wish to open their own liquor store. Rodney can help them fulfill this wish. Yes, with their money and Rodney's sweat, they may be business partners someday. Rodney would do well to stop thinking about Grey Goose and start thinking about his own goose.

Influence via Sweet Rye, Sunspots, and the Carpathian Mountains

While America is facing any number of serious problems today, it is comforting to know that there are over 300 brands of vodka available to suit any taste.[8] With so many brands on the market, some people have a difficult time selecting a suitable one. Part of this problem relates to the fact that in most instances, the physical properties of various brands of vodka differ very little, if at all. The federal government's definition of vodka illustrates the inherent difficulty marketers face in attempting to distinguish their offerings from one another:

> Vodka . . . without distinctive character, aroma, taste, or color[9]

Given this definition, how is it possible that 300 brands of vodka can coexist in the market today? Certainly, if one strictly adheres to the government's definition, vodka is essentially a commodity. Ah, but here is where the genius of the marketers comes into play. Marketing vodka is inherently more difficult than marketing, say, bourbon or scotch. These types of beverages are often positioned as "aged in oak barrels . . . for 10 long years . . . by masters from mountains high" and such. Vodka is not aged. Thus, manufacturers do not have to invest heavily in barrels or pay to inventory their offerings for 5, 10, and even 20 years. According to critic Eric Asimov, "Vodka does not necessarily benefit from artisanal manufacturing. The bearded bumpkin who minds the barrels in the ad campaign for bourbon has no place in the production of vodka."[10]

To some, the word "production" as used in the quote may connote fully integrated manufacturing starting from seeds and the fields of grain. Are all vodka manufacturers today out searching the world for special compounds with which to produce the basic ingredient, namely neutral spirits, aka alcohol? Not really. According to Asimov, "most so-called vodka producers do not even distill their own spirits."

Yet I do not recall any of the advertisements for vodkas mentioning this. Nor are you likely to see something else in any of these advertisements. This something else would certainly generate much attention and interest. It is about the alcohol. But not just any alcohol. "Archer-Daniels-Midland sells its 190 proof beverage alcohol (product code 020001) packaged one of three ways 'bulk truck, bulk rail, tanks.'"[11]

Picture the theme of the campaign. It is a portrait of a fleet of ugly, dirty, 18-wheel diesel tanker trucks carrying alcohol to a vodka manufacturer. Note that the trucks are blowing black soot out of their stacks and are being driven by tobacco-spitting guys sporting tattoos and undershirts. What about a theme that features freight train tanker cars? It is not a pretty sight. The cars are dirty and the background is strictly industrial park. On the sides of each rail car are bold painted letters:

> *Contents: Alcohol—The Basic Ingredient . . .*
> *Used in Producing Most Vodkas*

What if you saw this ad? What if you often find yourself trying to impress others at various cocktail bars via the favorite "call brands"? What if you discover that most of what is in your favorite call brand and many other brands of vodka once was inside of any ugly tanker truck or railroad car?

At the very least, you might stop buying those $15 vodka martinis at Juan Joseph's Vodka Bar and Oasis. In fact, you might stop drinking pricey vodka entirely. Maybe you might give up drinking vodka altogether. Or maybe you should write a letter to the company that produces your favorite vodka. Why not suggest that it ship vodka via tanker trucks to gas station–like outlets. If the law would allow it, people could just fill up their own bottles there.

But you know that you will never see tankers displayed or vodka fill-up stations in advertisements for vodka. Marketers in this business constantly associate prestige, status, and beauty themes in their promotional messages. But keep in mind what one sales manager for a vodka producer recently said: "Everybody [all vodka producers] buys their vodka [neutral spirits] from two or three people."[12]

And in America: ". . . almost all vodka producers buy neutral spirits that have already been distilled from grain by one of several big Midwestern companies like Archer Daniels Midland."[13]

And just imagine the sudden impact of a promotional theme for a premium vodka that emphasizes:

> *Our brand, like many of the 300 other brands of vodka,*
> *is made almost entirely from spirits produced by that*
> *"boutique" of commodity producers, Archer Daniels.*

If this message was broadcast, there might not be 300 brands of vodka in existence for too much longer. But it is not going to happen. On the contrary, some of the more aggressive, well-capitalized producers of premium and super-premium vodkas are doing everything imaginable to distance themselves from the crowd of 300.

Particularly interesting are some of the promotional messages that tout "ours is best" in various forms:

> *According to taste tests our brand is number one.*
> *Double platinum medal winner.*
> *Best of best in taste tests.*

Just review some of the recent print advertisements and you will get the point. It seems that there are almost as many brands of vodkas claiming to be number one in taste as there are sponsors of these messages. Consider some of the verbiage contained in advertisements found in the *Wall Street Journal*:

At a tasting of the experts of the World Beverage Championships . . . Pravda vodka was selected as the best luxury vodka. The finish: 1. Pravda . . . 7. Grey Goose. *Judge for yourself.* Simply call 1-800-xxx-xxxx for a special offer.

Handmade and distilled 6 times unanimous double gold medal winner for the World Spirits Competition. *Tito's Handmade Vodka* is designed to be savored by spirit connoisseurs.

In a blind taste test, the Beverage Tasting Institute of Chicago sampled seven cosmopolitans. . . . After careful consideration, all judges chose the cosmopolitan made with Grey Goose L'Orange. The best tasting vodka in the world with a whisper of orange. . . . Rank—Vodka cosmopolitans 1st Grey Goose L'Orange, 2nd Grey Goose . . . 5th Stolichnaya Gold . . . 7th Absolut Mandrin.

A particularly creative advertisement for Stolichnaya vodka appeared in *USA Today*:

1998 Monicagate begins

Gas is $1.06 per gallon

Grey Goose is rated best-tasting vodka

Sure seems like a long time ago.

2005 Stoli World's Best Vodka, Best in Show

2005 San Francisco World Spirits Competition

Would Grey Goose taste as good to your guests if you poured it out of a coffee can? Would Pravda be as appealing if you served it in specimen cups? Would that $50 bottle of Jean-Marc XO still be rated number one by your very sophisticated nose and taste buds if you found out that the fellow who picks up your trash twice a week, Ronald (a high school dropout with missing teeth), is a Jean-Marc XO man too?

But you will never see Ronald in advertisements for premium or super-premium vodka (not unless he gets his teeth fixed and goes for a total makeover). You will, however, get a rise out of your guests when you tell them, "Friends, you will be interested to know that Ronald, our trash collector, is also a Jean-Marc XO man!" Can anything worse happen to those who are trying to look rich when they learn the truth? They buy expensive, so-called high-status beverages because they need to tell people they are superior. They want so badly to do what the glittering rich do with their money. But then their trash collector's revelation dampens their enthusiasm.

From my experience, there is a strong positive correlation between the price of a particular brand of vodka and the visual appeal of its bottle. It does not take a designer's eye to be genuinely impressed with the bottles that house super-premium/super-priced vodkas such as Grey Goose, Wyborowa, or Pravda. Contrast these brands with the bottles that contain vodkas that cost considerably less, such as Gordon's, McCormick, Mr. Boston, or Popov.

Are you interested in enhancing the beauty of the interior of your home? Do you want to impress your guests via visual cues that denote sophistication? If you answered yes to these questions, then go with the beautiful bottles. That is what we do in our home. I tell our vodka-drinking guests that we offer four types of vodka: Smirnoff, served out of a Grey Goose bottle; Smirnoff, served out of a Jean-Marc XO bottle; Smirnoff, served out of a Pravda bottle, and Smirnoff, served out of a Smirnoff bottle. Yes, it is all Smirnoff, which sells for $12.99 (750 ml) or $18.99 (1.75 ml). I acquired the "expensive" empty bottles from a fellow who tends bar at a country club.

I suspect that if we did not tell our guests that it was Smirnoff, they would never detect the difference, if there is any. Besides having designer-grade bottles, how else could marketers of vodka influence our perceptions? They do spend heavily on advertising. Doing so is essential

> ... 120 new vodkas have been introduced in the last three years. Ads and barkeeps trumpet their superior quality to drinkers who usually can't taste much difference among them....Absolut Spirits [alone] spent $34 million advertising Absolut last year.[14]

Spending heavily on advertising is one thing that is important in marketing expensive vodkas. But it is the themes that are developed that often require genius. Imagine if you were given an assignment to write a paper describing how your brand of vodka is better, even vastly superior, to the other 300 brands on the market. Writing a grade A paper would not be an easy assignment.

It really helps if you closely consider the needs of your target market. Ideally it will be composed of young or middle-age adults who have good incomes. One must go beyond demographics to succeed in this very competitive game. You perhaps want to focus on charter members of the need-to-look-rich group, the aspirational segment. These people have a very strong need to display their superiority, intellect, and sophistication—call it high status or just plain image enhancement. In part, they do so by selecting and displaying certain brands they think will impress others. They have a demonstrated propensity to spend heavily on brands that give them the high-power ammunition with which to impress. Such brands provide their loyal followers key symbols with which they can use as ammunition in the battle to enhance their image.

Witness our aspirational friend Tony, in a tony bar. He sees Dusty, an attractive woman seated at the bar. According to the literature sent to me by Pravda (after responding to an ad in the *Wall Street Journal* and sent to "Vodka Enthusiast!"), the conversation would play out something like this:

TONY: May I treat you to a Pravda vodka martini?

DUSTY: Thank you. I enjoy vodka martinis.

TONY: Pravda . . . a luxury vodka from Poland now available in America for the first time in limited quantities.

DUSTY: I'll have to have one. But let me ask, how did you first find out about Pravda?

TONY: It happened when I was an operative with the CIA, assigned to Poland. A very hush-hush assignment. Most of the time there I was living in the heart of the world-renowned vodka-producing area of southern Poland.

DUSTY: Do you still work for the CIA?

TONY: No, now I work on Wall Street. I am an investment banker (aka stock broker). But I'm really more of a research type. Did a lot of research on vodka, Pravda vodka, production facilities, in the pristine Carpathian Mountain district.

DUSTY:	Sounds like you really know a great deal about vodka.
TONY:	People often consider me to be somewhat of an expert on the topic. Pravda, it's produced from "late harvest rye . . . untreated and natural giving a softer, mellower taste."
DUSTY:	How do you know so much about rye grains?
TONY:	I was trained as an astrophysicist. Studied the impact that sunspots . . . eruptions on the sun have on crop yields and of course the quality of grains.
DUSTY:	I'm really impressed with your credentials. (After sipping her martini) You were right in recommending Pravda, it's wonderful. I don't usually like a martini that's shaken, but this is truly exceptional, just as outstanding as the first time I tried Pravda.
TONY:	Did you say that you have already tried Pravda before?
DUSTY:	Oh, just once. Last month I responded to the advertisement for Pravda that was in the *Wall Street Journal*. They sent me a tasting kit. Also included was a brochure. It corroborates many of the research findings that you discovered about Pravda from your own research. You did say you were a researcher type?
TONY:	Ah . . . yes. But I forgot to ask what you do for a living.
DUSTY:	I'm an attorney.
TONY:	Working for . . . ?
DUSTY:	I work for the attorney general. I'm just one of many assistant district attorneys in this town.
TONY:	What is your area of expertise?
DUSTY:	Currently I'm assigned to lower Manhattan. Like you I'm associated with Wall Street, the investment industry. It's a bit hush-hush.
TONY:	Hush-hush?

DUSTY: Well, what can I tell you? I'm involved in prosecuting those in the investment industry who have difficulty telling the truth.

TONY: Ah, okay. Oh, oh, I just remembered I have to go to a PTA meeting tonight. Can't be late, got to run. Let me settle up with the bar.

DUSTY: Oh, don't be silly, Tony. Allow me. It's the least I can do to reward you for the information, all your original research you shared with me. Have a great evening at the PTA. Hope I will get the chance to cross-examine you again sometime. Do you come here often?

TONY: No, first time. Right. Oh, gotta go!

6

The Grapes
of Wrath

Wine and luxury are not the way to riches!

—Proverbs 21:17

Given all the press about wine and grapes, it seems as though we are obsessed about wine. Nearly every food magazine—from *Martha Stewart's Everyday Food* to *Gourmet*—includes articles on wine (picking the right wine for your meal, cooking with wine, special wineries, vineyard tours, etc.). Even the business press is in on the wine action. Consider, for example, just one line from an article from the *Wall Street Journal* (which features a weekly wine column).

> Just about all of us have that very special wine that we always mean to open, but never do.[1]

The press has been pressing grapes so much that even they believe that practically everyone (by "just about all of us," do they mean 80 percent or 95 percent of the more than 230 million adults in the United States?) have an altar that houses a "special" bottle of wine. For all the articles and references to wine in the press, it seems as though we are wine zealots of the highest order. If you do not have a "special bottle," you must be a rube freak in a population of wine worshippers.

Frankly, I started to worry that I was one of those non–wine-worshipping outliers and that something was amiss. Perhaps I had been touting frugality for so long and to such degree that I had denied myself something important and vital that everyone else had discovered. Perhaps I had missed something in my research, and wine could provide happiness. Cars and homes and watches wouldn't, but wine would.

I turned to the data from my national surveys of millionaires, and, lo and behold, it appears that not only can a person become an economic success without being a wine devotee, but that one doesn't turn into a wine spectator with success either. The profile of one affluent respondent is representative:

A Biographical Sketch of Sonny, aka Respondent #1051

Net worth: Eight figures

Motor vehicle: Six-year-old Cadillac sedan

Watch: Timex

Market value of home: $1 million

Number of wine cellars in home: 0

Number of bottles of wine in home inventory: 6

Average retail price of a bottle of wine in home inventory: $10.00

Average retail price of a bottle of wine served to guests: $10.00

Current occupation: Self-employed business owner, California-based
       winery

It was almost funny (the part about Sonny's occupation), but the data don't lie. It turns out that those with the most money, those who are in a position to buy their happiness, don't. And they don't buy expensive wine either. Anecdotally, my editor tells me that serious wine collectors and connoisseurs feel that most wine is terribly overpriced and rarely pay more than $10 a bottle; usually they look to buy it for even less.

Perception Is Everything, Unless It's Wrong

Arthur is one of the most delightful fellows I ever consulted for. At the time we met, he was a marketing manager for a large financial institution. Art came from a lower-middle/working-class background. The large public high school he attended, according to Art, had "a lot of rich kids." He traces his need to achieve in part back to his admiration of the lifestyles of his rich classmates and their parents. Art paid all of his college expenses by working. He earned both an undergraduate degree and an MBA by going to night school. Art was a success both in terms of educational achievement and occupational status, but his ambition extended beyond these basics. He wanted everything he thought that "rich" people had, including their activities and interests.

Art was not a snob by any means. He was not a show-off or elitist, but he was convinced that success and certain types of activities went hand in hand. He strongly believed that rich people, by definition, were connoisseurs. In his mind, millionaires were food experts as well as authorities on and patrons of gourmet restaurants. Art was also convinced that there is a very strong correlation between net worth and knowledge of wine.

As you might imagine, given Art's need to emulate the rich, he religiously studied wine, gourmet food, and the tonier restaurants in town. Art always kept a wine guide with him. It looked like a fat checkbook he kept inside his suit jacket pocket. With his job description and sizable expense account, he often "did lunch and dinner" at some of the best restaurants in New York City. Each and every time he sat down at a table, he first looked at the wine list and then he referred to his handy wine guide, back and forth. At the time, Art was not a millionaire, but he aspired to become one. No doubt about it, Art knew a lot about wine. He even had a burgeoning wine collection in the basement of his home. Art also had a great sense of humor. I affectionately referred to Art as "Arthur Grapes" or just plain "A.G."

I often told A.G. that most rich people don't study wine, and they don't collect it. What impact did these many discussions have on A.G.'s orientation toward wine? None. To this day, Art still thinks that most wealthy people are wine aficionados. No matter how hard I tried, I could not convince him otherwise.

In their insightful book, *Trading Up*, Michael Silverstein and Neil Fiske address the topic of "awakening the American palate to wine" by devoting an entire chapter to the topic.

> Not long ago, the palate of the American consumer was considered crude and unsophisticated, especially in comparison to the European palate; but the new American taste in wines has had a major influence on the flavor profiles of wineries around the world.[2]

Silverstein and Fiske further cite winemaker Tina Cola's statement that "the American palate is becoming the international palate. Most people everywhere now want richer, fresher, fruitier wines."[3]

Are "most people everywhere" really into wine? Did we really come to develop a "new . . . taste in wine"? It would be logical to conclude that those with modest or lower incomes could not afford to purchase a lot of high-grade vintage and costly wines. Plus, some promoters of wine may imply that these types of people might not be sophisticated enough to appreciate "richer wines."

So lower-income people don't buy expensive wine (though I haven't surveyed them so I can't make that claim definitively), and my surveys show that rich people don't buy expensive wine either. That leaves the nonmillionaire middle and upper middle class as the market for expensive wine.

The wine myth is one of the more interesting concepts that relates to the affluent population. As the data show, it is a myth that millionaires as a group have a strong orientation toward wine. My survey results indicate that only a minority of millionaires are wine oriented. Yes, most millionaires (more than 90 percent) consume wine. Yet only a minority of them regularly purchases costly wines, read about wine, and/or collect wine.

But what does it mean when I refer to "wine-oriented millionaires"? Those who are wine oriented answered yes to the following question: Do you collect wine and/or have you read about/studied wine at least once in the past month?

Only 16.5 percent of the millionaires I surveyed are wine oriented. Some might say that I am just not surveying the right kind of millionaires. What if some of those surveyed are in the lower-seven-figure millionaire class? What if some are the very frugal types of millionaires of the next-door variety? What if most do not live in or near upscale neighborhoods or affluent towns like Greenwich, Purchase, Rye, New Canaan, Lake Forest, Newport Beach, Short Hills, Sea Island, and the like? Sorry, but the 16.5 percent of millionaire wine collectors reflects the millionaire population nationwide. It includes those who live in homes valued under $400,000 and also includes those who live in homes valued in the seven and eight figures. It includes our friend, Mr. M, who has multiple Ferraris, and it includes Anna After, along with more understated millionaires.

What if a sample of millionaires was taken from only those who reside in the most affluent neighborhoods near and around the top-10 metropolitan areas in America?

What percentage of millionaires who reside in the most exclusive enclaves is wine oriented? About one in four (26.4 percent) versus one in three (32.9 percent) of glittering rich decamillionaires is so inclined.

What is particularly interesting is the percentage of the wine oriented among the high-income nonmillionaires who reside in Affluent Estates. Fully 23.0 percent of these aspirationals are wine oriented. No, they are not rich, but they act rich and live among the rich and glittering (or people who they think are rich).

Where you live has that pesky way of influencing how you behave. Live in or near those who glitter and you will start imitating them—even if you are not rich. But what if you look at the nonmillionaire/high-income-producing population nationwide, not just those who live in affluent communities? Only 9 percent are wine oriented. Yet these people are in the same income and age cohorts as those aspirationals who live in the exclusive communities.

Pressing Their Own Grapes

Imagine: Even most decamillionaires who reside in the most exclusive areas are not wine collectors. In fact, most never even read about wine. Yet the popular press, the gourmet press especially, and the wine industry all have done a wonderful job of conditioning us to believe that wealth and wine go hand in hand. Now you know that this is not the case (and by extension, perhaps you know not to believe everything you read).

Are you contemplating developing a wine orientation? Is this need based on your desire to emulate the rich, the successful, the owners of beautiful homes in upscale neighborhoods? If you are looking for accurate ways to emulate the typical multimillionaire, then you may want to think outside the boundaries of wine. Being a wine buff will not make you a millionaire. Nor will most millionaires likely be impressed with your knowledge of grapes. And if you are a wine buff among the masses of nonmillionaires, you will have something in common with only a minority of millionaires.

Silverstein and Fiske accurately report something quite interesting about wine fanciers:

> Respondents . . . who trade up in wine view it as a means of connecting and making affiliations with others . . . a way for consumers to express individual style-signaling that the are individuals of taste . . . sophistication, experience, and intelligence . . . drinking wine makes them feel . . . as if they're "living the best life."[4]

In spite of these revelations, most millionaires became wealthy—and even enhanced their fortunes—without ever becoming wine fanciers, let alone owning a wine collection. Most do not study wine. It should be self-evident that if one spends a lot of time studying wine, there is less time for other activities, including those that actually enhance one's net worth. Typically, when the rich buy wine, they do not expend time and money studying it. Instead, they rely on experts at their favorite wine shop. The vast majority of millionaires give high praise to these experts.

Correlates of Wealth: Real or Imagined

Why are millionaires millionaires? Because they involve themselves in activities that are complements to wealth: analyzing their investments, studying their businesses and product or service industries, and so on. This does not mean that a person cannot be a wine zealot and build wealth at the same time, but it does mean that the study of wine alone will not make anyone rich unless that study is turned into a profitable winery or wine store.

The relationship between one's orientation toward wine and building wealth provides some interesting discussions. Consider the following contrasts concerning the activities and habits of the rich. For every one

wine-collecting glittering millionaire (26.4 percent), there are nearly three
and one-half who "religiously plan their financial investments." That's cor-
rect; more than 90 percent of the millionaires surveyed from the wealthiest
neighborhoods in America (including 145 decamillionaires) have a habit
of planning and working on their investments. These same millionaires are
more than three times more likely to have a habit of studying/reading/
researching financial investments than studying grape juice.

What if you want to act wealthy and sophisticated overnight? Some
people think that this can be accomplished by reading the "grape"-oriented
literature, memorizing key buzz words and clichés, and then informally lecturing "on the grape." They might enroll in several wine-tasting "courses"
and related grape-type programs. What if you do not feel confident enough
to express your own grape-related thoughts in public? Then just memorize
the words and ideas of wine experts. You may want to practice first by lecturing to yourself in front of a mirror or to your spouse, dog, cat . . . then
show up at a social gathering and begin lecturing. Do it as often as possible
in as many settings as you can attend. Perhaps by doing so you will convince targeted audiences and perhaps even yourself that you are intelligent,
sophisticated, well educated, rich, and quite possibly a descendant of King
Henry VIII of England! If the people you associate with are true believers
in the power of the grape, they believe that people who display and ver-
balize a considerable knowledge of wines in social settings are very likely
intelligent and rich.

Here are some additional pieces of information that the Arthur Grapes
upwardly mobile types may be interested in learning. First, what percentage of the millionaires surveyed usually serve wine to guests? More than
four out of five (85 percent) do so. But if you go to their homes for dinner, don't expect to be offered wine from a special reserve collection.

Of those who do offer wine, what is the median price typically paid for
a bottle of wine that is served to guests? Just $13.09 ($14.54 less 10 percent
for case discount) is the answer (see Table 6.1). This means that 50 percent

Table 6.1   Price of Wine Served by Millionaires

Typical Amount Spent on Wine for Entertaining Friends/ Neighbors at Home		% Who Paid	
Per Bottle	Case Price per Bottle	Less than This Amount	More than This Amount
$ 8.49	$ 7.64	10	90
9.93	8.94	25	75
14.54	13.09	50	50
19.79	17.81	75	25
29.27	26.34	90	10
39.49	35.54	95	5
52.50	47.25	99	1

of the millionaires serve wine priced at $13.09 or less; the other 50 percent serve wine that was purchased at this price or more. Twenty-five percent typically serve wine that retails for $19.79 per bottle (or $17.81 with case discount). Yet another 25 percent serve wine that costs $9.93 per bottle or less. Only 1 in 20, or 5 percent, serve wine that exceeds $39.49 per bottle.

How much do millionaires pay for the wine that is inventoried in their homes? Hello again to all the Arthur Grapes upwardly mobile people out there. Take note of these facts about the affluent:

- Only 7 percent own a bottle of wine that cost more than $100 (see Table 6.2).
- Only 12 percent own one or more bottles that cost between $51 and $100; 30 percent own wine in the $26 to $50 range.
- Two-thirds (67 percent) own wine that costs somewhere in the range of $10 to $25.
- More than one-third (38 percent) have on hand at least one bottle of wine that costs less than $10.

Table 6.2   Prices Paid for Wine Contained Inside the Homes of Millionaires

Prices Paid for Wine	Percent of Millionaires Owning at Least One Bottle
No wine in home	9.8
$10 or less	37.7
$10–$25	66.7
$26–$50	29.8
$51–$100	12.0
More than $100	7.3

What if the wine that a millionaire serves his guests comes from his household's "on-hand" inventory? If it does, then his guests will likely be sipping wine in the $10 to $25 a bottle range. The reality is that there are many quality wines in this price range and even below.

"The price-equals-quality assumption has been squashed many times. At the San Francisco International Wine Competition in 2000, wines costing $10 or less won a third of the class contests."[5] Robin Goldstein, a wine expert, recently conducted taste tests on 540 wines that retailed from $1.50 to $150 per bottle. Five hundred testers participated in the tests. After tabulating the ratings of 6,000 glasses of wine, what did Goldstein's research reveal?

[The] results might rattle a few wine snobs . . . 100 wines under $15.00 consistently outperformed their upscale cousins . . . a $9.99 bottle of Domaine Ste. Michelle Brut outscored a $150 bottle of Dom Perignon . . . "two-buck Chuck" (Cabernet) bested the $55.00 version from Stags' Leap Artemis.[6]

Most millionaires usually go out and buy wine when hosting a specific social event. Most do not carry a lot of inventory. The median number of bottles the typical millionaire household has in inventory is just under 13

Table 6.3 Wine Inventory Owned by Millionaires

Number of Bottles of Wine in Home Inventory	Percent Owning Less than This Number of Bottles (%)	Percent Owning More than This Number of Bottles (%)
4.5	25	75
12.5	50	50
29.6	75	25
93.9	90	10
208.8	95	5
787.0	99	1

(see Table 6.3). Only one in 4 households has 30 or more bottles on hand, and fewer than 1 in 10 has 100 or more bottles in his "collection." Most millionaires just do not seem to have enough bottles on hand to qualify as actual wine collectors. But they do accumulate assets and have at least $1 million in their collection of financial investments.

Bon Appétit with that Wine

Arthur Grapes had it wrong about the wine consumption habits of millionaires. But he was also mistaken in his beliefs about several other food-related activities of the rich. Art often said that there were many benefits of being wealthy. Some of his favorites had to do with food, restaurant patronage, and food preparation and "delivery." Who memorized the names and addresses of every one of the top dining spots within every conceivable food type in New York City? Of course it was the gourmet Arthur Grapes. Who had a goal of dining at least once at each and every one of these restaurants? Our friend A.G. He assumed that being rich meant frequently dining at top-rated and, more often than not, very expensive restaurants.

After completing an assignment for Art's company, he would always say, "Stanley, I like what you did for us, so it's dinner tonight at a 'top restaurant.'" What is a 'top restaurant'? I define it as a place where there are at least a half dozen waiters in morning coats working each table. But even better is the type of credit card slips they employ. Most restaurants have a single line where you enter the gratuity, but the place Arthur Grapes selected had four categories of tips: one for the senior waiter, one for the maitre d', one for the wine consultant (aka sommelier), and one for the other waiters. In cases like this, you need a calculator to allocate the gratuities. And let's not even mention the prices: how about a club sandwich for $52.50? Dinner and fine wine for two plus tip(s) usually totaled over $600 at these types of establishments.

Art never blinked when the bill came. He wanted to dine where the rich frequently dine, and he was convinced that most millionaires dined frequently at expensive restaurants. "That's what rich people do in the evening . . . it's typical." However, spending big dollars in restaurants is anything but typical among the millionaire population. Nor are most millionaires enamored with the idea of gourmet dining that requires computer power to calculate the gratuities.

Millionaires in my latest national survey were asked about both their preferred restaurant and the size of the bill. How much do millionaires usually pay for the dinner that they order at their favorite restaurant? The median/typical price paid for dinner is $19.59 (see Table 6.4). In other words, half of the millionaires surveyed indicated that they paid this amount or less; the other half paid this figure or more. One in four reported spending $14.60 or less. Another one in four typically allocates $24.53 or more. Certainly these numbers are in sharp contrast to those that Arthur Grapes estimates. In fact, only three-tenths of 1 percent typically spends more than $100 for their dinner at their favorite restaurant.

What should Arthur Grapes understand as a marketer whose objective is to target millionaires? Most millionaires are not wine connoisseurs

Table 6.4   Price Typically Paid by Millionaires for Their Dinner at the Restaurant They Dine at Most Frequently

Typical Price Paid for Dinner	% Who Paid	
	Less than This Amount	More than This Amount
$11.79	10	90
14.60	25	75
19.59	50	50
24.53	75	25
39.24	95	5
87.12	99	1

or gourmets. Most do not spend near $100 for their dinner. Most prefer good food in nonpretentious settings. Want to treat a typical millionaire to a dinner? Demonstrate empathy for his needs. Ask him where he would like to dine, the type of atmosphere he enjoys, and the type of food and beverage he prefers. Even more basic, ask if he has any desire to break bread with you at all. Always ask first. Never assume what your wealthy prospect wants. Marketers who target the rich should always remember that me, me, me (my view, my preference, my needs) is especially dull, dull, dull to a millionaire.

Millions of marketing dollars have been wasted by those who misread the preferences of the rich. Time and time again marketers play the "I know what is best for both clients and prospective clients" game. Those who insist that all clients and prospects must be treated to dinner at a four-star restaurant often are surprised by the results.

What did one very wealthy business owner want from his New York City–based trust company? He wanted more than an estate plan drawn up. This Kansas native wanted to ride on the subway all day long and dine at an authentic New York deli. I am sure that the trust officer who accompanied him never had a more enjoyable experience.

Yes, the Arthur Grapes of the marketing-to-the-affluent population are usually thrilled to dine at four-star restaurants. But often millionaires find such an experience as a ridiculous excess and unproductive waste of time and money.

In Texas, Do as Texans Do

The worst thing marketers can do is to demonstrate zero empathy for the needs of their target audiences. Along these lines is a discussion I recently had with an entrepreneur from Texas with a net worth in the mid-eight figures. After our interview, he told me that he was pleased that his profile would be included in one of my forthcoming books. I insisted that I treat him to dinner; he countered with an offer that I could not refuse. But first he asked what type of food I liked. "Ah, Mexican," I said. Al and his wife then offered to take me to their very "favorite dinner spot," a Mexican place often frequented by "Texas-born and bred millionaires."

What an extraordinary difference existed between the four-star restaurants frequented by my client Arthur Grapes and the favorite dining choice patronized by Al and his wife and many other wealthy people. A few hours after interviewing Al, he and his wife picked me up at my hotel in Al's well-worn 10-year-old Lincoln. After a short drive, we pulled into a parking lot adjacent to the restaurant. It looked more like a small single-story factory than a restaurant. Unlike the four-star variety favored by Arthur Grapes, this place had no greeter, no palm trees, no maitre d', no morning suits, and no wine consultants. It did have a sign that read "Seat Yourself." The tables and seats, aka benches, all painted bright yellow, were of the picnic bench variety often seen in public parks. Also, several electric bug zappers (designed for outdoor use) were strategically hanging from the beams inside the restaurant.

Al noticed that I was a bit surprised by the décor and said, "Don't let the looks of this place fool you. It is the best Mexican restaurant in Texas."

Even with that comforting message, I thought to myself, "I wonder how Arthur Grapes and his cohorts in Gotham City would react if a prospective trust client insisted that they all have dinner in this place?"

I had confidence in Al, although it did waver a bit after looking over the menu. The most expensive item was priced at $9.95! Plus, I did not need an Arthur Grapes–type wine guide to help me select the ideal vintage. Just two types of wine were listed: red and white. In contrast, the variety of brands of beer offered was substantial.

Shortly after our waitress served us a large basket of tortilla chips and salsa, Al stood up and reached inside his jacket pocket. He proceeded to remove from his jacket a quarter-pound bar of "real" butter brought from home. He placed it in the center of the picnic table, then said something I will never forget: "I hate the synthetic stuff (margarine). That's the only problem with this place, no butter. Please help yourself."

You may wonder why a decamillionaire would carry his own spread to a restaurant. Why would a multimillionaire couple even consider dining at a restaurant filled with picnic tables and "synthetic stuff" that required patrons to byob (bring your own butter). Why would the financially secure Al and his wife dine at a place where the most expensive meal was $9.95? The answer to all of these questions is quite simple but something that many people do not understand. There is not a perfect correlation between how satisfying customers find the food offered and the price a restaurant charges for it. Al and his wife apparently were well aware of this fact. Plus, their judgment of the food offered by their favorite restaurant was not negatively influenced by picnic tables, a limited wine selection, or even the absence of butter. Al and his wife dine where they want to dine and not where food critics dictate they should. Certainly they could afford to eat at a four-star restaurant each and every night of the week. But according to Al, it has been many years since they last set foot in a so-called four-star restaurant. Some may argue that Al and his wife simply don't have taste (pun intended). They may be rich, but they have no appreciation for the finer things in life.

Al and his wife are not just rich (or rich rubes); they both graduated from a top-20-rated college. But they don't need to define themselves according to where they dine. Like most of the self-made rich, they do what they want to do and are not embarrassed by how they live. It is not a threat to their self-esteem to eat dinner off a picnic table garnished with a bar of brought-from-home butter.

Imagine if I had had the foresight to videotape my dinner experience that night! What if I then showed the tape to 100 marketers of trust/asset management services? How many of the viewers—including Arthur Grapes, his boss, Buffy Muffin Grapette, and her boss, Windsor Wellington Grapes, Sr.—would guess that Al and his wife were very wealthy? Probably none. Few would consider eating in such a joint or taking a wealthy client there.

Domestic Bliss

Arthur Grapes often talked about how the benefits of becoming wealthy extended beyond collecting vintage wine and dining at top restaurants. He firmly believed that most millionaires employed "domestic help" in their homes. Arthur Grapes envisioned that one day he would be truly rich and could hire a maid. In doing so, he reasoned that he could have his maid serve dinner and vintage wine. The domestic helper could also make and serve breakfast. (Neither Arthur Grapes nor his wife enjoyed making breakfast.) Making lunches for the kids and then driving them to school was getting "real old." "Why not have domestic helpers do these tasks as well?" he thought.

Ah, the benefits of being rich. Arthur Grapes's view on this topic differs from that of most millionaires, and Arthur may find that his reach exceeds his grasp if he continues to focus on consumption. In contrast, most self-made millionaires cite the freedom, security, and independence as important advantages of being rich. It's not about having hired help attend to daily tasks; it's about freedom from worry and financial obligations to others.

So what about Arthur Grapes's contention that the rich employ domestic help to prepare meals? Is he right?

What percentage of the meals that millionaires ate at home in the past month (30 days) was prepared, in part or in total, by paid for domestic help/maid/etc.? Let us first look at the extremes. Only half of 1 percent of the millionaires surveyed reported that all the meals they consumed at home were prepared by domestic help. Among this group were several who need "domestic help" because of health problems. In other words, some of those who have help are otherwise unable to do the work themselves.

What percentage of the millionaires report that none of their in-home meals was prepared by domestic help? The answer is 94 percent! Only 4.5 percent of millionaires report having 25 percent or more of their in-home meals prepared by domestic help. About 1 in 40 (2.6 percent) have more than half of their meals prepared by this method. In spite of the evidence, Arthur Grapes still believes that wealth and domestic help are close cousins. The good news for Arthur is that he has company, which is why so many high-income nonmillionaires employ such helpers.

Do you want to become rich someday? If you do, wait to build your large wine collections, to dine frequently at gourmet restaurants, and to employ domestic help until you become financially independent.

The Cellar Is Standard Equipment

As you can see from our friend A.G., often sales and marketing types are quite susceptible to persuasion themselves. This is especially true among those who market expensive homes. To stay current, many of these sales professionals attend seminars on how to market homes. The topics covered include recommended advertising themes and salient product features. One of the more prominent features touted over the last few years is the "wine cellar."

If you are a builder of expensive homes, should you include a wine cellar in them? Maybe, but many of the speculatively built million-dollar homes that have wine cellars were not jumping off the market before the real estate crash.

It may be foolish to conclude that a $2 million home is not selling because it is or it is not equipped with a wine cellar. But I did have an opportunity recently to interview a builder of luxury homes about this and related topics. At the time, all the homes he had in inventory were priced between $1.5 and $3 million. All contained wine cellars, and this fact was well emphasized in the promotional literature for the homes.

I discovered in the interview why the builder focused on the wine cellar feature. He spoke nonstop about several topics, especially wine. Ah, a wine rapper! He also explained that "even though I build homes, I am not really a home builder!" This builder defined his vocation as "senior executive" (akin to how trash collectors dubbed themselves "sanitary engineers"). He made repeated comments about how he was different from the blue-collar, hands-on builders who typify the industry. In fact, the day of our interview he was dressed in L.L. Bean country casual type clothing. His nails were manicured, and he drove a top-of-the-line Infinity sedan. He made it very clear that he had "never hammered a nail" in his entire life. He lived among his "clients," the surgeons, attorneys, and senior corporate types, and not in a neighborhood generally associated with the prototypical blue-collar home builder.

This builder has mastery of more than grape rap. He is in fact a very special type of rapper: a master of "legacy rap."

I should have suspected it. The builder inherited his wealth. He explained that his great-grandparents, his grandparents, and, accordingly, his parents were quite wealthy. He attended two prep schools and a variety of colleges. Plus he held a variety of positions before becoming a "senior executive."

If you were this fellow, how would you attempt to bolster your image with others? So what if you inherited much of what you own, including some of the property upon which you are building homes? If you are not a super-achiever yourself, tell others about your bloodline. It is all about your affluent ancestors, owners of railroads and steel mills, Civil War heroes, and Main Line Philadelphia, never just Philadelphia. You assume that people somehow will be honored just to be in your presence because of your noble heritage. Be sure to blend your grape rap with a good legacy rap. Constantly remind your audience that you are not a home builder. You are a crowned prince, a wine scholar, who lives among other nobles. You design castles and wine cellars, and you must never be mistaken for a home builder.

Perhaps this builder would have finished college if he spent as much time studying his textbooks as he does now studying wine. But who needs a college degree when your image is based on a grape and legacy rap? What is the problem with most wine-rapping, legacy-touting types? They lack empathy for the needs of other people. Just because you are into wine does not mean that everyone else shares your interest. But too bad; if you buy a spec home from this builder, it will be equipped with a wine cellar. Few if any of his homes are of the custom variety.

But it is not all the builder's (whoops, I mean senior executive's) fault. Several years ago he attended a marketing seminar. There he was told that "the rich collect wine" and "wine cellars are a must" for the affluent homebuyer. The problem is that only a minority of millionaires collect wine, and among those who designate themselves as collectors, only 10 percent have 100 or more bottles in their collections.

What if I had told the builder that rich people are much more likely to collect dividends and royalties than wine? It would have had no effect on his orientation about wine and wine cellars.

The Wine Rapper Next Door

If you want to impress your new neighbors, speaking fluent winese to them may not be the best way (as the next case study will show). The reality is that most people find "wine rap" more than a little annoying. In an excellent article, James Surowiecki alluded to wine speak and the frustrations of selecting the ideal wine.

> . . . too many choices . . . too much information, most of it unhelpful. WINESPEAK, the florid description of a wine's "sublime minerality" or its "caramel, prunes, and bourbon" taste, seems designed less to inform than to make you feel like a hayseed.[7]

Of course, some people cannot be convinced of this.

In a relatively new upscale development in Texas with homes in the $1.5 to $3 million range, one couple, Jane and Harry, decided to hold a homeowners' association party. Given the price of the homes, the educational backgrounds, and occupational status of the homeowners, one could conclude that this neighborhood was upper-middle-class Texas. Part of being upper middle class, however, does have its drawbacks. Often people in this league have extremely demanding schedules, so it is not unusual for neighbors on the same block to be strangers to one another. Realizing this, several members of the fledging homeowners' association decided to sponsor (pay for) a homeowners' "meet your neighbors" party. It was to be an informal affair featuring a buffet, wine, and dessert.

Jane not only volunteered to host the party at her home, she even insisted on underwriting the cost of all of the wine. The homeowners' association agreed to fund the catered food. Neither Jane nor Harry, however, is a wine expert, and they do not pretend to be. They may have one glass of some form of red wine, never white, with dinner. Jane usually buys it at the supermarket while Harry prefers membership warehouses. Jane "hates" to spend more than $10 or $12 for a standard size bottle of wine and sometimes chooses the more economical "bigger bottles." Harry is similar in his price preference points.

In order to be gracious as hosts, Jane decided to visit a wine shop for some expert help in choosing the right wine to serve. The proprietor recommended a fine wine suitable for entertaining important guests. With the case discount, the price was $12.59 per bottle.

Kev and his wife, Sheila, arrived at Jane and Harry's house fashionably late. But the couple stood out in the crowd. Harry described Kev as looking like something out of an Orvis clothing catalog. He had on a loud tweed jacket with leather elbow pads, a cashmere turtleneck sweater, a gold bracelet, a large watch, and stacked-heel dress boots. The boots helped him looked taller than his estimated natural five foot seven. His hair looked like it was melting caramel and was more painstakingly groomed than former football coach (now commentator) Jimmy Johnson.

As if Kev weren't overdressed enough, he was also carrying a large leather case on a strap. At first, Jane thought it contained an extraordinary large pair of binoculars. Could it be, she wondered, that Kev is into gazing at the planets? Or could it be something else? It turns out that the case contained two bottles of vintage wine that Kev selected after considerable research. Perhaps there should have been a warning on the case:

> Be careful removing contents. Guests may swoon or faint when first realizing the extraordinary quality of the wines contained herein.

Some people think that the best way to tell others about how important they are is to produce weapons that demand admiration: symbols, cues, brands, and vintage. Kev is likely one of these people. Perhaps he felt that he was going into an unfamiliar environment. Instead of being tagged as "the kid from blue-collar Queens, New York," Kev wanted to be sure he would be remembered as a fellow member of the upper-middle-class tribe. Given these possibilities, Kev may have felt the need to arm himself for the event. Yet he was the only guest who wore a bandoleer, the only one who carried his own wine to the party. No one else was armed with wine— not the surgeons, the lawyers, the CPAs, the successful entrepreneurs, not even the investment gurus. Kev came with and left with what remained. He was the only one who drank his wine, as he didn't offer to share with others. Most of the guests were more interested in talking about issues surrounding the pros and cons of buying a new home, the countless required redos, the quality of the schools, lifestyle activities, and so on. Kev just wanted to talk about wine. His wine.

Jane felt that Kev's wife was also "overdone." Her French manicure, top and bottom, her perfect hairdo, and the many rings on her fingers, including thumbs (and toes), made her look like one of the jewelry saleswomen on the cable shopping channel. Add to that the hint of a New York accent, enhanced tan, and the low-cut dress, and you could easily tell she was not "from around here."

Among toys, no other doll is so severe in appearance than the famous Ken and Barbie dolls. Yet Kev and Sheila wouldn't have even classified as dolls. Why not? According to Jane, it was because Kev and Sheila were too severe, even on the Ken and Barbie doll scale of severe. Kev and Sheila were almost a caricature from a *Saturday Night Live* skit.

It was supposed to be a very informal party. Most people were wearing country casual garb. Obviously, Kev and his wife stood out. Upon entering, Kev and Sheila sought out the hosts. Harry was near the threshold and introduced himself. Then he escorted the couple over to the bar where Jane was standing. After a minute or two of small talk, Jane asked the couple if they would like a glass of wine. Sheila nodded and said, "Yes," but Kev paused and picked up a bottle of the house wine being served. After examining the label, Jane noticed that Kev's facial expression changed from confusion to disgust. It was obvious to Jane that he was not impressed with her offering. On the contrary, Kev seemed almost offended that the label was in his presence.

Kev caught himself and realized that his face had given him away, covering his initial reaction with a quick comment to Jane, "It's brand X!" He continued, "Ah, yes . . . yes, I'm familiar with this. '02 . . . '02 is good, but '01 would have been better. Ah, '02 . . . good. I'll try some of my own."

With that he unstrapped his bandoleer and, with a flourish, pulled out a bottle and removed the cork. Obviously he had done this many times before.

When Jane told me about this experience, she asked about the meaning of Kev's "good" rating of the wine she and Harry served that night. I told her, in college testing parlance, that it probably ranked in Kev's mind as an 82 or 83 on a test, 100 being the highest. In order words, as I told Jane, her wine was in the low B range. We laughed about Jane's offering being grade "low B." She never felt insulted by the low-B handle. Rather, she thought it was all very funny and found Kev's performance greatly entertaining. She and Harry are very strong and confident people. But if you run into them the next time you are in Texas, ask them if they have improved their low-B grade in the course I call Wine Rap 101.

There is one thing in particular that Kev did not understand about most of his neighbors: They can live one more day, even longer, without consuming vintage wine. And in the hierarchy of important issues and concerns, choice of wine does not make it on to even the very longest of their lists.

Kev was intent on making the right impression at the neighborhood party, but he failed miserably. His "looking a gift horse in the mouth" routine reflected bad taste. But even worse was his insulting behavior. Those things combined with his dressed-to-kill outfit most likely had a negative effect on Kev's neighbors. Yet Kev assumed that they would be enthralled by his wine rap.

Living in a fine home situated in an upscale neighborhood does not automatically convert one to upper middle class. Neither does having the financial resources to buy (or at least finance) a million-dollar home. What if over the last 25 years you just got lucky? You bought and sold three homes. Each time you encountered appreciation. Most recently you especially got lucky when you sold that dull normal traditional three-bedroom home in Connecticut for nearly twice the original price.

What if it was not your education, training, social skills, or even performance on the job that explains how you and your family became "owners" of a $1.5 million home? You are determined to transform yourself into a member of upper-middle-class Texas. But class membership is much more than one's choice of clothing, accessories, cars, wines, and homes. For most members of the upper middle class, being an achiever is much more important than merely acting rich—whatever that may mean. And what about those who have moved up one, two, or even three rungs on the social class ladder in one generation? They should be proud of it, flaunt their success, and never be ashamed of it. Why try to mask stigma that is not a stigma at all? Communicate it, tell your Abe Lincoln story via English, not in the wine rap dialect.

The Real Kev, Un-Rapped

Kev is a member of the aspirational class. He is of the tribe that earns a high income (generally in the high five to low six figures) but has little real wealth independent of home equity. Kev has many of the characteristics that are high correlates of aspirationals. One of their more interesting habits relates to their orientation toward wine. Many are self-designated wine scholars, like Kev. But not all actually collect wine. Their rap is often so good that they convince themselves that they are economically successful by simply "acting rich." Acting rich leads to spending as if they have a lot more money than reality indicates.

How could you tell that the man who is giving you his wine rap is a member of the wannabe club? There are several significant correlates of the presence of these types of rappers.

Two occupational groups contain a disproportionately large number of pseudo affluent grape rappers. The larger of the two groups is the corporate middle/lower middle manager. The other group contains high-income–producing sales professionals. Please note that not all middle managers or sales professionals are members of the pseudoaffluent rapper team. Most are not. But nevertheless, in terms of relative probabilities, these two occupational groups stand out.

Often these types of rappers do not feel that their contributions at work are justly rewarded. Many feel they deserve to be paid more and promoted more often. So what if your efforts are not being recognized? You are still a winner, a much bigger spoke in the corporate wheel than your employer will acknowledge. What is the cure? Recognize yourself and tell others you are a socioeconomic success with symbols and signs you think denote success. You are firmly convinced that grape rap is a sign of those who are socioeconomic winners.

But what if you are in a similar corporate situation as is Kev the rapper? Kev and his family have relocated several times in the past 20 years. His most recent geographical moves were not associated with vertical status promotions but instead were (to use the "senior executive" term) "lateral changes." Each time Kev moved he felt a need to show his new neighbors and significant others that he was a socioeconomic success and a man of great taste, style, and sophistication. In other words, he had a compulsion to connect immediately and properly with "important people." He wanted to make certain that his new acquaintances would be favorably impressed with his "outstanding credentials." This is why Kev does the grape rap. No doubt it does impress people, but often with results that are at odds with Kev's intent.

7

The Road
to Happiness

See the USA in your Chevrolet.

—1949 jingle

Tony D. of the Washington Speakers Bureau called me shortly after my first book, *Marketing to the Affluent*, was selected by the Best of Business as a top-10 business book. He had two questions for me: first, would I speak at two of BMW's North American dealers' conferences, and second, if I preferred to be paid in BMW currency (use of a BMW for a year) or in U.S. dollars.

No doubt, BMW thought (hoped?) that I would be thrilled to drive a BMW. Perhaps they were surprised when I opted to be paid in cash. Why did I go for the dollars and not the barter deal? Several reasons: Driving a BMW would make me uneasy. It is at odds with my family's consumption patterns and beliefs. It could also have proven a slippery slope: Drive a car for a year and next thing you know, I just have to have one—that I would have to pay for—which would be harmful to my wealth. Most important, I know what a car can and cannot do for a person.

You can't drive your way to happiness. Yet some people believe otherwise. They may see some fellow driving a fully accessorized BMW, Corvette, or Cadillac and assume something about him. They whisper to themselves, "There goes a happy guy. If I had that car instead of my Toyota, I would be off the far end of the happy scale."

But . . . just what is the relationship between the car you drive and your level of satisfaction with life? According to my research:

> *There is no significant correlation between the make [brand] of motor vehicle you drive and your level of happiness with life.*

People who live below their means understand this. The data tell the story. Consider the results from my most recent national survey of high-income-producing households. Each of the 1,594 respondents was asked about the make of motor vehicles he had acquired over the prior 10 years as well as his most recent acquisitions. Guess what? Not one significant correlation was found between the make of motor vehicle acquired and overall satisfaction with life. That's right, not 1 of the 46 makes studied had any measurable effect on satisfaction with life overall.

It did not matter what measure of motor vehicle acquisition habit was studied. The results were the same. For example, those who bought and/or leased one, two, three, four, five, or more BMWs over a 10-year period were not significantly more satisfied with life than those who did not acquire any BMWs at all. And the same applies to all the other makes studied.

Independent of make, what is the relationship between the price paid for an automobile and overall satisfaction with life? There is a positive but not statistically significant correlation.

I have my own personal version of the Happy Story. An ABC *20/20* program producer called to ask me a number of questions in preparation for my appearance on the show. She asked: "Why does a bestselling author drive a 2005 Toyota (4Runner) and not a new BMW? The answer to this question is simple. My son bought my '97 4Runner so I had to get a newer car. More to the point, I would not be any happier driving a BMW. In fact, I would probably be less content if it cost $10,000 or $20,000 more than the $30,000 I paid for my four-wheel drive, sports edition 4Runner. And then there are the additional carry costs. (It costs more to insure a BMW than a Toyota.)

After the *20/20* interview was over, I did some additional calculations. From my survey data of high-income producers, I computed the average level of satisfaction with life overall by the make of motor vehicle most recently acquired. Those currently driving BMWs had an average level of satisfaction of 4.25 on a 5-point scale (5 being the highest). Those driving Toyotas had an average of 4.20. While there is a difference (one-twentieth of 1 point on the Happy Scale), it is not statistically significant. Yet some difference was expected, given the fact that 71 percent of the BMW drivers who were surveyed had annual household incomes of $200,000 or more. In contrast, only 46 percent of the Toyota drivers generated this much income. My surveys indicate that there is a significant correlation between income and satisfaction with life. In other words, earning more money may make you somewhat happier, but spending that money (particularly on cars) won't. If we make the appropriate statistical adjustments for income differences in life satisfaction, then we find that the average life satisfaction among Toyota drivers is higher.

But surely I could afford to drive the dressed-up version of my Toyota 4Runner, a GX470 Lexus. Yes, I can afford a Lexus. However, I prefer to allocate the extra $20,000 to conducting another survey of millionaires rather than to ride around with the money in traffic! (Is anyone happy in traffic, irrespective of the price and make of the wheel they are gripping?)

Not only is the V-6 engine in my Toyota 100 pounds lighter and more efficient, and provides superior acceleration than the V-8 in the gilded version, by allocating the $20,000 to the car the money is lost forever, but by allocating it to a survey, it will generate more income for me. The Lexus does have better paint (my Toyota has orange peel), a superior transmission, and a higher-quality interior, but are those attributes worth the extra $20,000? Not to me. Most of all, the people who are an important part of my life do not care if I drive a Toyota. Nor does my choice of motor vehicle have any influence on the number of people who respond to my surveys or buy my books.

Most people who are economically successful in objective terms do not need status brands to convince themselves or others in their social circles of this fact. Nor is their high level of satisfaction in life based on the make of vehicle they drive.

On the Inside

Much of my college tuition was funded by working summers in the parts department of a Chevrolet dealership. One day while I was working there, I came across a rather thick parts catalog, which I found fascinating. How could a catalog that listed thousands and thousands of part numbers be fascinating? It was no ordinary book that merely listed numbers. Some of us referred to it as "the cross" or X book. It referenced every Chevrolet part/number that was common to the other, more expensive, more prestigious makes of General Motors cars and vice versa. The X book often came in handy when I worked in the parts department. What if there was, for example, a Buick on the Chevrolet dealer's used car lot that needed a part? I could use the X book to see if a Chevrolet part in inventory could be substituted for the Buick part.

Years ago, General Motors came up with one of the most brilliant marketing ideas every conceived. Some call it the "trade 'em up" strategy.

During the time I worked in the parts department, the Chevrolet make was General Motors entry-level brand. It was assumed that adults in the early stages of their life cycle would first purchase a Chevrolet and then would trade up to a more expensive and prestigious model, such as a Pontiac, Oldsmobile, Buick, and eventually Cadillac as their social and economic situation improved. General Motors also realized if the quality and performance of the entry-level brand of car were impressive, then their customers would likely assume that the other more expensive GM makes were even "better" and thus worth the extra dollars.

I have a feeling that there is a much greater variation in the advertising themes associated with makes of motor vehicles than there are real differences in product quality across various brands. This is especially true among makes produced by the same corporation, such as General Motors, Toyota, Ford, and so on.

Imagine for a few moments that you are the CEO of the Toyota Corporation. You decide that the entry-level makes Toyota produces will have parts that wear out at, say, 75,000 miles. Call these parts "cheap," "inexpensive," or even "inferior." But your top-of-the-line models are manufactured with parts that will last for 150,000 miles. What a great idea: pricier models having higher-quality components! What is the problem? If Toyota's entry-level models/makes contained grade X components, what impact would it make on the sales of its premium models? The market success or failure of a premium make is a direct function of the quality of its entry-level cousins. In most instances, entry-level models/makes provide the best degree of quality for the dollars that drivers allocate.

I told my dad about the X book and that, in many cases, parts between makes were interchangeable. Did it have an influence on him? I can't be sure, but Dad never owned even one prestigious make of motor vehicle, even during his peak earning years. He always drove entry-level models.

The insight I gathered from the X book also had an influence on my family. The cars we have purchased over the years were all entry-level makes of motor vehicles that have high-quality parts. That is all we have wished to pay for, not the added marketing costs associated with touting the superficial superiority of prestige makes of motor vehicles. Given my experience with the X book, there never will be any of the gilded versions of what are essentially Chevrolets or Toyotas in our stable.

Chevrons with Wheels

If you study the automobile industry, you will learn a lot about American culture. Start your analysis by reviewing two important events that took place in 1927. In that year, General Motors head Alfred Sloan hired a gifted automobile designer named Harley Earl, who had attended Stanford and then worked for his father's Los Angeles–car customizing business. He quickly realized that increasingly affluent Americans would pay more for a symbol of wealth and status.[1] Also in 1927, GM began what we take for granted today, annual model changes. It would be very difficult and probably prohibitively expensive for car companies to make major changes in the performance of motor vehicles each year.

So how were buyers of automobiles persuaded to trade in last year's model for this year's?

> GM introduced annual model changes to lure motorists into dealer showrooms to see the latest styles and gadgetry . . .
>
> "The design of the car can be a persuasive tool for inducing car buyers to get rid of the old and buy the new," Earl said.[2]

As far back as 1927, both Mr. Sloan and Mr. Earl understood the desires of the automobile buyer: Consumers will pay big bucks for cars that symbolize wealth and status. Owning the latest, the new and improved, we really mean it this time, isn't this model hot will make a statement about the owner. Those who drive the latest model of prestige make of car are supposed to have more income, wealth, and status than those who do not. Statistically, this is true. There is a significant correlation between income and price paid for a motor vehicle. Also, the higher one's income, the more often one trades cars. Yet this correlation does not mean that those driving expensive, newer models are, in fact, wealthy. Many of those BMW drivers are only acting rich. They are substituting a car for real wealth. They drive new models of prestige makes of cars in an effort to enhance their status. In reality, they substitute "driving rich" for actually being rich. They have almost a desperate need to separate themselves from the so-called hoi polloi.

What if, for one reason or another, you cannot separate yourself from the crowd in terms of real wealth? Figure out how the rich behave and emulate their conspicuously displayed behaviors, the assumption being that all rich people have tasteful consumption habits for only the very best. Decode their habits and behaviors and you, too, can be a glittering person. Most important, avoid, at all costs, the consumption habits and behaviors of those who are not glittering (middle class, lower income, nonprofessional, and so on). You certainly don't want to emulate those who live in nondescript homes valued at under $400,000 or those who drive Toyotas, Hondas, Fords, Buicks, and Chevrolets. Note the absence of European makes, which is dominant among the glittering rich and their poorer aspirational cousins. It's almost as though some of us yearn for the very royalty our forefathers worked to overthrow in 1776.

Degrees of Separation

What makes of motor vehicles are in a statistical sense significantly more likely to be driven by the "beautiful people" and least likely to be driven by the "anything but beautiful" crowd? The Mercedes-Benz has the highest discriminant score, 3.6 times greater than the threshold of statistical significance. BMW scored very high as well with a 3.3. The other beautiful people—endorsed makes of motor vehicles and their scores are: Lexus (2.4); Jaguar (2.2); Land Rover (2.2): Porsche (2.1), and Audi (1.8).

Pity the poor American and Japanese automobile manufacturers. It must drive them crazy to suffer the illogical buying preferences of the glittering rich and aspirational market segments. How is it that some of their makes that are equal to or even superior in performance and reliability to certain European makes are rejected in favor of higher prices?

Well, let's think about who influences your buying decisions if you are at the top of the glittering rich scale. If you make a good income ($200,000 or more), then at least in the United States, you are at the top so there is no one to emulate. What to do? Do what your cohort has done since the days when the robber barons ruled: Take your consumption cues from your European cousins. If they drive German cars, you will want to have a German car. It's cachet. By driving a top-of-the-line Mercedes or BMW, you, in essence, are demonstrating that your behavior is approved by those Europeans who exude high status and prestige.

Given our proclivity to emulate the so-called European sophisticate, I should not have been surprised to learn that even though the Corvette Z06 received rave reviews, people did not jump to trade in their European models for this higher-performance car. Why didn't Porsche owners, for instance, make the switch?

In a road track comparison test, a $77,725, 505-horsepower, Chevrolet Corvette Z06 outperformed a $120,670 Porsche 911 GT3.[3] In fact, the same model Corvette outperformed just about every production sports car produced in Europe. But performance and cachet are not the same. Sure, the Corvette is fast, very fast. Plus, "you can't buy this much performance anywhere else for the price."[4] But under the heading of "the lows" or negative features of the Corvette, the same writer stated: "That gold-chain rep" [reputation].

Bottom line: The glittering rich and aspirationals who drive Porsches do not want to be associated with the gold-chain crowd. Perhaps that is why they will pay $42,945 more for a Porsche than the Corvette that out-performs it. Accordingly, the overall verdict given to the Porsche that was tested was:"The obvious pick for those with the means."[5]

Could it be that "those with the means" are the glittering rich and high-income producers who have a strong compulsion to emulate their European cousins?

Driving a BMW Does Not Make You a Millionaire

There are two types of people who drive prestige makes of motor vehicles: those who are rich and those who act rich. Who are these actors, the pseudoaffluent? Many of them think they are actually rich, even upper-middle-class rich. Others believe that they will soon be rich.

But, as I have pointed out throughout this book, there is a major difference between earning a high income and actually being wealthy (aka financially independent). Income is not the same measure as wealth. If you do not have investments (of which your home can be no more than 25 percent) valued at $1 million (at least), you are not wealthy. It does not matter what college you attended, for how long, or the number and types of degrees you have earned. Educational achievement is not wealth.

The acting-rich BMW crowd, more often than not, consists of college graduates who earn good incomes. They may be doctors, lawyers, corporate executives. They feel compelled to display the products and brands that they think many truly rich people own. In essence, they exaggerate their real level of wealth. Often they have to struggle, really struggle, to pay their club dues, lease payments on their prestige makes of automobiles, payments on the interest-only jumbo mortgages, private school tuition, and on and on. They are masters of deception who deceive themselves by thinking that they are much more than their balance sheets show. They surround themselves with neighbors whom they believe are wealthy and with artifacts and/or brands that connote success, wealth, and achievement.

The pseudoaffluent are insecure about how they rank among the Joneses and the Smiths. Often their self-esteem rests on quicksand. In their minds, it is closely tied to how long they can continue to purchase the trappings of wealth. They strongly believe all economically successful people display their success through prestige products. The flip side of this has them believing that people who do not own prestige brands are not successful.

Many people have a perverted notion about what it means to be wealthy. This is especially the case among those who are not rich. In a national study conducted by the *Wall Street Journal*, more than 2,000 adults (selected from the general population) were asked about the perceived benefits of being rich and the material artifacts that a person must have to be considered rich. More than one-third (35 percent) indicated that to qualify as rich, a person must own a motor vehicle that costs $75,000 or more.[6]

Now for the reality: If we applied this $75,000 threshold to the millionaires' survey, more than 90 percent would fail to qualify! Go inside the garages of millionaires and see what makes of cars are parked there. A minority drive true luxury motor vehicles. But it is not just about the cars they have parked in their garages today. It is also about history, the pattern of the makes of motor vehicles acquired by millionaires over the years. If you examine the data, it is clear that acquiring luxury makes among millionaires is much more about what they did not buy as about what they did buy.

Over the prior 10 years, what percentage of the millionaires surveyed *have not* owned/leased even one of the prestige makes of vehicles listed below?

Acura	88.9%	BMW	79.1%
Aston Martin	100.0%	Cadillac	88.7%
Audi	92.7%	Ferrari	99.7%

Infiniti	92.7%	Maserati	99.6%
Jaguar	92.6%	Mercedes Benz	75.1%
Lamborghini	99.9%	Porsche	95.1%
Land Rover	95.9%	Rolls-Royce/Bentley	99.6%
Lexus	78.9%	Saab	95.8%
Lincoln	93.0%	Volvo	90.4%
Lotus	99.9%		

Net worth is a significant yet not substantial correlate of the prices paid for motor vehicles that are purchased. But when it comes to predicting the acquisition of prestige motor vehicles, income is a superior variable to net worth. And so is the market value of one's home.

What can I predict about that fellow who just drove by in a luxury make of motor vehicle? Even if the car was bought as opposed to leased, I would not bet the farm on whether the driver has a high income, let alone a substantial net worth.

So what can one surmise about that fellow in the luxury car? Let's see. He is probably alive. He likely has a driver's license, a job, and possibly an annual household income of $75,000 or more. Plus he has a need to tell others that "I am successful." Whether he is, in fact, successful or anticipates becoming successful one day or merely is role-playing is not easy to predict by the make of car he drives. Within the millionaire population surveyed, a larger percent (27.7) acquired at least one Ford over the past 10 years than any luxury make of motor vehicle.

In America, 86 percent of all prestige/luxury makes of motor vehicles are driven by nonmillionaires.[7] Why do people who are not wealthy drive luxury makes of cars? For some, it's about acting rich ahead of the game. For others, it's about seeking to enhance their self-esteem and overall satisfaction with life by driving prestige makes of cars. Many believe that what you drive will determine whether the road takes you to a happy place. But all the data and every study show that there are no shortcuts to Happyville and that self-esteem can't be bought at a dealership.

Driving an expensive car ends up being a substitute, and not a very good one at that. The U.S. auto industry may be ready to fall over a cliff, sales may have plummeted indicating that we finally got the message that overspending is hurtful to our financial health, but I am fairly convinced that behavior will revert once the financial headwinds soften. If we had learned our lesson, we wouldn't have gotten to this terrible situation in the first place. Credit was easy and many took the credit and overextended themselves as part of a longer-term trend of buying up and of buying to replace real wealth and success.

Not only have we driven ourselves right to the poorhouse (though in a super-nice car), we have done so all the while thinking we've fooled our peers. Maybe. But anyone who follows the doings of the fabulously rich now or in times past understands something basic. Really rich people don't just have a Mercedes SUV, for instance, they have 10 other cars. Their consumption is over the top because their wealth is over the top—and still they spend below their means. What good is it to drive a Mercedes, live in an expensive home, belong to a country club, and pay up for wine and spirits if you are always living on the edge of financial solvency? If you can't weather an economic downturn? If there is any question that you might be unable to pay for the college of your daughter or son's choice? Or can't pay for healthcare services for your parents or grandparents?

Drastic times call for drastic measures. Maybe we should be required to file a statement of net worth when we file taxes with the government subsequently issuing us color-coded license plates that allow us to buy cars within a certain price range, based on our financial health. That would take care of the temptation to buy false badges of success.

The Decamillionaire and the Volkswagen

Why would someone with a net worth of over $10 million (which exceeds that of 99.7 percent of all households in America) drive what some would consider a dull, even mundane car? Mrs. Vivian Wells is not only wealthy but also reports that she is "extremely satisfied with her life." She is living proof that one can be very happy without ever owning a prestige make of motor vehicle. Mr. Wells drives a five-year old Saturn; Vivian drives a three-year-old Volkswagen Jetta. She paid $20,500 for her car. It replaced her 10-year-old Volkswagen. Even though Mrs. Wells hates to spend money on cars, she felt compelled to change horses. After all, the Volkswagen she traded in had over 130,000 miles on its odometer!

It is interesting to note that Mrs. Wells is the major financial force in her household. Ten years ago, the couple had a net worth of approximately $1 million. Today they are worth over $10 million. In spite of their considerable financial success, they drive a Volkswagen and Saturn. To Mrs. Wells, cars are like toasters. All toasters toast. All cars can get you from one place to another. She has no strong affection for toasters or motor vehicles. Therefore, she has no problem buying the no-frills versions of both.

It is not uncommon for people who enjoy a major upswing in their economic status to reward their success. One way to do this is to buy things. Not only do the successful reward themselves, but the purchase of luxury goods is a way to signal to others, to the world, about one's economic achievements. Not Mrs. Wells. She does not feel the need to use products, especially expensive makes of motor vehicles, to define herself. Why is this the case? Let's look at her background for some insight.

Mrs. Wells was raised by frugal parents. Even though they never earned much money, they were good at making ends meet by rigorous and disciplined spending and budgeting. Her parents were not college graduates, but Mrs. Wells received a full academic scholarship and graduated first in her "very competitive" college class. Interestingly, within the high-income population, I find that there is a negative correlation between one's grade point average and the amount one spends on motor vehicles. Those with the very highest grades tend to spend less on motor vehicles. This by no means suggests that people you see driving $100,000 cars all flunked out of college! Nor does it mean that all Phi Beta Kappas, like Mrs. Wells, drive subcompact cars. Could it be that people who receive recognition for extraordinary achievements feel less need to purchase symbols, brands, or makes of cars that supposedly denote success? Perhaps this is why Edmund S. Phelps, the 2006 Nobel Prize winner in economics, does not own a car.[8] Yet fully 85 percent of the households in America have one or more motor vehicles.

Mrs. Wells is a scholar, an intellectual, and a successful writer. This is her passion. Heavily marketed products, brands, makes of cars mean very little to her. Plus she knows that her readers do not care what type of motor vehicle she drives. Nor does her choice of make of car have anything to do with the products she produces. Call her a nerd, bookworm, tree hugger, granola, intellectual. But her kicks come from some deep feeling of pride of being published. She feels no need even to try to embellish her work, to decorate her accomplishments by driving a prestige motor vehicle or owning a second home. And certainly not even her $125 watch would indicate that she is a decamillionaire. But she does occasionally indulge herself in Stolichnaya vodka.

There is, however, another reason Mrs. Wells feels comfortable driving a Volkswagen. She weighs 113 pounds and is five feet five inches tall. She is well disciplined both in terms of her eating and exercising habits. She's petite and a petite car works nicely for her. Unlike Mrs. Wells, many people in the U.S. gain weight as they age through poor eating habits and a lack of exercise, causing a loss in flexibility. The result is that middle-age, overweight people prefer larger-size, roomier motor vehicles. The car companies know this. They also know that as people age, they generally have more money to spend. So the car manufacturers take advantage of these circumstances. Thus, you typically find that full-size motor vehicles, including SUVs and pickup trucks, are priced much higher overall than subcompact and smaller-size vehicles. Yet the differences in manufacturing costs across various size models are nowhere near the variations in retail prices charged. Call this age/weight price discrimination. Basically, those who buy full-size motor vehicles subsidize those who buy subcompacts. Often car manufacturers make no profit selling subcompacts, especially those designed as "starter cars for young drivers." But they typically make considerable profits from those who need full-size vehicles. They make even more from people who drive full-size, prestige makes of motor vehicles.

Mrs. Wells will have none of this. She does not subsidize; she does not need to do so. She is young of heart, mind, and body. And she could care less about what others might say about her choice of motor vehicles. What if you associate with friends who have the same set of values as does Mrs. Wells? Would they endorse your choice of car?

It is unfortunate that cases like Mrs. Wells's are not widely broadcast by the media. Instead of reading or hearing stories about Mrs. Wells, the media focuses on celebrity big spenders. Thus it has always been, but the proliferation of broadcast and Internet media outlets has turned up the volume on these types of stories. As recently as the 1970s, only a few magazines, for instance, focused on celebrities (and most of them were teen rags that offered cute pictures of young men whose personas were tightly controlled by their handlers). Today, there are no adults minding the young or handlers working to keep images squeaky clean. In fact, just the opposite. Anything goes and the more outrageous, the better. Britney and Paris in their Mercedes are the height of sexy. But what message do we send the children when we ooh and ahh over young women in European cars? That sex (literally, in the case of Paris) will make you rich and give you the trappings of wealth. And that's way better than any actual achievement. We may not believe that, but that's the message being transmitted. The question is: Who do you want your daughter to be, Paris or Mrs. Wells?

Extraordinary Wealth, Ordinary Cars

Mrs. Wells is not the only millionaire who drives an inexpensive car. I have come across many, one of whom is Tom. He loves to play golf at a local country club situated near a midsize city in the foothills of the Blue Ridge Mountains. The club was founded in the 1920s. It has a fine 18-hole course and a charming clubhouse. The initiation is a relatively modest $6,000 (versus $50,000 for NYC's CORE Club that has no golf course).

What types of motor vehicles are parked at the club on weekends? There are plenty of foreign and domestic luxury models, such as Audi, BMW, Cadillac, Lincoln, Mercedes, and such. Plus there are numerous SUVs from Chrysler, Ford, and Chevrolet.

There is one car in the lot that does seem a bit out of place in terms of its size as well as its sticker price. It is the four-door Honda Civic that Tom drives. Why a Civic? Was Tom hurting for money when he bought it? Did he have a sudden economic reversal that precipitated a trading down in status?

No, Tom drives a Civic because he is frugal. Plus, he is a rather successful mechanical engineer. Accordingly, he evaluates motor vehicles differently from most people. Tom believes that the Honda Civic epitomizes outstanding engineering, design, efficiency, and value. Plus Tom stands about five foot eight and has the ideal, slender build for a Civic.

Tom thinks for himself. He does not follow the crowd when it is briskly running down BMW Avenue or Mercedes-Benz Boulevard. Most people who are members of country clubs probably would feel at least a bit embarrassed to be seen driving a Honda Civic, the subcompact economy vehicle, to and from the club. Yet Tom never ever felt the least bit embarrassed by driving his Civic. He loves his Civic, as he loved the previous three Honda Civics he owned.

The irony of this situation is seen in the rankings of the members of Tom's country club according to their economic productivity and financial status. Who is at the top? Not the luxury and jumbo-size SUV drivers. You guessed it; Tom the Civic driver is the winner.

How can this be? Unlike the pseudoaffluent, it is Tom's values and his substantial achievements that underlie his high self-esteem. He just doesn't need to wrap himself or his achievements inside expensive automobiles. Tom and his cousin invented the Dumpster and other innovative products. He's made a lot of money. But, like many other real millionaires, he doesn't flaunt it by silly spending. He seeks out value.

Why do so many people who are country club members drive luxury makes of motor vehicles? Most of Tom's fellow members are college graduates who have moderate to high occupational status, but they are not millionaires. Although they may not be millionaires, they do have a high desire to be perceived a certain way.

Tom, however, because he is an engineer—and a true success in every sense of the word—is more focused on value and quality than showmanship. Within the millionaire population, engineers in general are among the most frugal. They tend to place more value on how well a product like a car is engineered and how well it functions than on style and fashion. In other words, engineers value good engineering more than excessive chrome, overaccessorized, glitzy motor vehicles. Engineers tend to be much more sensitive to variations in the physical characteristics of the things they buy and relatively insensitive to the marketing hype. Plus, Tom and many others in his wealth/occupational cohort do not need to communicate their socioeconomic successes by driving around town in prestige makes of motor vehicles.

Automobile manufacturers would have a difficult time making a profit if all of their customers followed the buying habits of engineers, but you would do well. Do you want to become rich someday? If so, emulate the buying habits of people like Tom. The buying habits of the engineers surveyed speak loudly: Buy what has value and good performance, is simple, and focus on the price paid for that value. Engineers also remind us not to confuse style for function. Those who need to accumulate style points via their product selections tend to be relatively insensitive to the variations in prices among makes of cars, for example, and less sensitive to genuine physical product quality.

Why do so many engineers like Tom drive Hondas or Toyotas? Both of these makes are among the best-engineered, best-performing, most reliable motor vehicles produced in the world. Engineers care less about turning heads and inciting envy than about performance. More broadly, how do engineers who are millionaires differ from the millionaire population in general?

- The Toyota make was found to be number one in market share among both engineers and millionaires in general. One in four (25.0 percent) of the engineers surveyed reported that the make of motor vehicle they most recently acquired was a Toyota. The most popular models were the Camry V6, Avalon, and Highlander. Toyota, as will be detailed later on, was also the number-one make selected among all millionaires surveyed (with a market share of 10.9 percent). But engineers are more than twice as likely to drive Toyotas as others in their wealth category.

- The Honda make was second in popularity among engineers, with a market share of 13.0 percent. In contrast, about 6.0 percent of millionaires in general drive Hondas. Thus, Hondas are more than twice as popular with engineers as with millionaires overall. The favorite models of Hondas among engineers are the Accord V-6 and the Pilot.

- Engineers are less likely to believe that the latest model of motor vehicle is always superior to earlier versions. Wealthy engineers tend to keep their motor vehicles longer—5 years and 7 months—than the median for the millionaire population in general—4 years and

4 months. Overall they pay about 11 percent (median) less for their vehicles than do typical millionaires.

- There may be another reason engineers do not feel uncomfortable driving Toyotas and Hondas. Within the same wealth, income, and age cohort, engineers who are millionaires tend to live in neighborhoods where the median price of a home is about 12 percent lower than for millionaires in general. Engineers, it seems, understate their wealth both in terms of their selection of homes/neighborhoods and by the cars they drive.

- The frugal nature of wealthy engineers is certainly reflected in their demonstrated superior ability to generate wealth from income. Overall, engineers produced about 22 percent more wealth per dollar of realized income than did millionaires in general.

- Estate data from the Internal Revenue Service also confirms that engineers have a high propensity to accumulate wealth. About 1 in 13 (7.6 percent) of all male decedents with a gross estate of $1 million or more was once an engineer. Yet engineers account for only about 2.3 percent of the male working population in this country. Thus, engineers are overrepresented by a multiple of 3.3 times the expectation, given their overall representation in the male working population.

Do you wish to enhance your economic productivity—transform your income into greater and greater levels of wealth? If you do, look to the buying habits of wealthy engineers. They are much more about function than style, more interested in the important physical attributes of competing brands than the high prestige and fashion that marketers often spend millions and millions of dollars trying to associate with their brands. But this is not only limited to motor vehicles. In fact, one of our friends who works in the clothing business suggests that we take a close look at the buying behavior of engineers.

Allan Griffith has a lot of respect for engineers. He has spent more than 25 years making a good living selling suits. He recently told me that engineers are by far his most discerning customers. No other group asks him more questions about a suit's construction, fiber content, quality of materials, and expected longevity than engineers. And, of course, as Allan emphasized, engineers never pay full retail! They appear at Allan's store almost en masse at "the end-of-season super sale."

The Frugality Hall of Fame

One athlete, in particular, stands out for his extraordinary record as a baseball player. But he was also extraordinary in another regard: He was very, very frugal. When he passed away, the value of his estate was estimated to be at least $45 million! During his rookie season in the major leagues, he hit .323. The next year he hit .346. His career batting average was .325. Plus he once had a 56-game hitting streak.

I was honored when I learned that this legend of baseball's favorite book was *The Millionaire Next Door: The Surprising Secrets of America's Wealthy*.[9] Yes, Joe DiMaggio, Mr. Baseball, the frugal of frugal millionaires, connected with all those budget-minded millionaires who were profiled in the book. Budgeting is made easier if one keeps detailed written records of one's expenses, no matter how small the expenditure. And Mr. DiMaggio detailed every expenditure.[10]

When it came to selecting a make of car, Joe DiMaggio was way ahead of his time. What make of car did Mr. DiMaggio drive during several of his peak earning years after retiring from baseball? Like many other millionaires, he drove a Toyota.

Why would a legendary ballplayer worth millions drive a Toyota? Besides being frugal, Mr. DiMaggio got a real good deal on his Toyota.[11] Think of all the professional ball players who drove BMWs, Mercedes, Cadillacs, and other luxury while Joe was tooling around in his Toyota.

Mr. DiMaggio's peers may have had nice cars, but his record, fame, status, and his net worth exceeded almost all of theirs. Clearly, it's not about the car.

Some may say, well, Joe, he was stingy. He died in 1999 of cancer and look at all that he could have had. He could have enjoyed a Maybach, for goodness sake! But for Joe DiMaggio, and Tom the engineer, and Mrs. Wells, the well-lived life isn't about the car they drive; it's about extraordinary achievement and about having their satisfaction come from those achievements—and the financial freedoms born from success.

The Mercedes Millionaire

The headline of the full-page advertisement for the new Mercedes-Benz E350 promised: "More horses. Bigger engine. Increased envy."[12]

Does the promise of increased envy sell cars? It must be a salient decision criterion for some car buyers. For them the need to be envied may override more practical considerations, although Mercedes-Benz has not always received high praise for initial quality:

> Last summer Daimler Chrysler recalled 680,000 vehicles . . . this month it had to recall 1.3 million vehicles to fix electronics and more braking problems—more than a year's total production.[13]

This major recall was not anticipated even by those in the automotive press.

> As recently as four weeks ago, senior executives were extolling recent improvements in Mercedes quality. "The situation" regarding Mercedes quality "is not as dramatic as has been reported," Daimler Chrysler CEO . . . said in a March 1 interview . . . "the highest Mercedes quality ever."[14]

Consumer Reports' reliability ratings of Mercedes are congruent with the reported problems. In both its "used car verdicts" and "new car prediction," several of the Mercedes models it studied received either "worse than average" or "much worse than average" evaluations.[15] A spokesperson for Mercedes responded to the evaluation the *Consumer Reports* made concerning the S430 model:

> Mercedes-Benz doesn't believe there's a problem, saying in a statement: "The data utilized by *Consumer Reports* is volunteered by [its] readers, not verified, and does not correlate to our own data or that of other surveys."[16]

J.D. Power and Associates evaluates the quality of makes of vehicles three years after they are produced. Mercedes-Benz ranked below average in regard to its 2002 model year vehicles.[17] According to Gina Chon in the *Wall Street Journal*:

> Mercedes has recovered some of the ground it lost in quality ratings. After dropping to 14th in the "initial quality" rating in J.D. Powers' annual survey in 2003, it rose to number 5 last year. . . . But its ratings on long term quality remain weak.[18]

What could hurt worse than receiving "weak" evaluations from American car buyers? Along these lines, where does the Mercedes-Benz brand rank among motor vehicle owners in Germany? J.D. Power and Associates recently surveyed 22,000 German car owners. Below are some of the results of that survey.

> Toyota Motor Corporation has the highest level of consumer satisfaction in Germany. . . . [The] Mercedes-Benz brand showed slight improvement, scoring more points than last year. But the company

ranked 11th and just beat the industry average by two points, a sign the company is still recovering after quality problems dented its luxury image.[19]

In spite of poor ratings both in the United States and Europe, the people at Mercedes didn't seem alarmed. What if people who buy Mercedes use a set of buying criteria that are not included in J.D. Powers' studies? Envy, prestige, emotional status, a legacy of quality and related variables may be key factors for certain types of buyers.

While the Mercedes brand was receiving ratings that were less than spectacular, U.S. sales increased.[20] In 2007 Mercedes took the lead in luxury motor vehicle sales (those with a sticker price of $42,000 or more, 189,576). About three of four (74.8 percent) of those Mercedes-Benzes sold in the United States in 2007 were true luxury. In contrast, only 40.6 percent of the BMWs and 32 percent of the Lexus vehicles sold were in this luxury category.[21] Mercedes was also the true luxury leader in 2008.[22] Obviously not all car buyers are equally influenced by the ratings:

> Ranking No. 1 in the J.D. Power and Associates' initial quality study may not be a priority for Mercedes Benz.... Eckhard Cordes, head of the Mercedes car group [stated] that the study's quality criteria may not be relevant to Mercedes' international customer base ..."one has to carefully analyze whether, as a global car. It is really advisable to be the J.D. Power No. 1."[23]

According to my survey data, millionaires who drive Mercedes are quite loyal to this make of motor vehicle. They drive rich and are by definition actually rich. For many of them, the image that Mercedes projects is highly congruent with their self-image as well as with many of their activities, interests, and opinions. There is a very strong bond between the Mercedes mystique and a certain type of millionaire. The "Mercedes

Millionaire" has a pattern of behavior that is predicated on his need to tell others of his wealth, power, and status. And the make of car he drives is a critical ingredient, a symbol, a display artifact, with which to do just that. To the Mercedes Millionaire, his car is part of an arsenal of weapons he uses to protect against being misclassified. Yes, in part, it is the make of car he drives that inoculates him from a dreaded ailment. It prevents him from ever being misclassified as being a plebian, just an ordinary person.

Ask a Mercedes Millionaire about all the other makes of motor vehicles he has acquired over the past 10 years. According to my surveys, what make is among the least likely to be mentioned? Ironically, it is the number-one brand among the millionaires surveyed: Toyota.

Clearly, what is more important to a Mercedes Millionaire is not car ratings published by *Consumer Reports* and J.D. Power but displaying success, status, wealth, and preventing social class misclassification. Nearly 7 in 10 (69 percent) of the 145 decamillionaires surveyed did not consult, not even once, *Consumer Reports* prior to making their most recent car purchase. When selecting a make of motor vehicle, is it possible to have one's cake and eat it too? The make of luxury motor vehicle that has received top reviews is Toyota Motor Corporation's Lexus. Lexus's promise is twofold: (1) it promises to provide high quality, such as having the fewest defects; and (2) it promises to help those who drive the Lexus brand to display high status. But millionaires surveyed who drive Lexuses are not like Mercedes Millionaires.

The Mercedes Millionaire is near the top of the elitist scale in activities and social characteristics among all the multimillionaires surveyed. Given their socioeconomic accomplishments, they have reason to be snobbish. In objective terms, they are the glittering rich. Many have some difficulty controlling their need to display as well as vocalize their importance. In fact, the Mercedes Millionaire is significantly more likely than the Lexus owner to agree with the following statement: "I have a nearly uncontrollable urge to succeed."

The Mercedes Millionaires surveyed also have a corresponding urge to display their success. For some millionaires, success is enough; for others, it is success and showing it. This urge manifests itself in a variety of ways, from the brands of alcoholic beverages they serve guests to the amount they spend on clothes and accessories and even haircuts. This type of millionaire wears expensive watches, shops at upscale clothing stores, spends more money on accessories, and entertains lavishly (with the expectation that the favor will be returned). Overall, in terms of prices paid for just about everything, they are significantly above the norm, even among other millionaires.

If you are having a party or wedding reception and plan to invite Mercedes Millionaires, get out your checkbook. This crowd expects high-grade beverages: Grey Goose, Pravda, Johnnie Walker Black, high-priced wines. The food should be equally as pricey and opulent. Mercedes Millionaires (even if they drive BMWs, Porsches, Land Rovers, or Jaguars) believe that they deserve more. They think of themselves as the chosen ones.

The Mercedes Millionaires deserve attention. Their consumption habits, preferences, and attitudes are congruent with their economic characteristics. Not only are they proficient spenders, they are also prodigious wealth accumulators. Even among millionaires in general, this group has more wealth and higher incomes than the norm. Nearly two-thirds (64 percent) of those surveyed have a high annual household income of $200,000 or more versus only about 3 percent of all U.S. households.

What about the millionaires who drive Toyotas? In terms of the income usually required to become a millionaire, the data suggest that it is easier to do so if you emulate the frugal behaviors of the Toyota Millionaire. Currently only 40 percent of Toyota Millionaires have annual household incomes of $200,000 or more. Toyota Millionaires are among the most productive in terms of transforming income into wealth. In this regard, consider the median realized annual income that was generated by

Toyota Millionaires during the year when they first reached the millionaire threshold. Their median income was $153,763. For Mercedes Millionaires, it was $198,432. In other words, Toyota Millionaires produced the equivalent of $6.50 of wealth for every $1.00 of income. For the Mercedes Millionaire, it was $5.04 in wealth for every $1.00 in income. While the Mercedes Millionaire has a great deal of wealth, he generates less wealth per dollar earned. What does this mean to "average" people of less fantastic income? It means that you have it within your power to generate more wealth, even if your income earning abilities are lower.

The percentage of Mercedes Millionaires who received less than 1 percent of their wealth from inheritance, gifts, estates, and/or trusts is 77 percent; it is 74 percent for the Toyota Millionaires. In both cases last year, fully 91 percent received less than 1 percent of their incomes from trusts, estates, or any other form of intergenerational transfer of wealth or income. Clearly neither of these groups could be considered members of the inherited wealth crowd. Essentially nearly all the Mercedes Millionaires as well as the "Toyota Millionaires" became economically successful on their own without being subsidized by relatives.

Those who only act rich have a goal: to look rich without having to pay the dues of hard work and sacrifice required to become millionaires. They drive prestige makes of cars, often entry-level models. They often lease the vehicles they can barely afford to operate. It does not seem to concern them that they are impostors, in full high-status-vehicle consume. Most (94.0 percent) of the millionaires surveyed bought their most recently acquired motor vehicle; they did not lease.

It is not always easy to recognize the differences between a Mercedes Millionaire and someone who is merely imitating him. But the Mercedes Millionaires surveyed are the real deal, the genuine millionaires who are not afraid to demonstrate their economic success. In essence, the millionaires whom I surveyed drive makes of cars they feel are in harmony with their personalities, achievements, activities, and interests.

Image over Substance

Ask the average person on the street, particularly anyone under the age of 30, what make of car they'd like to drive, and few will say "Toyota." You will hear a lot of Mercedes, BMWs, Jaguars, and so on. What's the big deal? Who wouldn't want to drive one of these "nicer" cars, and isn't the question really a proxy for the success people envisioned for themselves?

The problem is that people, particularly younger people, have come to focus on the trappings of wealth over everything else—including the work or savings to accumulate the wealth to be able to reasonably afford luxury brands. When we think about "rich," we think about acting rich over being rich.

The Mercedes Millionaire worked hard to achieve success. First it was about the success, and *then* came the high-consumption lifestyle—which is congruent with their level of success. Buying a Mercedes hardly puts a dent in their financial statement. Contrast them with the acting-rich actors who work to acquire brands with which to imitate the consumption life-styles of the Mercedes Millionaires. Not surprisingly, wannabes in general are less satisfied with their lives and have lower levels of job satisfaction than do millionaires. Driving a leased Mercedes, wearing an expensive watch, or filling up a heavily mortgaged home with Grey Goose will not make one rich or happy.

When an aspirational looks at a Mercedes Millionaire, he only sees what is on display. He focuses on the leaves of the oak tree, not its roots. But the values and work habits of millionaires, like the roots of the oak, are what support their lifestyles (the leaves), not the other way around. Who should the aspirational seek to emulate instead? The Toyota Millionaire. This advice may be painful for some hyperspenders. For them, a Toyota would never do. The very thought of a Toyota in the driveway makes them queasy. How do these people go about emulating Mercedes Millionaires?

The act begins with driving a Mercedes or other prestige make of automobile. Note I said *driving* one, not *buying* one. It is the aspirationals who keep the leasing companies in business in America. This is no path to wealth; to become rich, they should be following the Toyota Millionaire's example. But their real objective is to look rich, to drive rich, and to look like a real achiever. It is why they will never be financially independent.

But it doesn't stop there. To continue playing the part, you will most likely need a Rolex watch. According to my surveys, more than one in five (22 percent) Mercedes Millionaires wear Rolex watches. That is more than three times the proportion of Toyota Millionaires who wear Rolexes. One in four Toyota Millionaires wears a Seiko; one in seven wears a Timex. Only one in 20 Mercedes Millionaires wears a Timex. Overall, Toyota Millionaires are three times more likely to have paid less than $200 for the watch they most recently purchased.

You will also have to spend more on your clothing. When a Mercedes Millionaire is in need of a suit, dress, shirt, blouse, tie, scarf, coat, and/or dress/work shoes, they are two to eight times more likely to patronize Brooks Brothers, a custom tailor shop, Neiman Marcus, Nordstrom, Polo, and Saks Fifth Avenue than the Toyota Millionaire. Toyota Millionaires are more likely to shop at JCPenney, Kohl's, Sam's Club, Sears, Target, and Wal-Mart. Table 7.1 illustrates how the patronage behavior of millionaires corresponds to these and several other makes of cars they drive. That Mercedes gets more expensive by the day, and we haven't yet stocked up on Grey Goose or traded in the nondescript house in a pleasant but dull neighborhood for a more expensive home on beautiful land!

Poor Toyota. It has such a bad rap yet it is the number-one car among millionaires. Jim Farley, the vice president of marketing for Toyota Brand (USA), sums things up well:

> Toyota's problems . . . are matters of heart. Consumers like Toyota's cars and value its reputation for quality. But most don't have a passion for Toyota which has tended toward bland designs and middle of the road market positions.[24]

Table 7.1   Stores for Clothing and Accessories Patronized by Millionaires According to the Most Recent Make of Motor Vehicles Acquired

Store	Highest %	Lowest %	Ratio: Highest % to Lowest %
Banana Republic	BMW	Chrysler	5.8
Brooks Brothers	Mercedes Benz	Ford	2.3
Costco	Toyota	BMW	1.7
Custom tailor	Mercedes Benz	Toyota	2.9
Dillard's	Lexus	Chrysler	2.0
JCPenney	Ford	BMW	4.7
Kohl's	Ford	Mercedes-Benz	3.5
Neiman Marcus	Mercedes-Benz	Ford	6.0
Nordstrom	Mercedes-Benz	Ford	2.8
Polo	Mercedes-Benz	Toyota	5.1
Men's Wearhouse	Chrysler	BMW	3.3
Saks Fifth Avenue	Mercedes-Benz	Toyota	8.3
Sam's Club	Chrysler	Lexus	2.5
Sears	Chevrolet	Mercedes-Benz	3.5
Steinmart	Toyota	Chrysler	1.9
T.J. Maxx	Toyota	BMW	2.1
Target	Toyota	BMW	1.7
Wal-Mart	Chevrolet	Mercedes-Benz	3.0

I might ask why anyone has a passion for any car so much so that they buy based on prestige and not value, but it does explain how it is that Porsche has "the best profit margin (17 percent) in the auto world"?[25] If you are a Mercedes (type) Millionaire and drive a Porsche, for example, you might feel superior. That's great. But how superior do you feel if you are only acting rich, driving a leased Porsche, knowing that Porsches have a terrific profit margin while your net worth suffers for it? Now, who do you want to be? The Toyota Millionaire or the acting-rich Mercedes driver? Gordon Wangers, a marketing consultant, sums up the problem:

> Toyota. . . . It's the ultimate vanilla automobile . . . it has a silly name. The styling is invisible. It does not give you bragging rights at the valet, to put it mildly.[26]

But it is not only marketing consultants and amateur critics among the acting-rich crowd who downgrade Toyotas. A professional car critic referred to the Toyota Camry's "lows." Included was the "curse of blandness."[27] *Webster's* defines blandness as lacking in special interest, liveliness, individuality, insipid, dull, unemotional and indifferent.

Good grief! Who wants to be accused of driving a car that is bland! But what is really lacking is individuality. The marketing message of a car may conjure up excitement, passion, and even visions of superiority, but if your balance sheet is in the red, how special, lively, and exciting will your life really be?

Why We Buy What We Buy

Evaluating motor vehicles has become a big business. The quality ratings of the various makes and models generate great press coverage. People wait with considerable anticipation each year for the April edition of *Consumer Reports*. I am certainly among this crowd. This issue is devoted to motor vehicles. J.D. Power and Associates also provides considerable insights about the initial quality of new motor vehicles as well as evaluation of makes at certain intervals (years) after they are produced. No doubt this type of information can be extremely valuable to those who purchase motor vehicles. But ranking the makes and models of motor vehicles based upon criteria such as the frequency that certain problems occur, defects, and/ or initial quality has never been the full story. Is buying a car all about the number of black or red balls *Consumer Reports* gives out for each new model of motor vehicle produced?

No.

Most car buyers employ multiple criteria when making their auto purchases. But what if we bought only on quality as defined by *Consumer Reports* or J.D. Power? If this were the case, we might all be driving vehicles produced by the Toyota Corporation. Yet many other issues factor into the decision of which car to buy, including price, dealer service, location, and convenience. In fact, according to a regression analysis I computed, the share of dealers (relative number of dealers) accounts for more than 40 percent of the market share (sales) of new cars. Never underestimate the importance of location, location, location in explaining retail market share.

Overall, the Toyota Corporation produces high-quality cars. But given the number of Toyota-defined dealers compared to those of Chevrolets, who has the marketing advantage? According to *Automotive News* in terms of convenience, in 2007, Chevrolet had about three times the number of dealers as did Toyota (4,063 versus 1,224). Thus, in a crude calculus, the typical car buyer must pass by three Chevrolet dealers (potential interceptors) before he gets to a Toyota dealer.

Dealer service, location, product quality, design, price, fuel economy, and a variety of other variables all contribute to explaining the variations in market share among manufacturers of motor vehicles. Market share, in terms of unit sales, is an excellent composite indicator of how buyers evaluate cars across a variety of choice criteria. Along these lines, what can be learned about the desirability of various makes as seen through the eyes of millionaires? These people are not frivolous about how they spend their dollars. Yet they usually do not wear themselves out trying to find the lowest price either. Millionaires were asked to indicate the actions they took during the past five years to receive the "best deal" when buying a motor vehicle. Of the 30 choices offered, the most frequent action mentioned was "Determining the dealer's cost prior to entering into negotiations with him."

This should not be interpreted as meaning that all millionaires relentlessly shop and aggressively demand the very lowest price. Most millionaires know that buying a car involves certain trade-offs. Thus, consider the second most mentioned action taken by millionaires: "Buying from a dealer I dealt with previously since my time is more valuable than shopping for so-called big discounts."

Fully 46 percent of the millionaires tend to be very dealer loyal. Accordingly, they tend to be loyal to a particular make of automobile. It is the high-income-producing nonmillionaires, aka the only acting rich, who most aggressively price shop dealers as well as status makes of cars. Only 34 percent of these types are dealer loyal as defined above.

Most millionaires are an astute group of people who are excellent judges of quality in terms of both product and service. If they are not satisfied, they will make changes and vice versa. The millionaires in my survey were asked to report the makes and numbers of motor vehicles within each make that they had acquired over the past 10 years. This question was designed to uncover which makes had the highest retention rates (loyalty) among millionaires. The retention rate is a simple yet useful measure of how millionaires judge competing makes.

Over the 10-year period, the make with the highest retention rate (45.5 percent) among millionaires was Chevrolet (see Table 7.2). This means that of all those who acquired at least one Chevrolet in the prior 10 years, 45.5 percent acquired at least one more, usually the same model. Ford was a close runner-up with a retention rate of 44.8 percent. Seven of the top 10 makes with the highest retention rates among the millionaires surveyed were also listed on the J.D. Power and Associates' Customer Retention Study: Toyota, Lexus, Chevrolet, Ford, Cadillac, Mercedes-Benz, and BMW.[28] R.L. Polk and Company also studies customer retention. It gives annual loyalty awards for the model, make, and manufacturer based on the level of consumer loyalty. To do so it analyzes consumer transactions from more than 6 million households throughout America.[29] These

Table 7.2 Makes of Motor Vehicles Acquired by Millionaires

Customer Loyalty Retention Rate— Past 10 Years	Market Share— Past 10 Years	Market Share—Most Recent Acquisition
1. Chevrolet (45.5%)	1. Ford (9.5%)	1. Toyota (10.9%)
2. Ford (44.8%)	2. Mercedes-Benz (8.0%)	2. Lexus (10.8%)
3. Chrysler (41.0%)	3. Toyota (7.6%)	3. Mercedes-Benz (9.6%)
4. Lincoln (40.0%)	4. Lexus (6.6%)	4. Ford (8.3%)
5. BMW (39.7%)	5. Chevrolet (6.4%)	5. BMW (7.9%)
6. Toyota (39.7%)	6. BMW (6.3%)	6. Chevrolet (7.0%)
7. Cadillac (39.1%)	7. Honda (4.5%)	7. Honda (5.9%)
8. Lexus (37.9%)	8. Jeep (4.4%)	8. Chrysler (3.1%)
9. Mercedes-Benz (37.2%)	9. Cadillac (3.8%)	9. Cadillac (3.0%)
10. Buick (37.0%)	10. Chrysler (3.7%)	10. Volvo (3.0%)

retention rates and those among millionaires are fairly congruent with each other.

Among the millionaires surveyed for this book, Ford had the highest market share (9.5 percent) for the 10 years combined. The Ford make was also found to be number one in market share (9.4 percent) in the 1995–1996 National Survey of Millionaires that served as the base for *The Millionaire Next Door.*[30]

What makes of motor vehicles did millionaires most recently acquire? Toyota emerged in first place with 10.9 percent of the millionaire market, followed by its luxury make, Lexus (mostly entry-level models), with 10.8 percent. Millionaires share something in common with other car buyers in this country: Most do not drive luxury makes of cars. A nonluxury make occupies the top spot in both categories of market share.

The Ford F Series pickup truck is popular among millionaires *and* is the number-one bestselling vehicle in America. In fact, in 2008 Ford sold 78,896 more of its F Series than Toyota sold Camrys, its bestselling model.[31] But market share figures for various makes do not tell the whole story about the car-buying habits of millionaires. Many are cherry pickers when it comes to selecting models among various makes of motor vehicles. In other words, they tend to acquire and acquire again the best-of-breed model within various makes of motor vehicles. In political terms, only a minority vote the straight party ticket.

Why do millionaires cherry pick? Most millionaire households own multiple vehicles. And, in most cases, these vehicles are acquired with different purposes in mind. What typically happens in cases where household needs dictate having a full-size SUV and a midsize car? It is not unusual to see a full-size SUV, probably a GM or Ford make, parked next to a Toyota Avalon or Camry, a Lexus ES 300, a Honda Accord, or a BMW 3 or 5 Series. All of these types of vehicles are winners, best of breed.

My Favorite Model

I am often asked a puzzling (to me) question: How can these people be millionaires if they don't drive top-of-the-line luxury cars?

It appears that it is difficult for most people to believe that most millionaires do not drive prestige makes of motor vehicles and that when they do, it's usually the entry-level model (see Table 7.3). The marketers have done a fabulous job training us to believe just the opposite. What is true is that glittering rich people and high-income earners (who most likely are not truly millionaires) do buy the top-of-the-line models produced by European manufacturers. The median price paid by millionaires for their most recent acquisition was only $31,367. The typical price paid by decamillionaires was $41,997, nowhere near the $75,000 figure it is assumed that rich people spend on cars. Not only do many millionaires drive so-called common, nonprestige makes of cars; some drive makes that are not rated tops in quality in exchange for conveniently located dealers with reliable service.

Table 7.3   Popular Models of Motor Vehicles Acquired by Millionaires

Make of Motor Vehicle	Popular Models
Acura	MSX
Audi	A6 Sedan V6
	A4 Sedan V6
BMW	5 Series Sedan 6 Cylinder
	3 Series
Buick	LeSabre
Cadillac	Escalade
	Deville
Chevrolet	Suburban
	Tahoe
Chrysler	Town and Country
Dodge	Grand Caravan
Ford	Explorer V6
	F Series Pickup
	Escape V6
	Expedition
GMC	Yukon/Yukon LX
Honda	Accord
	Odyssey
Infiniti	G35 Sedan
Jaguar	S-Type
Jeep	Grand Cherokee 6 cylinder
Land Rover	Range Rover
Lexus	RX 300, RX 330, ES 300, ES 330
Lincoln	Aviator
Mercedes-Benz	E Class Sedan V6
	S Class

(Continued)

Table 7.3   Popular Models of Motor Vehicles Acquired by Millionaires (*Continued*)

Make of Motor Vehicle	Popular Models
Mercury	Mountaineer V6
Nissan	Maxima
	Pathfinder
Porsche	911 Carrera
Toyota	Avalon
	Camry V6
	Highlander
	Sequoia
	Sienna
Volvo	S60, XC90

I admire people who drive Buicks. They show wisdom in buying a car that ranks high in both quality and value. In terms of vehicle dependability, Buick tied with Jaguar as the highest-ranking brand.[32] Even better, people who trade in Buicks are the least likely to be upside down (owe more on the trade in than the vehicle is worth). About one in three (33.6 percent) of all new car buyers in the United States is upside down.[33] Only 13.1 percent of those trading in Buicks were found to be upside down. Contrast this with those who traded in Mitsubishis, where 56.1 percent were in this unenviable category.[34]

I also have an affinity for those who own Buicks because these people seem to me to be among the least pretentious among all of millionaires who drive motor vehicles. They typically understate their wealth via the middle-of-the-road brands they select. They understate even more than Toyota Millionaires. From suits to shoes, from watches to vodka, as well as the stores they patronize, Buick drivers who are wealthy are anything but flashy. Plus it is nice to know how they judge the quality of the people who host parties. To them it is much more about the people and not the price of the beverages and foods being served. Millionaire Buick owners are among the least likely to have ever received any inheritance from their parents, grandparents, or any other source. In other words, they earned their wealth, the old-fashioned way: work and thrift. Accordingly, most are from lower-, middle-/working-class backgrounds. In essence, theirs is somewhat of an Abe Lincoln story.

After looking over all the correlates of Buick ownership, I recalled a personal experience that brought home what the data show: Those who have a strong need to display high status may not have a lot of interest in associating with Buick types. For several weeks, I drove a Buick, my father-in-law's. During this time, my family was in the process of building a house. The weekend before ground was to be broken, we visited the lot to make plans for our future in the neighborhood. One of our new neighbors, Buff, introduced himself, and we chatted for a few minutes. Buff then asked us for our current address and telephone number, "just to keep in touch."

Later that weekend, we received a telephone call from another new neighbor, Dell, who introduced himself as the "chairman" of the Architectural Review Committee in the neighborhood. He said that he understood we were planning to build a new home but that we had not submitted our house plans for evaluation by his committee. He also informed us that we could not break ground until the plans had been approved. We wanted to get the approval quickly so we agreed to meet him at his home the next day.

After looking over our plans and the Buick in his driveway, Dell made the comment that "these are not custom plans." He said that most of the homes in the neighborhood were custom homes. Later I discovered that the existence of an "Architectural Review Committee" and the claim that most homes were "custom" was so much baloney, but at the time I was concerned if not offended. I assured Dell that our builder was outstanding and that he had suggested using these stock plans. I paid $175 for seven copies of W.D. Farmer Company's "Stock Plan #2727-A." Our builder was familiar with the house because he had built it a dozen times and had worked out all the problems. As Dell reviewed our plans, he spotted something else that disturbed him. "What! No Jacuz? I don't see where you are going to put your Jacuzzi," said Dell. I informed him that we didn't want a Jacuzzi; we would not use it, and we would prefer to spend the money to help fund a 40-year roof and 44,000 bricks. Finally, Dell gave the "official" approval, but we could tell he was not particularly happy about doing so.

What was this all about? I have a theory that Buff, our future neighbor, panicked when he saw us drive up to the lot in a green, nondescript Buick. (It was also missing its hubcaps, but that's another story.) Furthermore, as we were just running out to a construction site after spending the day cleaning out our basement, we weren't exactly dressed for success. Our entire "aura" must have been offputting. Good grief, who knows what kind of house we planned on building since, clearly, we had no taste whatsoever.

Unknown to Buff, we were also concerned. Buff was driving a Porsche, and his wife was driving a Mercedes. Had we inadvertently stumbled into a community where we would be surrounded by people who earned and were worth significantly more than we were? Were we about to see our expenditures increase significantly in keeping up with these new Joneses? It turns out that was not the case. We never did become close friends with Buff or Dell, though when my book, *The Millionaire Next Door*, made the *New York Times*' Bestseller List, Buff's wife called and wanted to host a book signing party at her house! It is amazing what a little success can do. It can even transform the Buick-based opinion once held by an aspirational.

Getting Out of
the Poorhouse

The strength of a nation derives from the integrity of the home.

—Confucius

About a month after moving into the home we had built, my wife and I attended the annual neighbor cocktail party. It did not take the attendees long to start quizzing me about who has the money in America and how affluent our neighborhood is. One woman asked an interesting question.

"How can you, Dr. Stanley, a professor, live in this neighborhood?"

I asked her for clarification. "What do you mean by 'how can'?"

Her response was that this was an affluent neighborhood. In fact, she stated, "Our children are the richest kids who go to our local high school!"

"How do you know that this is an affluent neighborhood?" I asked her.

"Look at the size of the homes, Professor."

I then said, "The size of a home is a better predictor of the size of one's mortgage than the size of one's net worth." Plus, the homes were not mansions; they were spacious at 3,500 to 4,500 square feet, but not overly huge.

I explained that I had purchased a lot in the neighborhood not for prestige but in order to be 10 miles closer to downtown and that I had made the purchase when the real estate market was at its lowest level. During an interview in the early 1980s, millionaires in the real estate business had told me, "Now is the time to buy." In addition, we had built our home and thus saved about 40 percent of what it would have cost if already built by a developer. I also explained that I had had my students survey the neighborhood before we moved into it. Sure enough, I found that we would be out of place moving into that neighborhood. Why? Because we were a lot better off financially than the norm (even though we drove modest cars). At the time of the study, only about 1 in 10 of the homeowners was a millionaire.

Most of the households in the neighborhood had incomes under $100,000, including the family that lived in the classic colonial (her house!). I pointed out that often well-educated people with good incomes feel compelled to live in middle- to upper-middle-class neighborhoods even if they can barely afford the payments.

Her response to these revelations was "Well, you obviously inherited your money." I told her that the only thing I had inherited was a bunch of college loans. Our conversation ended.

Clearly, my neighbor, like most people, did not understand the point I was making. Conspicuous symbols of wealth, such as homes and motor vehicles, are better indicators of one's credit use than of the size of one's investment portfolio.

How Would You Live?

Remember our millionaire friend Carlton, back in Chapter 5, he of the decamillionaire flavor? If you had his wealth and income, how would you live? Would you feel the need to trade up to fit in with your rich neighbors? Dump your Toyota for a BMW, lose the dull Seiko watch and go for a $20,000 Breitling? Dig out the basement and build a wine cellar? Pour your Crawford's scotch and $10 Merlot down the drain, go to the top liquor and wine shop in your area, tell the experts that you repent of your frugal ways, and give them carte blanche to select the brands of beverages that will fill your liquor cabinets? It is only money, after all, and you have plenty.

If you make all of these changes, you might think that your consumption lifestyle would be congruent with that of your wealthy neighbors. And it might well be, but that doesn't mean that your income or net worth will be equal to or greater than that of your neighbors. In fact, you may well find yourself living among those who are higher-income earners and who may or may not have a high net worth. The bottom line is that your choice of house and neighborhood will have the biggest impact on your balance sheet. Your choice of home, more than anything else, will have the greatest impact on your spending—either a lot or not so much.

If you buy up to live in a tony neighborhood and reside among the rich, you will spend like the rich on everything else. You may well be able to afford the mortgage. You may have even calculated that you can handle the carry costs of higher property taxes and insurance. But the unseen carry costs will increase the burden more than you can possibly imagine. The mortgage may be doable, but what about the high-prestige car such as a Mercedes or BMW (and not the entry-level models), the expensive watches for you and your spouse, the high-priced clothing, and the ridiculously priced spirits and wine? And please don't forget your Neiman Marcus shoes before you run out of the house to drop your children off at private school, or leave a check for the maid and tell her to let in the contractor who is coming to start building you a Jacuzzi.

What if you are not rich now but expect to receive a sizable windfall soon? If you are like most people, visions of high-ticket purchases are dominating your dreams. Why not spend before the bird is in the hand? You have two in the proverbial bush. Perhaps this was how a middle-age couple in Florida felt. They were scheduled to receive $1 million for their mobile home, lot included. In anticipation, they bought a boat for $52,000 and a $40,000 truck. But shortly thereafter the real estate developer withdrew his offer.[1] Perhaps this couple should have waited until after they were rich before they began acting rich.

My most recent survey paints a clear picture: Those who live in pricey neighborhoods are too often aspirationals who do not have the income or wealth of their neighbors. The gravitational pull to spend like their high-income neighbors is a force that exceeds even the strongest willed.

But what if most of your neighbors are not rich? Carlton doesn't live among the glittering rich or aspirationals who hyperspend. Carlton's net worth isn't adversely impacted by taking on expensive car leases; recall that he drives a $28,000 Toyota Avalon. He doesn't serve his guests overpriced wine or spirits, yet he entertains generously. Smartly, Carlton lives in a neighborhood that encourages him to keep his spending down. The gravitational pull works to his net worth's advantage.

The Millionaire Next Door, Alive and Well Today

More than a dozen years later, the millionaires next door are alive and well. My interest in looking at the current population of this segment was piqued by Deidre, a producer from ABC's *20/20* news magazine television show. She asked if I could identify neighborhoods where millionaire next door types live. After checking my database, I pinpointed several neighborhoods where these people resided. The resulting televised program certainly raised eyebrows. Most of the homes depicted were in the $200,000 to under $400,000 price range. All of the millionaire next door types who lived in these neighborhoods had an investment portfolio of at least $1 million. Yet the median price they typically pay for a bottle of wine is just over $10.

After the program was televised, I did a statistical analysis of my database and ultimately a profile of millionaires who live in homes currently valued at between $125,000 and $395,000. What is particularly interesting is that most of their neighbors had less than one-fifth the financial wealth that these affluent respondents had accumulated. A more detailed examination of the data brought to mind another television episode. It took place while I was promoting *The Millionaire Next Door* on the Oprah Winfrey Show. A rather well dressed woman from the audience asked me the same question I had heard a thousand times before: "What good does it do to have all this money if you don't spend it?" The woman was agitated, even indignant, that I was touting frugality. She further indicated that "these people couldn't possibly be happy." She, like most people who are not wealthy, believed that the more one spends, the more satisfying life is. Thus, more money translates into more spending and therefore more happiness. But she does not completely understand the benefits of being wealthy. It has much more to do with being financially independent and secure than owning prestige brands. High self-esteem is related to achieving financial independence. Both the sense of achievement that comes from success and financial independence lead to happiness and life satisfaction, not meaningless badges.

What percentage of the millionaires who live in homes valued at under $400,000 are happy? More than 9 in 10 (91 percent) indicate that they are extremely satisfied with life. Yet only 1 in 20 has a wine collection. Happy people tend to live well below their means. I have found this to be the case in all of the studies I have conducted.

Most of the people who make up this low-profile millionaire segment never earned very high incomes. In fact, their median household annual realized income (from all sources) of this group was $113,334 at the time they first reached millionaire status. However (as I have said repeatedly), most people will never earn enough money to become wealthy and to be hyperconsumers at the same time. Do you want to become wealthy? If you do, you might follow the ways and means of this affluent group. Their consumption lifestyle goes beyond merely living in a modest home in a nondescript middle-class neighborhood.

The demographics of this group, millionaires who live in homes valued under $400,000, are quite similar to those of the millionaire next door profiled nearly 14 years ago. Ninety-two percent are married. In 90 percent of the cases, the male head of household is the major breadwinner. Fully 62 percent of those who are married have never been divorced. The median value of their home is $293,214. Their median realized household income from all sources in 2006 was $152,193, or more than one-half the current value of their home.

Not all regions of the country are equal in producing these low-profile millionaires. I first discovered this in 1979. At that time I was asked by Rick, a former student, to analyze the data from a large national survey of investors conducted by his employer, the New York Stock Exchange. Rick also asked me to write up my findings and present my paper at the national conference of the Securities Industry Association. In the speech I pointed out that most marketers of investment services were wasting their time targeting prospects in America who only acted like they were wealthy. Instead, I suggested they should focus more on what I called at the time blue-collar millionaires. In essence, I introduced them to the low-profile millionaires next door:

[T]hese wealthy, blue collar prospects . . . members of "the really big segment" don't need to purchase the expensive artifacts that are part of the white collar worker's status knapsack. The symbols that are associated with most brokerage firms are indicative of the upper-middle and upper classes. The language, cues, atmospherics, architectural style, advertising, and dress may indicate that the broker is not interested in the investment needs of blue collar millionaires that I have found among captains of fishing vessels, materials handlers (especially operators of crane and pile driving equipment), farmers and ranchers, scrap metal dealers, dry cleaners, and auctioneers.[2]

I also pointed out that as a proportion of their respective populations the Midwest had a higher concentration of these high-net-worth people. These findings are congruent with those of my most recent national survey. In it, the concentration of millionaires next door in the Midwest is 1.65 times greater than what is expected, given the size of its overall population. The South is also above the norm with a multiple of 1.2, while California and especially the Northeast areas of the United States have less than half the expected number, given their overall household population. These concentrations are inversely related to the respective proportions of wine zealots found in each region. The traditional values of thrift and modesty in spending are still alive in many parts of the Midwest. If I were to open an exclusive wine bar or luxury car dealership, the last place I would consider to place it in would be the Midwest. Apparently, my presentation on behalf of the New York Stock Exchange hit a nerve among the audience. As a result, I had so many requests to make the same presentation that I had to train two of my former graduate assistants to give my speech verbatim.

The most memorable occurrence that followed my presentation was a conversation I had with the head of an investment company. At that time, John's firm operated only in the Midwest. Also, he emphasized that his company developed a success formula that was very effective in penetrating the blue-collar millionaire, aka the millionaire next door, segment. As a result, the firm became one of the most successful and well-managed brokerage firms in America. A typical office was staffed by one registered representative and one assistant. At the time, all of the company's offices were strategically located in small towns. Its strategy of becoming the dominant supplier of investment products within a narrowly defined geographic area proved extremely successful.

John explained that among his firm's clients was a high concentration of frugal, low-profile farmers and ranchers, owners of small businesses, teachers and professors, and auctioneers. The surveys I later conducted for the firm confirmed that its clientele was indeed an affluent group.

Not only was the firm's client base a frugal, economically productive, low-profile, and unpretentious group, so were the partners who ran the company. As an example, take my key contact, the partner in charge of marketing at that time. Mr. T, as I will call him, was just 30 years of age. He was already a millionaire and very, very frugal. He spent very little money (none on wine) while investing a lot. He was so good at relating to blue-collar millionaires as a broker in the field that the firm sent him new recruits to train, and he took it upon himself to write a manual on how to market investments to the blue-collar millionaire segment. The manual alone proved so valuable to the firm that Mr. T was made marketing head for the entire firm. What kind of car did this young millionaire drive? I recall it vividly; it was a 10-year-old Ford sedan with 150,000 miles on the odometer. Blue smoke poured from the tailpipe as the engine light flashed on. ("Not a problem, Tom, it just went on last Monday!") Can you say small-town, midwestern values? This was the car he drove around while prospecting affluent investors. At the time, his trade area was in and around a rural community of 25,000 people that contained many more hogs than people. But not even one wine bar.

Mr. T's trade area was known as the hog-raising capital of America, and Mr. T had a good number of clients who were affluent hog farmers. His wealthiest client, a hog farmer, was a bit unusual even among the blue-collar millionaire crowd. He first prospected this fellow via a cold call. It was just after the noon hour at the farmhouse. The farmer's wife invited Mr. T into the parlor. There he found the farmer dressed in bib overalls snoozing in a full-size barber's chair. He took a 30-minute catnap every day after lunch. The barber chair was the only piece of furniture in the room and clashed with the floral design on the linoleum floor. But, as Mr. T commented, highly coordinated interior design and wealth are often negatively correlated. Not all decamillionaires in America have rugs in their parlors or wine collections in their cellars.

An even more memorable scenario from my association with this firm took place just prior to making a presentation to the firm's managing partners. Almost all were young, in their 30s and 40s. And all were already millionaires. As I was preparing to profile their customer base at the luncheon meeting, John told me we would be having "prime steaks and vintage wines" catered by "Rojar." Wow, I thought. Maybe these folks are not as frugal as I thought. At that point, in walked Mr. T with two assistants carrying two very large bags of Steak 'n Shake double cheeseburgers. Shortly thereafter, the milkshakes arrived.

What happened to "catered by Rojar"? Turns out that "Rojar" was actually Mr. T, Roger being his first name. When he handled lunches, he was called "Rojar."

No one complained about the Steak 'n Shake lunch; on the contrary, the menu reflected the values of these people. It was unpretentious food for unpretentious, down-to-earth people. Plus, the cheeseburgers were quickly consumed, leaving plenty of time for the important business at hand. After the meeting, John spoke with me.

> Thank you . . . fine job. I hope you were not turned off by the burgers . . . Actually we like you and what you have done for us. That's why we went for the double cheeseburgers and shakes. . . .
>
> Yesterday some VPs from a big New York investment bank were here making a presentation. They were fed McDonald's (single patty) burgers with Cokes . . . no shakes! But in your honor we upgraded to Steak 'n Shake.

These folks understood that what is served at luncheon meetings should never be the main focus. The purpose of the meeting was to disseminate information and ideas that would make the company and its partners more productive. The partners didn't feel degraded because steaks and vintage wines were not on the table. On the contrary, being frugal and becoming financially secure actually enhanced their self-image and esteem. Call it what you like, but it finds its roots in traditional values found in the adages "Waste not, want not" and "You reap what you sow." High self-esteem and wealth building comes about by setting goals and achieving them, not from a certain kind of wine bottle on the lunch table.

Was there anything these partners were missing? At the time they believed that all the low-profile, high-net-worth investors lived in small towns, in rural America, but eventually they began to see that the majority of millionaires, including those who reside in large metropolitan areas, live well below their means. Today the firm has more offices in the United States than any other investment company, and its offices are located in towns and cities of every size. You do not to have to live in a small farming community to nurture rural values. According to one writer, part of this value structure is to have "a deep suspicion of consumption."[3]

Shopping for Happiness

Imagine for a moment that today you are "somewhat happy" with your life overall and that last year your annual income was $50,000 or even $100,000. This year you will generate an income of $200,000. Given this scenario, you might predict that your satisfaction with life would also increase, perhaps placing you in the "extremely satisfied" with life category. Don't count on it, though.

Not all high-income producers are satisfied with their lives. Who are these seemingly financially rich people who tell me "I'm not satisfied with my life?" Even though they possess the basic factors that all studies find as important ingredients to happiness—health, loving families, enjoyable jobs—they are still not happy. How can this be?

Much of their dissatisfaction is found in certain choices they have made. Two key choices are neighborhood and house. Both of these elements influence consumption patterns. What if you earn $200,000 a year but spend like neighbors who earn $300,000? You are likely living above your means. As my surveys and studies have found, those who live above their means tend to be dissatisfied with their lives. Conversely, those who live below their means are significantly more likely to report that they are happy.

Those who find it hard keeping up with higher-income-earning neighbors like the Joneses, and ahead of the Struggling Smiths, are anything but happy. I have examined the income and wealth characteristics of high-income producers who are unhappy. Most have an identity problem. They identify with and take their consumption cues from their neighbors, the Joneses. But the Joneses have both significantly higher income and wealth. Members of this dissatisfied segment are not ahead of the Smiths in their respective neighborhoods. In cold, hard objective terms, they *are* the Smiths. Throughout America, where do the dissatisfied Smiths typically rank in regard to both income and net worth compared with their neighbors? They are highly concentrated in the bottom quartile. And, typical of the Smiths, their home has a market value below the neighborhood norm. Yet they can have difficulty paying for it and the consumption habits that are dictated by their wealthy neighbors. In essence, the Smiths are only acting like the people in their respective neighborhoods who are actually rich.

How can these Smiths find happiness? Get out of Jonesville! This is an especially urgent message now with real estate prices plummeting and some tempted to grab a so-called bargain in or around an exclusive neighborhood. Never forget that that nice house in that prestigious community will cost you considerably more than the price of the mortgage, real estate taxes, and insurance. Your ego may take a bit of a bruising by admitting that you don't have the income to live among the glittering, but bruises fade with time, and it's almost guaranteed that your satisfaction with life will increase once you are no longer fighting to keep up with those who can simply run faster. Should your self-worth really be defined based on the neighborhood you live in, the car you drive, the vodka you drink, or should you define yourself and your value according to achieving a good deal of financial independence that will allow you all sorts of freedoms? Is it downgrading to achieve a higher net worth?

Most people who are in the six-figure or above income bracket are satisfied with their life overall. Yet Rob Smith is not among them. Although he believes he can spend his way into Happyville, it seems that the more he spends, the less satisfied with life he becomes.

What is it that Rob does not understand about the relationship between satisfaction with one's life and spending money? Those who live below their means tend to be significantly happier than people like Rob. In sharp contrast, Henry Jones understands why he is satisfied with his life. Henry lives below his means. As a result of keeping his spending in line with his income, plus prudent investing over the years, he is financially secure.

Unhappy Rob and Happy Henry are archetypes, labels given to high-income-producing baby boomers. Nationwide, they are the typical/representative characters from two subsamples of 300 high-income-producing baby boomers culled from my national survey of 1,594 households. They both, as you will see, have much in common. Both started working at nearly the same time and today are in their mid-50s. On a national basis, they live in homes worth just under $800,000 (median dollars). In the Northeast, their homes are valued at over $1 million (median dollars) and even higher in California.

Happy Henry's household has both a significantly higher annual income and net worth than does Unhappy Rob's. Rob is not happy because he is trying to keep up, in terms of consumption, with the higher-income-producing Happy Henry. But Rob is delusional. He identifies with and attempts to emulate the consumption behavior of his neighbors who are much more able to support a high-consumption lifestyle. Also, he thinks that he is a twin or at least a close cousin of Henry. But in reality, most of his neighbors are much higher on the happiness scale and on the economic productivity scale.

Rob has kept pace with Henry in one very telling category. In spite of earning considerably less income, Rob's adoption of prestige brands and other expensive artifacts matches, and in some cases even exceeds, Henry's. Rob lives a treadmill existence. He earns in order to spend. But the more he spends, the less satisfaction he receives. He also thinks that if he had more money to spend, he would reach Happyville. Unfortunately, not only is Rob wrong about what makes for a satisfied life, his train is moving in the wrong direction.

What motivates Rob to spend so much? As we have seen throughout this book and as the statistics show starkly, the number-one factor is his housing. Rob lives in a high-income, high-consumption neighborhood surrounded by dozens more even higher-consuming neighborhoods. Rob and his cohorts live in Fairfield, Westchester, North Fulton County, near Palm Beach, Cambridge, the North Shore, Shaker Heights, and minutes from Palo Alto.

How did all the Unhappy Robs end up in these places? The market value of the homes people select to reside in is heavily influenced by their occupational status. Those with high occupational status but relatively lower incomes than their neighbors often live above their means. They struggle to keep up with the consumption norms of their high-status neighbors. Dissatisfaction with life overall is typically the result of this treadmill existence. Among the high-income baby boomers surveyed, is there one occupational group that contains a higher proportion of people who are in the not-satisfied category? Yes! Middle-level corporate managers and executives tend to spend at a level more congruent with their occupational status (high) than with what their incomes should allow them to spend. In other words, there are more middle managers in the Unhappy Rob category than any other occupational group. Perhaps these Robs try to emulate the consumption behaviors of another occupational group: the senior corporate executives for whom they work.

Satisfaction and Money

Professor Glenn Firebaugh is a leading authority on the influence that income has on happiness/satisfaction. Dr. Firebaugh has found that there is a significant correlation between income and overall satisfaction in life. He has found that "relative income" is a better predictor of happiness than "absolute income."

> Richer [higher income] people tend to be happier. Experiments suggest, however, that what matters most is not income per se but income relative to the income of one's peers. . . . Americans compare themselves to other Americans the same age, resulting in a hedonic treadmill because incomes in the United States rise over most of the adult lifespan . . . rather than promoting overall happiness, continued income growth in rich countries could promote an ongoing consumption race where individuals consume more and more just to maintain a constant level of happiness.[4]

If you have a higher income than most of those in your circle of friends, neighbors, and/or fellow workers, guess what? You are then likely to be higher up on the happiness scale than those of your social cohorts who earn relatively less.

> [T]he group you likely compare yourself with are folks Harvard economist Erzo Luttmer calls "similar others." . . . If you compare two people

with the same income, with one living in a richer area than the other the person in the richer area reports being less happy.[5]

What if you study only those who live in what Professor Luttmer calls "richer areas"? You will find that some residents of "Richville" are very satisfied with their lives while others are not.

What factors account for this variation? In order to answer this question, I examined two groups of high-income-producing baby boomers, the Robs and the Henrys. All were born between 1946 and 1964 and had annual realized household incomes of $100,000 or more. Those who rated their satisfaction in life overall as a 5 (the highest degree of satisfaction) on a 5-point scale were contrasted with those who reported not being satisfied. The Happy Henrys ranked in category 5. At the other end of the happy continuum were the Unhappy Robs.

Who Are Rob and Henry?

There is no question that research has consistently shown that people with high incomes tend to be satisfied with their lives overall. But income is not the only factor that is a correlate of happiness. This is especially the case when the variation in income is narrowed by focusing on those who earn a minimum six-figure annual income.

Spending patterns also account for variations in satisfaction in life. Insights can be gained in this regard by examining both the demographic and housing characteristics of Henry and Rob. As mentioned, both Henry and Rob are in their mid-50s (see Table 8.1). Henry bought his first home for $68,000. At that time he was 26 years old, and his annual realized household income was $36,600. The ratio of the purchase price of his first home to his household annual income was 1.86. Rob was 27 years old when he bought his first home. He paid $74,100 for it, and, at that time,

Table 8.1   Profile of Happy versus Unhappy High-Income-Producing Baby Boomers

	Not Satisfied with Life (the Rob Types)	Very Satisfied with Life (the Henry Types)
Demographic Characteristics		
Age (mean years)	54	55
Marital status		
Married, never divorced	62%	61%
Now married	29%	35%
Education		
Graduated college	91%	90%
Attended graduate/professional school	57%	62%
Rank in college class (top 5%)	25%	19%
Economic Characteristics		
Annual realized household income (median/$000s)	$203.3	$307.4
Percent of income received from trusts, estates, or gifts from relatives (1% or more)	17%	12%
Household income donated to charitable causes last year (5% or more)	38%	60%
Financial assets (median/$000s)	$303.8	$1,383.0
Ratio: Financial assets/household income	1.49	4.50
Primary Home: Then and Now		
Purchase price of first home (median/$000s)	$74.1	$68.0
Age when purchased first home (median years)	27	26
Annual realized income at time first home purchased (median/$000s)	$40.1	$36.6
Ratio: Purchase price of first home/annual realized household income at time of purchase	1.85	1.86
Current market value (median/$000s)	$798.1	$785.3
Ratio: Current market value of home/annual realized household income	3.93	2.56
Ratio: Current value of financial assets/current market value of home	0.38	1.76

his household's annual income was $40,100. Similar to Henry's, Rob's ratio of the purchase price of his first home to his household's annual income was 1.85.

Looking back 30 years or so, Rob and Henry's households were generating annual incomes that were fairly similar. At that time, both had nearly an identical purchase price of home to annual income ratios.

Where do things stand 30 years later? Both Rob and Henry have moved twice since they purchased their first homes. You may be surprised to learn who lives in a more expensive home today. Given the fact that Henry is happy and Rob is not, you might assume that it is Henry. Don't we all assume that the nicer, more opulent, more ideally located home will make us happiest? Rob certainly assumed that was the case. His home is valued at $798,100, or nearly five times the median value of existing homes in America today. The current market value of Henry's home is $785,300. While this difference is not substantial, their relative positions along the happy scale are significantly different.

It is not the value of the home that explains the variations in satisfaction among high-income producers; it is something more basic. Henry understands that the key rule concerning homes and happiness is as follows:

Happy people tend to live in homes that they can easily afford.

So, financially speaking, it is the ease which Henry can afford his home and all the expenses related to owning and operating it that contributes to his happiness.

Thirty years ago, Rob and Henry started out as fellow members of the same income group, but things have changed over the decades. Last year, Rob's household generated an annual realized income of $203,300; Henry's, $307,400. Given their respective incomes, the ratio

of home value to income is 2.56 for Henry and a whopping 3.93 for
Rob. Rob, again typical of his cohorts, lives a neighborhood where he
is on the lower end of the income and wealth scale. It is just the opposite for Henry.

How can it be that Rob is not happy when his annual household
income places it in the top 3 percent in America? He lives in an expensive
home situated in an expensive neighborhood. More than half the homes
in his area sell for over $1 million. Could it be that Rob feels that he and
his family are economically deprived, relative to his neighbors? It is likely,
given the fact that for every Rob who agrees with the following statement, there are two who disagree:

We are financially better off than most of our neighbors.

In sharp contrast, the ratio is just the opposite for the Henrys: Two
agree for everyone who disagrees. Accordingly, Henry has more than
four times as much in his investment portfolio as does Rob ($1,383,000
versus $303,800). Plus the ratio of the current value of financial assets/
the current market value of the home is 0.38 for Rob versus 1.76 for
Henry. To date, since Rob and his wife have been working, they have
generated over $3 million in income but have saved or invested only
$120,000, or about 4 percent of their total income. The balance, approx-
imately $180,000, came from the appreciation of other financial assets.
Rob has a bad case of the big house, small investment portfolio problem
so common today. As Rodney was defined in Chapter 5, he's "big hat,
no cattle."

There are more high-income-producing Rob types than ever before
in our history, even with the economic downturn and layoffs. At this
moment, some are contemplating buying even more expensive homes in
even pricier neighborhoods because there are such good deals to be had!
They will struggle, perhaps not to pay the mortgage, but to pay for all

the other things that their wealthier neighbors like Henry enjoy. Why do people follow the path taken by the Unhappy Robs? Because they think that owning in an exclusive neighborhood will significantly enhance their level of satisfaction with life overall. But it will not do so. After the initial euphoria and the temporary feeling of superiority wears off, what then? What then will occur is the realization of having to pay for the home and the hundreds of items and activities that are all complements of living in or near "luxury land." From the high ever-increasing property taxes to private school tuitions, it is all about living in a high-consumption neighborhood. More than 40 percent of the school-age children in Rob's neighborhood attend or have attended private school.

Fully 42 percent of those in Rob's group versus 43 percent of those in Henry's acquired at least one Mercedes-Benz and/or BMW in the past 10 years. But there are plenty of other makes of motor vehicles in "Robville": Audi, Cadillac, Infinity, Jaguar, Lexus, Lincoln, and Volvo. Overall, the Rob types have spent more (approximately 11 percent) for the motor vehicle they most recently acquired than did the Henry types.

Living in "Robville" can cause disharmony among family members. Some people who live in mansions have a difficult time explaining to their children why they cannot afford to pay for their band uniforms, let alone school trips to Europe. Not all people who live among the glittering are ecstatic about life. Not by a long shot. Many are struggling to pay bills, all for the joy of living in a certain prestige area. Conversely, there are many people, like Henry, who live in homes they can afford. They are happy. The Robs and Robins should understand that within the high-income population surveyed nationally, there is no statistically significant correlation between the market value of a home (and by extension, neighborhood) and level of overall satisfaction with the life. Within every upscale residential area in the United States, some homeowners live well below their needs and, as a result, are satisfied with life overall. Conversely, some live above their means and are not satisfied.

What if you purchase an expensive home in anticipation of "making it big," financially speaking? Rob thought the same thing. Anticipation will not make house payments! Nor will that inflated level of status you ascribe yourself. The bank holding your mortgage does not give special dispensation to those whose inflated self-image greatly exceeds their objective economic means (although the government is trying to do so). Always remember the key rule concerning homes and happiness:

Live in what is below your means.

Bad Influence

Most Robs realize that they are, in relative terms, among the poorest families in the richest neighborhood. The Robs know they are living well above their means. But they have convinced themselves that it is worth the price to be able to live near the glittering rich.

Many Robs have also convinced themselves that they are somehow related to their more economically productive neighbors. Their neighbors' success and prestige somehow translate into theirs. The Robs enjoy telling people that they live near, around, and/or in the same area as do "a whole lot of very rich, exceedingly successful people." Unfortunately for Rob, his wealthy neighbors cannot pay his bills with their sizable incomes. The income that Rob does get from his wealthy neighbors is psychic income. Rob uses this form of imagined currency in an attempt to bolster his self-esteem. Rob is not rich, but he is a member of a very wealthy team (if only in his mind). He wants to be thought of as being part of the team and not judged on his individual economic batting average.

The Robs believe that some kind of a giant superiority halo hovers over affluent communities. Because Rob is under the halo, he thinks that he is entitled to think of himself as superior to others, even higher-income/higher-net-worth others who do not live in affluent communities. Rob admits that he is not as rich as his neighbors. He accepts this. But how does Rob feel about those who do not live in exclusive estates like he does? He believes that people, even multimillionaires, who do not live in upscale, wealthy areas like he are both socially and economically inferior to him and his rich team members.

But here is the harsh reality: Living in a so-called high-status area does not make a person wealthy. Rob is not rich relative to his neighbors, and he's not rich relative to the millionaires who inhabit more modest homes in less glittering communities. But try convincing Rob of this. Consider how Rob and his type responded to the following question:

Do you have more or less wealth accumulated than most people (not neighborhood specific) in your age/income group?

On average, for every 100 Robs who answered "less," there were 270 who answered "more." Yet most of those who answered "more" were wrong, very, very wrong. Just what is the affluent world according to Rob? He believes that most high-income/high-net-worth producers who do not live in high-status areas like he does are socioeconomically inferior to him and his ilk.

Rob is fooling himself. What if we gave Rob a truth serum and then asked a key question? The truth will emerge:

QUESTION: Rob, do you believe that you have a higher income and more wealth than people who objectively have more income and wealth than you but live in modest homes situated in dull, normal, middle-class neighborhoods?

ANSWER: Yes, yes. Absolutely.

Perhaps the delusional Rob thinks that there are two types of currency in the world. One dollar earned by Rob—call them Rob dollars—must be worth at least two or three earned by, say, a blue-collar multimillionaire who lives in a lower-middle-class area. Clearly, if you don't live in Rob's community, by definition you must have less wealth, success, prestige, and status than Rob and his brethren. So if you follow Rob's logic, you can become socioeconomically superior almost overnight. All you need to do is to move into an exclusive community. Then the value of all those dollars of income you generate, all your wealth, will instantly double or triple in value. Rob's dollars are clearly the gold standard.

Perhaps you think I'm being a bit too harsh on poor Rob, but surveys show that there are too many Robs, deluded souls:

> Many believe they already are [rich]: A poll in 2000 found that 19 percent [of Americans] thought they belonged to the richest 1 percent of U. S. households.[6]

What can be said of these millions of people who believe they are rich but are actually not? In essence, they are imitators of their neighbors who actually score much higher on both the income-producing and net-worth-building dimensions of productivity.

Happy, Wealthy, and Generous?

There is a strong correlation between donating to charitable causes and overall satisfaction with life. Researchers have consistently found that happy people tend to contribute a higher percentage of their incomes to noble causes than do people who are less satisfied with their lives. In fact, a significantly smaller proportion of Unhappy Rob types donated at least 5 percent of their annual income to noble causes than did the Henry types.

In other words, for every 38 Robs who gave 5 percent or more, there were 60 Henrys who gave 5 percent or more.

Does giving produce happiness or does being happy underlie giving in the first place? Some people, especially those involved with noble causes, indicate that charitable giving enhances one's level of happiness. I have a somewhat different view about the relationship between charitable giving and happiness. Along these lines, consider the following analogy. Have you ever wondered why people with higher incomes pay a disproportionately large share of the income taxes in America? The government says it is because high-income producers reaped more from our economy than did other income producers. Do not buy into this explanation.

There is a reason why the top 1 percent of the income producers in America pays 37 percent of the entire federal income tax bill, why the top 5 percent pays 57 percent, the top 10 percent pay 68 percent, and the top 25 percent pay 85 percent. High-income producers are the only ones who earn enough money to do so! The bottom 50 percent of the income producers contributes less than 4 percent of the total tax bill.

How are paying high taxes and charitable giving and happiness related? As with the income tax analogy, those who give more have more to give. But when I say "more" in this case, I am not talking about income. I am referring to net worth, that is, wealth. Those people who accumulate more wealth tend to give a larger percentage of their incomes to charitable causes. Even within homogeneous income groups, it is the accumulator type who gives more and the spender, like Rob, who gives less.

We also know that people within the same income cohorts who have more wealth have greater levels of overall satisfaction with life. They have more wealth because they are not enamored with consumption, with keeping up with the Joneses, and with displaying expensive brands.

But it is more than the variations in giving, more than wealth or income that is needed to explain happiness. It also has much to do with lifestyles, values, and needs. In an earlier work, I also found that giving to charitable causes and wealth are complements, not substitutes, as logic might seem to dictate.[7] Two groups of high-income producers were studied. Both groups were statistically identical in terms of income and age. The first group (TPs, or ten percenters) contained those who gave at least 10 percent of their annual realized income to charitable causes each year; the second group (OPs or one percenters) gave 1 percent or less. In terms of average dollar amounts, the TPs significantly outpaced the OPs, $41,500 versus $2,600.

How is it possible that the group which donated significantly more money was able to accumulate more wealth? People allocate their dollars in ways they feel will give them the greatest satisfaction. I believe that these people feel that giving is a substitute for spending more on products and pleasure-related services. They seem to get more satisfaction from accumulating wealth and giving than from consuming more. If you spend a large proportion of your income on prestige brands of products like the Rob types do, you have fewer dollars remaining with which to save, invest, or even donate. And those who gave 1 percent or less of their income to noble causes were, in fact, found to spend significantly more and invest much less than their more generous counterparts.

The more generous group was found to have spent fewer dollars on the impediments to building wealth: income taxes, homes, clothing and accessories, motor vehicles, mortgages, interest on personal loans, club dues, and vacations. Those who gave more also had a history of allocating more money to the foundation stones of accumulating wealth, including investments, pension or annuity contributions, and fees for professional financial advice and asset-management services. Most of the members of the generous group credited their parents for instilling in them the habits of accumulating wealth and sharing that wealth.

Can the Unhappy Robs transform themselves into Happy Henrys by giving more? Not if they continue to believe that spending is what will make them happy. Giving will take away from spending and consuming and, presumably, put a dent in their happiness. Giving to noble causes and consumption habits is likely to be influenced by where you live. This is especially true for high-income producers. Those who live in high-consumption areas tend to give less. The opposite is true for those who reside in areas where people spend less on products and services.

Where can the highest concentration of the high-income-producing, hyperconsuming Robs be found in America? According to my national surveys, the highest concentration can be found in the Northeast, especially within the tristate-metropolitan area of New York. This includes areas of southern Connecticut, northern New Jersey, and the New York counties of Westchester and Nassau. Now guess what areas, in terms of counties in America, have the highest average annual expenditure rates per household? Seven of the top 20 ranked counties also happen to contain among the highest concentrations of the Rob types. These counties and where they rank among the top 20 are:[8]

2. Fairfield, CT
5. Morris, NJ
6. Somerset, NJ
7. Westchester, NY
10. Nassau, NY
11. Hunterdon, NJ
15. Bergen, NJ

Where are the Rob types least likely to be found? The Midwest and southern regions contain the majority of areas that have the lowest levels of consumption in America. Adjusting for population variations, a disproportionately large share of high-income producers (those with annual realized household incomes of $200,000 or more) who give generously to noble causes are found in these types of areas. The New Tithing Group conducted research in which it ranked the 50 states according to the average percentage of wealth donated to charitable causes by high-income producers and found "the top of the list . . . dominated by a group of states that run from the Rockies through the Plains and down into the Southeast."[9]

The top five most generous states were (1) Utah, (2) Oklahoma, (3) Nebraska, (4) Minnesota, and (5) Georgia; ". . . states with beaches and museums . . . generally failed to crack the top 20 in ranking . . . the average affluent resident of New York (ranked) 23rd on the list."[10]

What if we could convince all the Unhappy Robs to move to a more charitable area or at least downsize? They might end up imitating their neighbors, consuming less and giving more. Some may even move into the happy range of the satisfaction with life scale.

9

All that Glitters Is Not the Millionaire's Goal

That man is richest whose pleasures are cheapest.

—Henry David Thoreau

There is something else about wealthy people that sets them apart from others. Most wealthy people have a wide variety of interests and activities. In fact, there is a substantial correlation between the number of interests and activities that people are involved in and their level of financial wealth.

Some wealthy people feel that owning a vacation home, for instance, would restrict them, obligate them to spend a lot of time there. And if they do not spend much time there, they feel guilty for allocating lots of dollars on something that is underutilized. Most millionaires came to this realization without first having to make the mistake of purchasing a vacation home. Many respondents have told me about the emotions associated with owning vacation homes. First, joy and euphoria, shortly followed by a loss of interest, and then resentment at having to pay for something that is rarely used but drains financial resources. Many rich people, however, rank high on the cosmopolitan scale. They like variety and change in their lives. Being tied down to a vacation home is "just so parochial." (They say the same thing about owning a boat.)

So if millionaires don't own vacation homes, what do they do? I asked the decamillionaires I surveyed about some of the activities that they engaged in during the prior 12 months. Here are some of the more popular activities reported:

- Visiting museums (83 percent)
- Raising funds for charities (75 percent)
- Consulting tax experts (75 percent)
- Attending fundraising balls (75 percent)
- Participating in civic activities (69 percent)
- Attending major league sporting events (69 percent)
- Vacationing overseas (69 percent)
- Attending Broadway plays (67 percent)
- Participating in trade/professional association activities (56 percent)
- Shopping for original art (56 percent)
- Gardening (55 percent)
- Attending antique fairs/sales (55 percent)
- Fishing (33 percent)
- Skiing in the Rockies (33 percent)
- Vacationing in Paris (28 percent)

Popular activities that decamillionaires listed in their diaries over a 30-day period included:

- Socializing with children/grandchildren (95 percent)
- Planning investments (94 percent)
- Entertaining close friends (87 percent)
- Watching their children/grandchildren playing sports (66 percent)
- Studying art (63 percent)
- Playing golf (60 percent)
- Attending religious services (52 percent)
- Jogging (48 percent)
- Praying (47 percent)
- Attending lectures (44 percent)
- Caring for elderly relatives (44 percent)
- Playing tennis (30 percent)

What do these wealthy people know that many vacation homeowners, boat owners, and seekers of prestige brands have overlooked? You cannot be in two places at one time. Mostly, what they know is that it is life activities that give pleasure and satisfaction, not the watch on your wrist.

The following letter exchange is a reminder that we should all take time to stop and smell the roses.

Dear Dr. Stanley,

I have finished your book, *The Millionaire Next Door*. I have some experience with some millionaires, and I'd say you have them down real well. They know who they

(continued)

are . . . frugal, cheap. I sure don't believe in living beyond my means and never have. It is a great idea to invest in your own business or in stocks or real estate. The only error I see in your book is that this is the end all and be all of life.

Owning… cars…The expensive model looks better, lasts longer, runs faster, needs less repairs, has better resale value, and generally a lot nicer to own. I've owned both type cars. A nice Mercedes costs more [than] a Ford because [it's] a better car.

A number-one Oxford or Hickey Freeman [man's] suit is better [than] a Sears off-the-rack suit. The material is better, the workmanship is better, the style is better, and it lasts at least five times longer. I've had both. A cheap golf shirt from Wal-Mart costing six to ten dollars will last about one or two years with proper care. A fifty-dollar Ralph Lauren golf shirt is a lot better quality and with good care will last about twenty years. I know, I've had both.

A [Casio] twenty-dollar watch from Wal-Mart will keep just as good a time as a [Gubelin] watch from Switzerland but, I hope you don't think [it's] just as good a watch. I've got both, and I don't think so.

A vacation in Emporia, Kansas . . . Athens, Georgia [or] . . . going through the south of France, or to Athens, Greece . . . I don't think they are all equal vacation spots and I've been to all of them. Shopping at Wal-Mart or Sears is not quite the experience as shopping at Neiman Marcus or Saks Fifth Avenue is.

It is great to make money and save money, but if these types don't let up after while and "smell the roses," they are a little bit nutty aren't they? As I recall it, Mr. Sam Walton lived a life pretty much like you seem to feel is great. Unfortunately for Mr. Walton, I seem to recall him getting some terrible form of cancer and meeting [an] early death. I wonder if he said to his doctors and close ones on his deathbed, "Gee, I wish I would have spent more time at the store." What do you think?

Sincerely yours,
Mr. H.
Affluent, Florida

Dear Mr. H:

Accumulating wealth is not the "end all and be all" of life. Yet it is considerably easier to accumulate wealth if you get great satisfaction from elements in your life that do *not* require hyperspending. Far too many people believe that in order to smell the roses, in essence to enjoy life, they must purchase prestige brands. Yet the data indicates that there is little correlation between this type of spending and happiness. But those who spend with the hope that happiness will result will be disappointed.

Basic to happiness are factors such as health, family, job, and values. If you have good health, a loving family, are surrounded by a network of caring friends, have a job you enjoy, doing without certain luxury items is not painful. But what if your work pays well but is not satisfying? You may think that loading up on luxury goods will cure your discontent. But hyperspending will only make things worse. Displaying luxury brands may (or may not) impress your neighbors, but it will not transform an unhappy person into a happy one. Or, as many millionaires have told me, "money makes life easier, not better."

Most millionaires were happy even before they became financially independent. They set goals and achieved them. One of their goals was to accumulate wealth. They built their wealth slowly but steadily and controlled their spending, instead of the other way around. These are confident people, people in control of their lives. Products and homes do not control them.

Certainly smelling the roses has something to do with being married to a wonderful spouse. Most millionaires (91 percent) are married (on average for thirty-six years to the same spouse). Fully two-thirds have never been divorced. I have often said that if you want to live forever, marry the wrong spouse. Do so and every day will be an eternity. No amount of luxury goods will make you happy if each day is an eternity. But marry the right person and every day will be a joy.

(continued)

Millionaires are not misers, especially when it comes to funding the educations of their children and grandchildren (and even nieces and nephews) or donating to noble causes. Certainly part of smelling the roses is the realization that you helped finance your son or daughter's business school, medical school, or law school education. This variety of rose has an aroma superior to owning even dozens of expensive cars, watches, suits, boats, or even vacation homes.

Those who are frugal in spending tend to be the most generous in terms of donating to charity and other so-called good causes. But those who are hyperspenders, including many high-income/low-net-worth types, have few dollars, if any, to give. Generous givers smell the aroma that emanates from the flowers produced by helping others who are not so fortunate.

You mention that the founder of Wal-Mart, Sam Walton, may have not smelled the roses. I never had the honor of meeting Mr. Walton, but from my reading I have a different view of the man. I have come across his profile and picture more often in sports periodicals than in the business press. From his profile, I can only surmise that Mr. Walton was not an "all work, no play" type. Often he was depicted on a bird shooting hunt, along with his pickup truck, Remington shotgun, and favorite hunting dog, Ol' Roy. In honor of Ol' Roy, you might note the brand name on Wal-Mart's private label dog food. Yes, it is the Ol' Roy brand in a wide variety of sizes and textures.

It was not only Mr. Walton's choice of motor vehicle, a Ford pickup truck, that impressed me. His shotgun was a Remington 870 Wingmaster pump. I purchased the same gun because I figured that if it was good enough for a billionaire, it was certainly good enough for me. I do not know how much he paid for his Wingmaster, but I paid $449.92 for mine at a Wal-Mart store.

You can pay $2,000, $5,000, $10,000, or even $50,000 for a shotgun, but you can't buy a better shotgun than an 870 Remington. To date they have sold more than 10 million 870s. It is strong and extraordinarily reliable. It gives me all the rose I need, and I have a feeling that Mr. Walton felt the same way. Yet the aspirationals at my gun club (a small minority) refer to my shotgun as obsolete, an iron boat anchor. They own gilded shotguns, European brands of the four- and five-figure variety. Their comments about my Remington never bother me in the least. In fact, I think of them as humorous. Plus they provide input for my research.

The clay pigeons that I shoot at do not seem to care how much I paid for my shotgun. It shoots straight and has never jammed. I bought mine to shoot and not in an effort to display status among my fellow club members. (My status comes from my score, not the gun.) Plus being around my good friends (all are frugal) when shooting is much more important than the price of the gun. This is in sharp contrast to those people who feel the need to own the gilded version of every gun they shoot, every suit they wear, and every car they drive. These types of people think that anyone with means who acts otherwise is suffering, never smelling the roses. Nothing could be further from the truth. Yes, even some billionaires and many decamillionaires prefer to drive pickup trucks. And there are plenty of wealthy people who shoot Remingtons.

In contrast, I recently read an article that mentioned the sale of a shotgun for $287,500. It was originally made for Czar Nicholas of Russia (S. P. Fjestad, "The Czar's Parker," *Field and Stream*, October 2007, p. 28). The gun not only had a lot of history, but it also had hand engraving all over it. To me it looked really ugly, like the gilding of gildings. I understand that most things that the czar once owned were top-of-the-line brands. He used these "things" to tell his subjects and himself that he was superior. Well, we know what happened to him. In contrast, most of the self-made rich in America do not have the same urgent need to document their superiority via the display of prestige brands.

What does this tell us about people who try to act rich by spending and displaying but are not? While searching for roses to smell, they overdress, overdrive, and overact. No, they are not Wal-Mart-type shoppers. But they would enhance the probability of actually becoming rich if they would patronize stores of this type.

America is a nation of excesses. And these excesses, especially when it comes to consumption, have a profound influence upon our young. They are constantly told that spending is the American way. Often their role models are highly compensated

(continued)

professional athletes and entertainers. Day after day, the public relations machinery keeps cranking out stories about the multimillion-dollar mansions that this athlete has purchased or the fleet of exotic cars that this movie star owns.

By sensationalizing and glorifying these powerful role models, the press sends a message. It says that happiness is obtained by spending freely on cars, homes, and parties. But in reality, spending will not make people happy. And very few people grow up to become star athletes or movie celebrities.

Recently our local newspaper published an article that featured in glowing terms the home of a professional baseball player. The article mentioned that the interior space of the highly decorated, nine-bedroom home was 25,000 square feet (Jennifer Brett, "Home of Brave a Comfy Expense," *Atlanta Journal-Constitution*, September 30, 2007, p. F3). Apparently this fellow is an all-star in terms of spending.

What else is so interesting about this home? Nationwide, only 3 percent of America's decamillionaires live in a home that has nine or more bedrooms. The square footage of this baseball player's home is four and one-half times larger than the median square feet (5,600) of the primary homes owned by the chief executive officers of Standard & Poor's 500 firms (Judith Burns, "Sell Signal: When Boss Buys Trophy Home," *Wall Street Journal*, April 12, 2007, p. D6). These are America's major league–caliber business leaders who run companies that generate billions in sales revenues and employ millions of Americans.

Could it be that many of these CEOs do not feel the same need as the baseball player to display their success, and supposedly enhance their status, via homes, car, and accessories? Perhaps just being the head of a major corporation has a lot of status attached to it all by itself. And in terms of making a real contribution to our economy, these CEOs have a much higher batting average than the baseball player. In fact, in this regard, he probably belongs in the minor leagues. Nonetheless, he is still a role model, a poster child for the "smell the roses" society of hyperconsumers in America.

We cannot count on the press to paint an accurate picture of how carefully most achievers allocate their dollars, yet most achievers are very satisfied with their lives.

Their satisfaction has little to do with the brands that they own. We would do well to adopt the values of the majority of the real achievers in America and not those who are of the "star" variety. The big-house baseball player, a one-in-a-million young phenom, was born with his extraordinary talent. But most achievers know that their type of success was not predetermined. Often it takes twenty or thirty years before they break into their own version of the really "big league."

What happens when owning "the better brands" takes priority over achieving? When it's about having money just to spend? People can't survive. It is one thing to enjoy an increased standard of living; it is another when it is all about money for spending on prestige brands. Individual achievement, small and large, today and tomorrow, is what leads to an increased standard of living. It is about the Bill Gates of the world creating firms that make products that make our lives better and more productive; it is about the teacher who labors to teach a class of fifth graders math. These are the things and activities that lead to improvements in life. In short, when it becomes about brand, less energy and money is spent on things and activities that will actually benefit people (which may explain why America has to import its engineers from India, a place where academic achievement is highly valued). It is not easy to break bad habits, but doing so will make us happier and, ultimately, lead to richer lives for all—now and tomorrow.

Sincerely,

Thomas J. Stanley, Ph.D.

Appendix A

The Nationwide Search for Millionaires

For each of the 208,790 Census Block Groups/neighborhoods in the United States, an estimate of the incidence of millionaire households was made. "Millionaire households" were defined in terms of the net value of investments. The proportion of millionaire households in each neighborhood was estimated by adjusting unearned income for underreporting, capitalizing it with a rational rate of real return, and estimating net worth through a nonlinear fit to a Lorenz curve expressing the proportion of net worth attributable to the sources measured by the Census as a function of the size of unearned income (dividends, interest, net rental income, royalty income, etc.). The empirical basis for the model is derived from the Survey of Consumer Finance (Federal Reserve) and its wealth over sample. Internal Revenue Service Statistics of Income series and studies provide the basis for estimating the real rate of return.

Using this methodology, a rank ordering was generated of all 208,790 neighborhoods in descending sequence of the incidence of millionaire households. This step permitted a specific selection of the highest incidence areas for identifying a sample of households within them as prospective survey respondents with a high likelihood of being millionaires, as defined above.

Potential respondents were selected randomly from neighborhoods nationwide that had a high estimated incidence of millionaires.[1] Commercial list organizations were able to supply head-of-household names and addresses for approximately 95 percent of the number of Census-tabulated homes in the neighborhoods selected. Addresses with more than three lines and with more than one name at the same telephone number were purged because of the high probability that they were commercial organizations. In total, 5,000 households were selected at random for use in surveys from the enumerated households within the designated neighborhoods.

The national geodemographically based survey for this book was specifically conducted from October 2005 to June 2006 by the University of Georgia Survey Research Institute. Each head of the 5,000 households received a 10-page questionnaire containing 220 questions, a form letter asking for his participation, and a one-dollar bill as a response incentive. Also included was a business reply envelope in which to return the completed questionnaire. A total of 1,594 surveys were completed in time to be included in the analysis. Overall, the response rate was 31.9 percent. Out of the 1,594 respondents, 944 or 59.2 percent of the total were millionaires.

Appendix B

The Millionaire Profile

Age (median years)	57

Marital Status	
Married, never divorced	59.0%
Now married	32.0%
Never married	2.2%
Separated/Divorced	4.0%
Widowed	3.0%

Total household annual realized income (median)	$212,888

Net value of household's investments (median)	$2,229,690

Percent who received 0.0 percent of last year's income from trusts, estates, or gifts from relatives	87.0%

Percent who never received any inheritance, gifts, estates, and/or trusts	68.0%

Home and Neighborhood

Homeowner	98.0%
Market value of home 2006 (median)	$827,249
Market value of home 1996 (median)	$453,238

Educational Background

Graduated college	90%
Graduated in top 5% of college class	22%
Paid for 100% of all college expenses	32%

Primary Occupation

Business owner/self-employed	28%
Senior corporate executive	16%
Middle manager/executive	11%
Engineer	9%
Physician	8%
Marketing/sales professional	7%
Attorney	5%
Education[1]	3%
Accountant	2%
Homemaker	2%
Other, including: tradesman, craftsman, artists/entertainers, clergy, economist, financial advisor, real estate investor, consultant, programmer	9%

Parents of Millionaires

Parents divorced prior to respondents eighteenth birthday	11%

Mother's Primary Occupation

Full-time homemaker	61%
Secretary/clerical worker	8%
Blue-collar worker	7%
Educator	6%
Sales/marketing professional	3%
Nurse	3%
Business owner/self-employed	3%
Other, including: executive, physician, financial advisor, civil servant, middle manager, engineer, attorney, artist/entertainer	9%

Father's Primary Occupation

Blue-collar worker	24%
Business owner/self-employed	19%
Senior executive	9%
Middle manager	7%
Sales/marketing professional	7%
Engineer	5%
Civil servant	4%
Educator	4%
Physician	3%
Attorney	2%
Military	2%
Accountant	2%
Other, including: financial advisor, farmer, scientist, real estate investor, entertainer, clergy, service provider, consultant, economist, chemist, banker, clerk	12%

Mother attended college	40%
Father attended college	47%
Respondents who believe that, in comparison with the parents of students they attended high school with, their parents at that time ranked in the bottom 50% in terms of annual household income	32%

Notes

Chapter 1 The Difference between Being Rich and Acting Rich

1. Number based on my laborious number crunching from IRS data.
2. The Stanley Wealth Equation is the copyrighted (1987) property of Dr. Thomas J. Stanley.
3. In this analysis, augmented net worth was used because the wealth equation was developed and validated numerous times using this measure.
4. Shari Roan, "It's the Activities That Make Us Happy, Not Money," *Chicago Tribune*, March 8, 2009, section 9, p. 6.
5. Pamela Paul, "The Luxury of a Large Family," *Atlanta Journal and Constitution*, April 9, 2008, p. A11.

Chapter 2 Everything You Think about Rich Is Wrong

1. Lucius Beebe, *Big Spenders* (Garden City, NY: Doubleday, 1966), p. x.
2. Harley-Davidson, Inc. Form 10-K, December 31, 2006, p. 4.
3. Louis Uchitelle, "American Wins Nobel in Economics," *New York Times*, October 10, 2006, P. C9.
4. Jonathan Clements, "Forget the Mansion: Why Buying Bigger Doesn't Guarantee a Rich Retirement," *Wall Street Journal*, August 23, 2006, p. D1.

Chapter 3 Do the Shoes Make the Man?

1. The most preferred brand of shoe, reported by millionaires, was defined as the one suitable "for dress" and/or "for work."
2. Thomas J. Stanley, *The Millionaire Mind* (Kansas City, MO: Andrews McMeel Publishing, 2000) p. 291.

3. Note that several other "quality" brands did have a popular following, but not enough to make it onto the top-five list. Among these brands were: Alden, Bally, Brooks Brothers, Ecco, Ferragamo, Gucci, and New Balance.
4. Ray A. Smith, "A Decent Suit at a Good Price," *Wall Street Journal,* September 9, 2006, pp. 1, 5.
5. *Automotive News,* January 30, 2006, p. 22.

Chapter 4 Brother, Do You Have the Time?

1. Bruce Nussbaum, "Who Cares What Time It Is?" *BusinessWeek,* May 22, 2006, pp. 88–89.

Chapter 5 Keeping Up with Your Spirits

1. W. Lloyd Warner et al., *Social Class in America* (New York: Harper Torch Books, 1960), p. 123.
2. Thomas J. Stanley, *Marketing to the Affluent* (New York: McGraw-Hill, 1988), p. 136.
3. Deborah Ball, "As Vodka Sales Skyrocket, Many New Comers Pour In," *Wall Street Journal,* January 26, 2007, pp. A1, A8.
4. Ibid., p. A1.
5. Michael J. Silverstein and Neil Fiske, *Trading Up* (New York: Portfolio, 2003), p. 203.
6. Ibid., p. D6.
7. Eric Asimov, "Spirits of the Times: A Humble Old Label Ices its Rivals," *New York Times,* January 26, 2005, p. D1.
8. Ibid.
9. Eric Felten, "The Emperor's New Vodka," *Wall Street Journal,* January 7, 2008, p. 14.
10. Asimov, "Spirits of the Times," p. D6.
11. Eric Felten, "How's Your Drink," *Wall Street Journal,* September 1–2, 2007, p. 5.
12. Felten, "The Emperor's New Vodka."
13. Asimov, "Spirits of the Times," p. D6.
14. Matthew Miller, "Booze Battles: Absolut Chaos," *Forbes,* December 13, 2004, pp. 85, 86.

Chapter 6 The Grapes of Wrath

1. Dorothy J Gaiter and John Brecher, "Sprucing Up for Wine's Night," *Wall Street Journal*, January 26, 2007, p. W4.
2. Michael J. Silverstein and Neil Fiske, *Trading Up: The New American Luxury* (New York: Portfolio, 2003), p. 178.
3. Ibid., p. 179.
4. Ibid., p. 180.
5. James Surowiecki, "A Fine Glass of Hooey," *Money* (January 2006): 100.
6. Roxana Popescu, "Wine: Tastes Great, Less Billing," *Newsweek*, April 7, 2008, p. 12.
7. Surowiecki, "A Fine Glass of Hooey," p. 98.

Chapter 7 The Road to Happiness

1. Scott Stoddard, "The General of Colorful Cars," *Investor's Business Daily*, June 15, 2007, p. A3.
2. Ibid.
3. Barry Winfield, "Comparison Test: Hardcore," *Car and Driver* (March 2007): 41–51.
4. Ibid., p. 47.
5. Ibid., p. 45.
6. June Fletcher, "When a Million Isn't Enough," *Wall Street Journal*, March 16, 2001, p. W1, W14.
7. This means that 14.0 percent of prestige/luxury makes are driven by millionaires, or four times the expected proportion, given the size of their population.
8. Louis Uchiteke, "American Wins Nobel in Economics," *New York Times*, October 10, 2006, pp. C1, C9.
9. Buzz Bissinger, "For the Love of DiMaggio," *Vanity Fair* (September 2000): 363–376.
10. Richard Sandomir, "The Detailed Life of DiMaggio, Minus Some Juicy Details," *New York Times*, July 16, 2007, pp. D1, D3.
11. Bissinger, "For the Love of DiMaggio," p. 371.
12. *New York Times*, May 11, 2005, p. A5.
13. Jens Meiners, "Mercedes Now Is Weak Link in DCX Chain," *Automotive News*, April 25, 2005, p. 43.

14. Stephen Power, "Huge Mercedes Recall Dents Daimler," *Wall Street Journal*, April 1, 2005, p. A3.

15. See "2006 Cars: Detailed Reliability Ratings," *Consumer Reports* (April 2006): 82–93.

16. Jonathan Fahey, "Over-engineering 101," *Forbes*, December 13, 2006, p. 62.

17. Gail Kachadourian, "Lexus Keeps J.D. Power Dependability Crown," *Automotive News*, July 4, 2005, p. 10.

18. Gina Chon, "Mercedes Seeks to Reverse Damage to Its Image," *Wall Street Journal*, January 30, 2006, p. B4.

19. "Toyota Leads Poll of Driver Satisfaction in Germany Again," *Wall Street Journal*, June 30, 2005, p. D1.

20. John K. Teahen, Jr., "Mercedes, Lexus Zip Past Cadillac in True Luxury Race," *Automotive News*, July 17, 2006, p. 10.

21. John K. Teahen, Jr., "Mercedes Again Is True-Luxury King," *Automotive News*, March 17, 2008, p. 10.

22. John K. Teahen, Jr., "Mercedes again leads true luxury class," *Automotive News*, February 16, 2009, p. 14.

23. Jens Meiners, "Cordes: Top Power Rank Isn't a Mercedes Priority," *Automotive News*, May 9, 2005, p. 57.

24. Gina Chon, "Toyota's Marketers Get Respect—Now They Want Love," *Wall Street Journal*, January 11, 2006, p. B1.

25. Jerry Flint, "The World's Best Car Company," *Forbes*, July 4, 2005, p. 62.

26. Chris Woodyard, "Toyota's Dynasty Has a New Ruler," *USA Today*, January 10, 2006, p. 3B.

27. Aaron Robinson, "Familiar Four Door," *Car and Driver* (February 2007): 64.

28. J. D. Power and Associates 2004 Customer Retention Study.

29. Polk Automotive Loyalty Award Winners, January 18, 2005.

30. See Thomas J. Stanley and William D. Danko, *The Millionaire Next Door* (Atlanta: Longstreet Press, 1996), p. 115.

31. John K. Teahen, Jr., "Good Riddance to a Bad Year," *Automotive News*, January 12, 2009, p. 31.

32. Chris Woodyard, "Buick, Jaguar Tie for Most Reliable," *USA Today*, March 20, 2009, p. 3B.

33. Leslie J. Allen, "The Downside of Upside Down," *Automotive News*, April 17, 2006, pp. 31–32, 36.
34. Ibid., p. 31.

Chapter 8 Getting Out of the Poorhouse

1. Paul Davidson, "Millionaire Hopefuls' Cash Gone with Breezes," *USA Today,* August 14, 2007, p. 3B.
2. Thomas J. Stanley, speech, national conference of the Securities Industry Association, October 10, 1979.
3. Kevin Helliker, "The Corn Belt Gets Rich, Quietly," *Wall Street Journal,* August 17, 2007, pp. W1, W2.
4. Glenn Firebaugh and Laura Tach, Relative Income and Happiness: Are Americans on a Hedonic Treadmill? *Working Paper,* August 22, 2005, p. 2
5. David Futrelle, "Can Money Buy Happiness?" *Money* (August 2006): 129.
6. Alexandra Star, "America's Right Turn," *Business Week,* June 7, 2004, p. 26.
7. Thomas J. Stanley, *Millionaire Women Next Door* (Kansas City, MO: Andrews McMeel Publishing, 2004), p. 139.
8. Marco R. della Cava, "Spending Is Hotter than the 4th of July," *USA Today,* July 3, 2007, pp. D1–D2.
9. David Leonhardt, "Philanthropy from the Heart of America," *New York Times,* November 22, 2006, p. C4.
10. Ibid., p. C4.

Appendix A The Nationwide Search for Millionaires

1. Also see Thomas J. Stanley and Murphy A. Sewall, "The Response of Affluent Consumers to Mail Surveys," *Journal of Advertising Research* (June/July 1986): 55–58.

Appendix B The Millionaire Profile

1. About one in eight (12.2 percent) of the respondents were educators and/or married to an educator.

Acknowledgments

Most important, I acknowledge my wife, Janet, for her strong guidance, patience, and assistance in the development of this manuscript.

Many thank-yous are accorded to my children for their contributions to this project. Dr. Sarah Stanley Fallaw did an outstanding job in searching and interpreting much of the current literature that served as an important base for the measures and concepts included in this work. Bradford T. Stanley's perceptive inputs and comments about the topic selected were invaluable. And for the second time in a row, his recommendation for a title for the book won first place!

I cannot offer enough thank-yous to all those who shared their case histories.

The Survey Research Center, Institute for Behavioral Research, at the University of Georgia once again did an outstanding job collecting and tabulating the survey data for this book. I commend Dr. James J. Bason, director of the institute, for his leadership and commitment to excellence in carrying out this project.

Acknowledged are the extraordinary patience, effort, and brilliant statistical and computer analysis shown by Kathleen J. Shinholser. Also, special thanks go to Linda White, who yet again did an outstanding job in formatting the questionnaire used in the national survey. Lesly McCollum's work in coding and Mallory Abramson's data entry must also be commended. These tasks were carried out with great effort and painstaking accuracy.

A million thank-yous go to my editors, Pamela van Giessen and Emilie Herman, who—based on their efforts—are surely the best and brightest stars in the publishing business.

I greatly appreciate the efforts of my agent, Raphael Sagalyn, whose suggestions and expertise have been invaluable to me.

Also, I owe a great debt to my good friend and attorney David J. Hungeling, whose sage advice, tenaciousness, and professionalism have been most encouraging and inspirational throughout this project and beyond.

I am very grateful to and most appreciative of Frank "Proven" Bulloch and his colleagues at the Edwards Institute for Social and Political Research for helping to prioritize hundreds of concepts and measures that were proposed during the early stages of this project.

I owe a deep debt of gratitude to Chantel Dunham, director of development, University of Georgia Library, for her wonderful brand of encouragement and keen interest in this work.

Also, Mr. John Prechtel, Data Services Librarian, the University of Georgia, did a consistently outstanding job in crunching the mountains of Census data that were essential in constructing a conceptual foundation for this book. And a thank-you goes to Michael Schmidt, aka Mr. Numbers.

A very special thank-you is in order to all the fine scholars at the University of Minnesota's Population Center for providing information from the Integrated Public Use Microdata database. In particular, I appreciate the significant contributions made by Steven Ruggles, Matthew Sobek, Trent Alexander, Catherine A. Fitch, Ronald Goeken, Patricia Kelly Hall, Miriam King, and Chad Ronnander.

About the Author

Thomas J. Stanley, America's foremost authority on the affluent, is a respected researcher, advisor, and author of several highly regarded, award-winning books on America's wealthy population.

Dr. Stanley is the author of *The Millionaire Next Door* and *The Millionaire Mind*. These books spent more than 170 weeks combined on the *New York Times*' Best Sellers list. His *Millionaire Women Next Door* was selected as a finalist for the business book of the year by the Independent Publishers Association and was on several business bestseller lists. Dr. Stanley's first three books, *Marketing to the Affluent, Selling to the Affluent,* and *Networking with the Affluent and Their Advisors*, were all designated as outstanding business books. In total, more than 3 million copies of Dr. Stanley's books have been sold worldwide.

Dr. Stanley has authored more than 40 published articles that deal with the affluent in America. His most significant, groundbreaking articles include: "America's Affluent,"*American Demographics*; "How to Live Like a Millionaire,"*Reader's Digest*, originally published as "Why You're Not as Wealthy as You Should Be"; and "The Doctor who Manages His Own Investments Has a Fool for a Client,"*Medical Economics*.

Dr. Stanley has also published numerous articles on the topic of marketing professional services to the affluent, including: "Ways to Add Value for Clients,"*Journal of Accountancy*; "How to Network with Affluent Client Prospects,"*Marketing for Lawyers*; "Marketing Trust Services to the

Affluent," *Trust and Estates*; and "Investment Management and the Affluent Customer," *The Bankers Magazine*.

Dr. Stanley has appeared as a featured guest numerous times on *The Today Show, 20/20,* and *The Oprah Winfrey Show*. His work has been cited in the national media, including the *Wall Street Journal*, the *New York Times, Forbes, Fortune, Time, Money* magazine, *U.S. News & World Report*, and *USA Today*.

In 1979, Dr. Stanley first conceptualized the "blue collar affluent" segment, a precursor to the millionaire next door typology, in a speech given on behalf of the New York Stock Exchange; the text of his speech later was published by the American Marketing Association. In 1980, Dr. Stanley conducted a national survey of America's multimillionaires—the first ever of its kind. Since that time, he has conducted numerous studies of the affluent and focus group interviews with high-net-worth respondents for a majority of the top 50 financial institutions in America.

Dr. Stanley has served as a top-rated main platform speaker for the American Bankers Association, the Society of Certified Public Accountants, the Securities Industry Association, the International Association of Financial Planners, the Association of Estate Planners, and the Million Dollar Round Table.

Dr. Stanley is also chairman of the Affluent Market Institute through which he has developed research-based marketing and selling strategies for identifying, attracting and retaining wealthy clients. Dr. Stanley received his doctorate in business administration from the University of Georgia. He was a university professor for 20 years, leaving to pursue a career in research and writing about America's millionaires. At Georgia State University, he was named Omicron Delta Kappa's Outstanding Professor.

Visit Dr. Stanley at www.thomasjstanley.com.

Index

A

Absolute income, happiness predictor, 222
Accessories, stores, 199t
Achievement, badge, 105
Acting rich
  attempts, 133
  class identification, 26
  ease, 33–34
  problem, 30–31
Advertisers, classical conditioning usage, 132
Advertising
  influence, 29–30
  message, confusion, 64
  targeting, 109
Affluent communities, superiority halo, 228–229
Affluent neighborhood, recognition, 209–210
Affluent people
  facts, 153
  Grey Goose, popularity, 126–127
  insecurity. *See* Pseudoaffluent marketing, 158
Age/weight price discrimination, 185
Alcoholic beverages
  income/wealth, relationship variations, 117–118
  serving container usage, impact, 140

Alcoholic beverages, preferences, 117
Allen Edmonds, shoe brand, 68
Ancestry groups, home ownership/occupation, 57t
Annual income
  increase, 220–221
  realization, 110–111
  wealth predictor, 24
Annual realized income, alcoholic beverage preferences, 117
Appearance-enhancing products/services, overspending, 25
Archer-Daniels-Midland, beverage alcohol sale, 137
Asimov, Eric, 137
Aspirationals, 2–6
  frugality, 5–6
  income/wealth, absence, 212
  membership, 168–169
  Mercedes–Benz millionaire viewpoint, 197
  Porsches, driving, 178–179
  rich behavior, 5
  spirits consumption, example, 142–144
  success, absence, 64
Asset value, exaggeration, 9
Attorneys, income occupations, 55–56
Augmented net worth, 8–9

Automobiles (cars)
  driving, substitute, 182
  happiness, relationship, 172–174
  manufacturers, profit (difficulty),
    187–188
  models, trading, 176–177
  ordinary cars, wealth (relationship),
    186–190
  ownership/leasing, survey, 180–181
  parts, 174–176
  price, life satisfaction (relationship),
    172–173
  purchasers, criteria, 201
  road track comparison test, 178–179
  separation, degrees, 177–179

B

Baby boomers
  archetypes, 220–221
  happy/unhappy contrast, profile,
    224t
Badges, 96–100, 105
  purchase/sale, 100–102
Balance sheet affluent (BA), 17–18
  characteristics, 19
  habitual differences, 27–28
  homes, characteristics, 25–26
  socialization process, 20–21
Bargain, grabbing, 219–220
Beverage alcohol, Archer-Daniels-
    Midland sale, 137
Beverage purchases, price
    sensitivity, 117
Big house strategy, 46–47
Blue-collar customers
  means, level, 2
  service, 1–2
Blue-collar millionaires, 214–215
  investments, marketing, 216

BMW
  acquisition, 227
  driving, millionaire status
    (relationship), 179–182
  preference, 173
  satisfaction level, 173
  score, 177–178
  selection, 171–172
Bourbon, marketing, 137
Brand choices, 12–14
Brand preferences, 132
  conditioning, 37
  spirits, 118–119
Brand selection
  habits, 136
  trading down, 134
Brooks Brothers
  patronage, 198
  suit brand, 75
Budgeting, notion (dismissal),
    22–23
Buicks
  admiration, 206–207
  ownership, correlates, 207
Business owners, characteristics, 6

C

Caddying, experience, 2–5
Call brands, usage, 138
Carpathian Mountains, 136
Cars. *See* Automobiles
Cash rich households, interaction, 2
Celebrities
  behavior, 34
  media focus, 185
  prestige purchases, 80
Cereal trap, avoidance, 29–32
Charitable giving, taxes/happiness
    (comparison), 231–232

Chemical engineers, product
   viewpoints, 121
Chevrolet
   dealers, number, 201
   millionaire retention rate, 202–203
Chon, Gina, 192
Cinderella syndrome, 76–79
Classical conditioning
   impact, 131–132
   keys, 132–133
Clothes
   financial resources, allocation, 73
   impact, 59–63
   purchase, 70–75
   stores, 199t
Cole Haan, shoe brand, 68
Conspicuous consumption, 15
   wealth, relationship, 94
Consumption
   behavior, brand category, 97
   continuation, 6–7
   lifestyle, 63–66
      neighbors, congruence, 211–212
      purchases, relationship, 106–107
   suspicion, 218
Consumption items, frugality, 5–6
Content, change, 108–109
CORE Club, 186
Corporate middle managers, income
   occupations, 55–56
Country club members, ranking,
   186–187

D

Darden, Bill, 115
Debt reduction strategy, 64–65
Decamillionaires
   activity, 237
   example, 61–63

Volkswagen, relationship,
   183–185
DiMaggio, Joe, 190–191
Dinner, millionaire price payment, 157t
Domestic help, assistance, 160–161

E

Earl, Harley, 176
Economically productive neighbors,
   relationship, 228
Economic elite, Grey Goose
   symbol, 125
Economic productivity
   consideration, 110
   enhancement, 189
Economic status, increase
   (enjoyment), 183
Economic success
   achievement, 121–122
   wine devotee, absence, 146
Educators
   on-campus socialization process, 25
   wealth indices, 23–25
Embellished net worth, 8–9
Emotional energy, usage, 99
Engineers
   frugality, 187, 189
   Honda, popularity, 188–189
   incomes/wealth accumulation,
     54–55
   motor vehicles opinions, 188–189
   product viewpoints, 121
   success, 187
   Toyota
     market share, 188
     popularity, 188–189
   wealth
     accumulation, propensity, 189
     indices, 23–25

Entertainers, average annual net
        income, 63
Estates, IRS data, 189
European sophisticate, emulation, 178
Expensive automobile, driving
        (substitute), 182

F

Family members, disharmony, 227
Farley, Jim, 198
Farmers, wealth, 54
Fear, experience, 6–7
Financial crisis (2008–2009)
    impact, 6–7, 31–32
    spending, decrease, 7–8
Financial flu, symptoms (impact), 6–7
Financial freedom, 191
Financial independence, long-term
        goal, 98–99
Financial resources, drainage, 236
Fiske, Neil, 138
Florsheim, shoe brand, 69
Ford F Series pickups, millionaire
        popularity, 203–204
Four-star restaurants, entry, 159–160
Frugality, 120–121, 135. *See also*
        Engineers
    groupings, 216
    Hall of Fame, 190–191
    touting, 213

G

General Motors
    marketing ideas, 174–175
    models, changes, 176–177
Generosity, happiness/wealth
        (comparison), 230–234
Germany, car owners (J.D. Power and
        Associates survey), 192–193

Giving, value, 231
Glittering rich, 9–10
    affection, 130–131
    behavior habits, spirits purchase,
        127–128
    brand purchase, propensity, 13
    buying behaviors, 12
    collection, 111
    compromise, 16–17
    conditioning, 131–132
    consumption patterns, emulation
        (absence), 6
    entertaining frequency, 14
    Grey Goose purchases, 131
        reduction, 134
    high-status brand, consumption
        elements/language, 126–127
    imitation, 5
        goal, 11–12
    importance, examination, 10
    outliers, 30
    Porsches, driving, 178–179
    prestige brands, purchases, 129–130
    role model, 12
    scale, buying decisions, 178
    spirits, consumption, 15–16
    stores, score, 72
    Texas, 106–108
    trophy vehicle ownership, 14
Goals, distinctions, 11
Gold course, work environment
        (advantages/disadvantages),
        3–4
Grade point average, motor vehicle
        purchase price (negative
        correlation), 184
Grape-oriented literature,
        examination, 152
Grapes, wine conversion, 146

Grey Goose (vodka)
  automobile purchases, relationship,
    135
  behavior habits, 127–128
  brand, value, 123–124
  buyer statistics, 133
  customer purchases, observations, 128
  devotion, 126
  expectation, 195
  per-ounce payment, 133
  popularity, 126–127
  purchasers, characteristics, 128
  purchases, 131
  success, increase, 124
  taste preference, 129
  usage, 129
Griffith, Allan, 190

H

Habits, cessation, 27–28
Haircuts, price, 60t
Happiness, 171
  automobiles, relationship, 172–174
  contrast, 223–228
  experiences, relationship, 31
  giving, relationship, 231
  income, correlate, 223
  predictor
    absolute income, usage, 222
    relative income, usage, 222
  purchases, impact, 89–92
  scale
    comparison, 222–223
    relative positions, 225
  shopping, 218–222
  taxes/charitable giving, relationship,
    231–232
  wealth/generosity, comparison,
    230–234

Hart Schaffner & Marx, suit brand, 75
Hickey Freeman, suit brand, 75
High-income nonmillionaires, wine
    orientation, 150
High-income producers
  dissatisfaction, 219
  home values, 44–45
  life satisfaction, absence,
    218–219
  satisfaction, variations, 225–226
  survey data, 173
High-income producing baby boomers
  archetypes, 220–221
  happy/unhappy contrast,
    profile, 224t
High-income-producing households,
    national survey, 172
High-income producing
    hyperconsumers, concentration,
    233–234
High-net-worth/high-income
    households, study, 12–14
High-net-worth people,
    concentrations, 215
High-net-worth success, example,
    107–108
High occupational status, 5
High realized annual income, earning,
    110–111
High-status area, living, 229
High-status neighborhoods, millionaire
    concentrations, 120
Homeowners, income/net worth
    (contrast), 44t
Homes
  living cost, impact, 42–43
  size, mortgage (relationship), 210
  values, 213–214
    explosion, 8–9

Honda
    Civics, ownership, 186–187
    engineer popularity, 188
Hosts
    graciousness, 165
    self-designation, 119
Households
    earnings, 11
    income level, 210
    investments, net value, 247
    market value, 47–48
    millionaire category. *See* United
        States
    purchase, efficacy, 46–47
    total realized income, impact, 26
    wealth level, 8–9
Hyperconsumerism culture, 7
    socioeconomic mobility, impact,
        21–22
Hyperconsumption habits, 106–107
Hyperspending, reasons, 22

I
Image
    bolstering, 163
    substance, contrast, 197–200
Income
    earnings, attainment, 219
    happiness, correlate, 223
    life satisfaction, correlation, 173
    net worth, division, 110
    tax, impact, 28–29
    transformation, 17–19
    watches, relationship, 96
Income generation
    ability, 8
    importance, 17
Income statement affluent (IA), 17–18
    habitual differences, 27–28

median age, 19
    millionaires, ranking, 19
    socialization process, 20–21
Influence, problems, 228–230
Informal party, attendance, 166–167
In-home meals, 161
Intellectual property, 120
Internal Revenue Service Statistics of
        Income series, 245–246
Inventory, absence (sales problem), 101
Investment strategy, examination, 110

J
J.D. Powers and Associates, Customer
        Retention Study, 202–203
Johnson & Murphy, shoe brand, 68–69
Jos. A. Banks, suit brand, 75
JCPenney, patronage, 198

L
Liabilities, underestimation, 9
Life creed, 99–100
Life experiences, impact, 31
Life satisfaction, 132–133
    absence, 218–219
    automobiles, price (relationship),
        172–173
    income, correlation, 173
    money, spending (relationship),
        220–221
    spending patterns, impact,
        223, 225
Liquor industry
    frugality, 135
    marketing efforts, 116
    patronage, appearances, 134
    product knowledge, 130
    serving container usage, impact, 140
Living lifestyle, selection, 211–212

Living standard
  decrease, 8
  enjoyment, 8
Lower-income people, wine
    purchases, 149
Low-profile millionaires, 213–214
  introduction, 214–215
Luttmer, Erzo, 222–223

M
Marketing
  dollars, waste, 157
  efforts, 116
  propaganda
    insensitivity, 116
    sensitivity, 116–117
  success, 115–116
Marketing to the Affluent (Stanley), 17,
    79, 122, 171
Men's Wearhouse Private Label, suit
    brand, 75
Mercedes-Benz
  acquisition, 227
  discriminant score, 177–178
  driving, 197–198
  purchasing criteria, 193
  ratings, receipt, 193
  reliability ratings (*Consumer Reports*),
    192
Mercedes-Benz millionaires, 191–196
  aspirational, viewpoint, 197
  attention, 195–196
  consumption habits/preferences/
    attitudes, 195
  driving, 193–194
  elitist scale, 194
  median income, 196
  survey, 195
  wealth, receipt, 196

Middle class, impact, 95
Millionaire Mind, The (Stanley), 2
*Millionaire Next Door, The: The Surprising
    Secrets of America's Wealthy*
    (Stanley), 190
Millionaire Next Door, The (Stanley)
  findings, 72
  National Survey of Millionaires, 203
  promotion, 213
Millionaires. *See* Decamillionaires
  accessories, stores, 199t
  activities, 108
    ranking, 236
  assets, accumulation, 155
  augmented net worth,
    examination, 47
  automobile purchases, 38–39, 104
  BMW, relationship, 179–182
  boat purchases, 39–40
  buying behaviors, 12, 77
  characteristics, 35–37
  Chevrolet, retention rate, 202–203
  clothes
    purchase, 70–75
    stores, 199t
    usage, 80–81
  commonality, 43
  concentration, 120
    small business proprietors, 122
  consumption spectrum, 13
  contrast, 93–100
  custom-made suits, avoidance, 76
  database, statistical analysis, 213
  demographics, 214
  dining, location, 156
  dinner, price payment, 157t
  domestic help, assistance, 160–161
  educational background, 248
  emulation, selection, 34

Millionaires. (*continued*)
  father, primary occupation, 249
  food, pretension (absence), 217–218
  Ford F Series pickup popularity,
    203–204
  fraternization, 120
  frugality, 120–121, 135
  generosity, 120–121
  goal, 235
  haircuts, price, 60t
  homes, 248
    average value (augmented net
      worth), 48t
    market value, 45–46
    value, 213–214
  host, self-designation, 119
  households
    definition, 245
    investments, net value, 247
    number, 43–44
  income
    generation, 10
    receipt, 247
  in-home meals, 161
  luxury items, avoidance, 80
  marital status, 247
  median household annual realized
    income, 213–214
  men
    shoes, preference, 68–69
    stores, patronage, 71
    suit brands, preference, 75
  Mercedes, driving, 193–194
  modest homes, 45
  modesty, 122–123
  mother, primary occupation, 249
  motor vehicle
    acquisition, 199t
    favorites, 204–208

  judgment ability, 202
  makes, acquisition, 203t
  median price, 204
  models, acquisition, 205t–206t
  price demand, 202
national geodemographically based
  survey, 246
nationwide search, 245–246
neighbor characteristic,
  212–218
neighborhoods, 248
parents, characteristics, 248–250
party, hosting, 164–165
population, continuum, 9–10
primary occupation, 248
profiles, 95–105, 247–250
  location, 109
purchase consistency, 35–42
recognition, importance, 36–37
responses, 237–243
restaurant preferences, 156–160
role model, 108
shoes
  preference, 67
  purchase, 66–70
  quality, importance, 70
spirit purchases, 37–38
student introductions, 112–114
suits, purchase, 72–73, 76–77
targeting, marketer objective,
  156–157
term, usage, 8
total household annual realized
  income, 247
Toyotas, usage, 195–196
transformation, 78–79
vacation homes
  avoidance, 236
  purchases, 40–41

vehicle ownership/leasing, survey,
  180–181
vodka, consumption, 123–125
watches
  brand usage, 91t
  gifts, receipt, 105
  ownership, 104–105
  purchases, 36
wines
  cellars, 161–163
  cellars, focus, 162
  enthusiasts, household
    concentrations
    (relationship), 215
  inventory, 155t
  inventory, amount, 154–155
  orientation, 149–150
  price payment, 153–154, 154t
  serving, percentage, 152–153
  serving, price, 153t
women
  stores, patronage, 71
  suits, preference, 76–77
Millionaire Women Next Door
    (Stanley), 65
Miser
  definition, 65
  lifestyle, 130
Money
  democratic ability, 135
  financial philosophies, 22–27
  impact, calculations, 42–47
  renewability, 23
  requirement, 98
  spending, life satisfaction
    (relationship), 220–221
Mortgages, home size
    (relationship), 210
Motor vehicles

acquisition, 199t
best deal, 201
buyers, criteria, 201
driving, substitute, 182
evaluation, 200–201
favorites, 204–208
glitziness, 187
happiness, relationship, 172–174
makes, millionaires acquisition, 203t
manufacturers, market share
    variations, 201
median price, 204
models, millionaire acquisition,
    205t–206t
ordinary cars, wealth (relationship),
    186–190
ownership/leasing, surveys, 180–181
prestige/luxury makes,
    nonmillionaire usage, 181–182
product/service, millionaire
    judgment ability, 202
purchase
  price, grade point average
    (negative correlation), 184
  reasons, 200–204
quality evaluation (J.D. Power and
    Associates), 192

N

National Survey of Millionaires, 203
Nature, nurture (contrast), 20–22
Negative correlates, 135–136
Neighborhoods, 248
  affluence, impact, 43
  consumption lifestyles, 50t–52t
  homes, sociological forces, 43
  quality, wealth (relationship), 122
Neighbors, misunderstanding,
    167–168

Net worth
  definition, 8
  embellishment, 8–9
  factors, 107
  impact, 212
  increase, 220–221
Neutral spirits, vodka producer
      purchase, 138
Nonmillionaires, prestige/luxury makes
      (usage), 181–182
Non-wine-worshipping outliers, 146
Nordstrom's
  patronage, 198
  Private Label, suit brand, 75

O

Occupational status
  characteristics, household location
      (relationship), 55
  net worth, negative correlation, 49
  societal assignation, 48–49
Occupations, wealth-producing
      characteristics (high income/
      high net worth contrast), 53t
One percenters (OPs), 232
Oprah Winfrey Show, 213
Ordinary card, wealth (relationship),
      186–190
Outliers. See Non-wine-worshipping
      outliers
  types, 116–117
Overcompensation, 65–66

P

Pavlov, Ivan (conditioning), 131
Perception, importance, 147–150
Phelps, Edmund S., 184
Physicians, annual realized income, 49,
      52, 54

Plastic Bottle Affluent, 118
Poorhouse, 209
Porsches, driving, 178–179
Poverty, impact, 95
Premium vodkas
  impressions, 140–141
  producers, 139
Prestige brands
  adoption, 221
  classical conditioning methods,
      impact, 132
  preferences, conditioning, 130–131
  promotion, 131
Prestige brands, selection, 129–130
Prestige/high-status artifacts,
      millionaire perspective, 93–94
Price discrimination. See Age/weight
      price discrimination
Primary occupations, 248
Private course golfers
  characteristics, 3
  tipping levels, 4
Product categories, symbols, 129–130
Productivity, recognition, 105
Pseudoaffluent
  insecurity, 180
  values, contrast, 187
Public course golfers
  characteristics, 3
  tipping levels, 4
Purchases, reasons, 19–20, 200–204

R

Real estate prices, decrease,
      219–220
Recognition, 105
  necessity, 100–102
Relative income, happiness
      predictor, 222

Restaurants. *See* Top restaurant
   appearance, 158–159
   differences, 158
   entry. *See* Four-star restaurants
   preferences, 156–160
   Texas, 158–160
Return on net worth (RON),
   differences, 110
Rich
   acting. *See* Acting rich
   appearance, necessity, 124
   benefits, 160–161
   compromise, 16–17
   discipline, absence, 11
   looking/being, contrast, 2
   variation, 223
Rich people (wealthy people)
   automobile purchases, 38–39
   behaviors, 30–32
   boat ownership, absence, 97
   boat purchases, 39–40
   characteristics, 4–5
   emulation, 147–148
   examination, 3–5
   imitation, 5, 133
   interests/activities, 31
   preferences, misreading, 157
   spirit consumption, 37–38
   vacation homes, purchases,
     40–41
   watches, purchases, 36
   wine collection, 163
Rockport, shoe brand, 69
Rolex
   ownership, 103–104
     differences, 105
   popularity, 89–92
   status brand, achievement, 96
Rolls-Royce customers, 79–80

S
Sales
   customer orientation, 130
   experience, 100
   problems, 101
   success, 100–101
San Francisco International Wine
   Competition (2000), 154
Satisfaction. *See* Life satisfaction
   money, relationship, 222–223
   variations, 225–226
Scotch
   marketing, 137
   preferences, 118–120
Second homes market, growth, 41
Seiko
   gifts, 105
   popularity, 89–92
   usage, 119, 135, 198
Self-esteem, bolstering, 228–229
   Grey Goose, usage, 129
Self-made millionaires,
   commonality, 43
Self-made millionaires, values/lifestyles
   (adoption), 11
Senior corporate executives,
   entertainment, 134
Shoes, purchase, 66–70
Silverstein, Michael, 138
Sloan, Alfred, 176
Small businesses, proprietors
   (millionaire concentration),
   122
Social cohorts, happiness scale,
   222–223
Social expectations set, existence,
   34–35
Society, change, 6–7
Socioeconomic dream, cessation, 133

Socioeconomic mobility
  encounter, 29–30
  impact, 21–22
Socioeconomic status, judgment, 84
Socioeconomic success,
      communication, 187
Sommelier, usage, 156
Specialty stores, patronage, 13–14
Spending
  contrast, 223–228
  history, 7
  life satisfaction, relationship.
      See Money
  motivation, 221–222
  patterns, 223, 225
Spirits (alcohol)
  brand preferences, 118
  brand purchases, sales influence,
      127–128
  consumption, 15–16
  distillation, 137
  marketing, 116
  per-ounce payment, 133
  preferences, 126–135
  serving container usage,
      impact, 140
  store-sponsored credit cards,
      usage, 128
  taste factor, 126–127
Status
  impact, 47–58
  items, avoidance, 123
  symbols, usage, 96–97
Status brands
  millionaire perspective, 94
  substitutes, 94
Stolichnaya vodka
  advertisement, 140
  indulgence, 184

Stores
  patronage habits, measure
      (importance), 13–14
  personnel behavior, 85–89
Substance, image (contrast), 197–200
Success
  achievement. *See* Economic success
  acknowledgement, 122–123
  badges, 96–100, 107
  creed, 99–100
  display, necessity, 98
  level, achievement, 63
  rewarding, 183–184
  symbols, 97–98
Suits
  JCPenney ad, example, 74
  purchase, 72–75
Sunspots, 136
Super-premium vodkas
  impression, 140–141
  producers, 139
Surowiecki, James, 164
Sweet rye, 136
Symbol traps, 30–31

T
Taxes, charitable giving/happiness
      (relationship), 231–232
Ten percenters (TPs), 232
Texas
  glittering rich, 106–108
  restaurants, 158–160
Timex, popularity, 89–92
Top restaurant, definition, 156
Toyotas
  blandness, curse, 200
  entry-level parts, 175
  high-quality cars, production, 201
  Lexus, reviews, 194

market share, 188
millionaires
    economic success, 196
    median income, 196
    usage, 195–196
misperception, 198
selection, 135
Trading Up (Silverstein/Fiske), 148
Trophy vehicles, ownership, 14

U
United States
    homeowners, income/net worth
        (contrast), 44t
    households, millionaire category, 7
    spending history, 7
University of Georgia Survey Research
    Institute, 246
Upper-middle-class membership,
    demonstration attempts, 122
U.S. weight gain, 184–185

V
Vacation homes
    avoidance, 236
    ownership, restrictions, 235–236
    purchases, 40–41
Vanity
    concept, 79–80
    definition, 79
Vehicles. *See* Motor vehicles
Vodka. *See* Grey Goose
    advertisements, 139. *See also*
        Stolichnaya vodka
    advertising dollars, 141
    brands
        multiplicity, 136–137
        price, visual appeal (positive
            correlation), 140–141

commodity, 137
consumption, 123–125
    cessation, 134–135, 138
    enthusiasm, 142–144
    expensive brands, marketing,
        141–142
    favorites, reasons, 138
    federal government definition, 136
    marketer influence, 141
    marketing, difficulty, 137
    number one status, claim, 139
    producers, neutral spirits purchases,
        138
    production, 137
    promotional theme, 138–139
Volkswagen, decamillionaire
    (relationship), 183–185

W
Wall Streeters, productivity, 114
Wangers, Gordon, 200
Wannabes, 111–114
Watches
    brand usage, 91t
    gifts, receipt, 105
    income/wealth, relationship, 96
    price differential, 89–90
    selection, reasons, 109–110
Watches, purchase, 36, 83–84
    happiness, result, 89–92
    store personnel behavior, 85–87
Wealth
    accumulators, characteristics, 56
    acquisition, difficulty, 28–29
    bloodlines, relationship, 56
    building, wines (relationship),
        151–152
    correlates, 151–155
    embellished level, attainment, 9

Wealth (*continued*)
  happiness/generosity, comparison,
    230–234
  high-status area, relationship,
    229–230
  income transformation, 17–19
  measure, 8–12
  millionaire perspective, 94
  notion, perversion, 180
  ordinary cars, relationship, 186–190
  predictor, annual income (usage), 24
  separation, 177–179
  substitutes, 94
  symbols, credit indicator, 210
  watches, relationship, 96
Wealth accumulation
  correlates, 25
  donation ability, comparison, 232
  problems, 56, 58
  response, 239–243
Wealth-building productivity, ratio, 46
Wealth index (WX), 18–19
  engineers/educators, 23–25
  income, relationship, 21
White collar customers
  cash, search, 2
  service, 1–2
Windfall, expectation, 212
Wine-oriented millionaires, 149

Wines
  articles, 145–146
  cellars, 161–163
    focus, 162
  collection, ownership, 151
  collectors, millionaires (relationship),
    149–150
  consultant, usage, 156
  descriptions, 164–168
  fanciers, characteristics, 151
  image, bolstering, 163
  inventory, 155t
  literature, examination, 152
  median price, 152–153
  myths, 149
  on-hand inventory/availability, 154
  orientation, development, 150–151
  preferences, 117–123
  price-equals-quality assumption,
    154
  price payment, 153–154, 154t
  rap, 164–168
    receipt, 168–169
  selection, limitation, 159–160
  serving price, 153t
  study (absence), 148
  terminology, knowledge, 164–168
  wealth building, relationship,
    151–152